中国饭店服务补救实证研究
归因、预期和满意度

FROM SERVICE FAILURE TO BEHAVIORAL INTENTION:
THE ROLE OF ATTRIBUTION, RECOVERY EXPECTATION AND SATISFACTION
AN EMPIRICAL STUDY IN THE CHINESE HOSPITALITY INDUSTRY

杨富荣 著

浙江工商大学出版社
ZHEJIANG GONGSHANG UNIVERSITY PRESS | 杭州

图书在版编目(CIP)数据

  中国饭店服务补救实证研究:归因、预期和满意度 / 杨富
荣著. —杭州:浙江工商大学出版社,2020.1
  ISBN 978-7-5178-3641-4

  Ⅰ．①中… Ⅱ．①杨… Ⅲ．①饭店—商业服务—研究—
中国 Ⅳ．①F726.93

  中国版本图书馆 CIP 数据核字(2020)第001602号

中国饭店服务补救实证研究:归因、预期和满意度
ZHONGGUO FANDIAN FUWU BUJIU SHIZHENG YANJIU: GUIYIN、YUQI HE MANYIDU
杨富荣 著

责任编辑	王　英	
封面设计	林朦朦	
责任印制	包建辉	
出版发行	浙江工商大学出版社	
	(杭州市教工路198号　邮政编码310012)	
	(E-mail:zjgsupress@163.com)	
	(网址:http://www.zjgsupress.com)	
	电话:0571-89995993,89991806(传真)	
排　　版	杭州朝曦图文设计有限公司	
印　　刷	虎彩印艺股份有限公司	
开　　本	710mm×1000mm　1/16	
印　　张	20	
字　　数	401千	
版 印 次	2020年1月第1版　2020年1月第1次印刷	
书　　号	ISBN 978-7-5178-3641-4	
定　　价	68.00元	

谨以此文感谢我的家人和朋友的支持，

感谢Alain JOLIBERT教授和Agnès HELME-GUIZON教授的指导

CONTENTS

目　录

LIST OF TABLES

LIST OF FIGURES

CHAPTER 1

INTRODUCTION

In the past forty years, the service sector has become a dominant power in many economies. As a result, there have been numerous researchers focusing their research on service and customer behavior in the service industry. For instance, Zeithaml (1981) indicates the four unique and distinctive characteristics of services: intangibility, inseparability, perishability and heterogeneity. Clearly, comparing to physical product, these attributes of service make it a riskier item to manage (Kuenzel et al., 2011). As a typical representative of service industry, hospitality gains its appeal for the easy access and the high level of employee-customer interaction.

Moreover, the market of China is experiencing an unprecedented growth in various aspects, including tourism and hospitality industries. Academic researchers and market practitioners are not only facing domestic but also international customers from all over the world. Chinese market serves international tourists and Chinese customers leave their footprints across every continent. On the other hand, the world's leading hotel brands and groups have seen the great potential in China. The American hospitality company Marriot (include Starwood) hotel group, is currently the biggest among its competitors—it has nearly 500 hotels in China. Other world-leading brands in China include Intercontinental, Accor, Four Seasons, Hyatt, and so on. Their main customers come from Chinese domestic market. Therefore, studying Chinese hospitality industry could benefit both Chinese and international markets.

Unsolved problems remain while the hospitality industry evolves over time. For example, service failure is often seen even in present days. It is why we, like many other researchers, focus on failure recovery. We concentrate on the most confusing part—why customers still choose to act undesirably [exit or negative word of mouth (NWOM)], after receiving service recovery. What's more, consequences continue that those customers would affect not only the loyalty of existing customers but also the preference of potential customers.

Specifically, there are some gaps in the existing research. The first one is regarding customer attribution, that is, when the service failure occurs, customer attribution can affect the customer's recovery expectations, and further affect the effectiveness of the service recovery provided by the hotel in terms of satisfying customers. But there are only a handful of studies in the existing literature that deal with the relationship between these three concepts: service failure, customer attribution and customer's recovery expectation. Thus, we are not aware of (1) when a customer encounters a service failure, is it the severity or the type of service failure that affects the customer's attribution to the hotel? (2) is it the magnitude or the type of customer's recovery expectation that is mainly affected by customer attribution? (3) is it the severity or the type of the service failure that affects the customer's recovery expectation? (4) is it the magnitude or the type of customer's recovery expectation that is affected by service failure? Secondly, according to expectation-disconfirmation paradigm (Oliver, 1980, 1997; Parasuraman et al., 1985), it is shown that customer satisfaction stems from the perceived difference between what they expect to be compared with the obtained recovery. However, there is a lack of attention to the study of the difference between customer service recovery expectation and the obtained recovery. Thirdly, in the past, most studies have considered customer satisfaction as a whole concept when they have studied their impact on customer behavioral intention. However, in practice, customer satisfaction with recovery may differ from satisfaction about overall service process.

Therefore, this study is assigned to achieve two goals: the first one is to research if customer attribution affects recovery expectation, then satisfaction and future intention, in the process from service failure occurring to customer behavioral intention prediction; the second one is to research if service failure matches recovery expectation, and if recovery expectation matches obtained recovery (align with matching hypothesis).

To start off, for a better understanding of customer behaviors after experiencing service failure, we add two key variables (customer attribution, recovery expectation) into the research model, with reference to classical frameworks like attribution theory (e.g. Kelley, 1967; Weiner, 1980, 1985a, 1985b), justice theory (e.g. Adams, 1965;

Tax et al., 1998) and expectation-disconfirmation paradigm. Such practice helps manifest the influences that customer attribution has over recovery expectation; also, it clarifies that customer satisfaction after recovery is influencesd by the result from self-comparison between recovery expectation and what is obtained. Here, customer satisfaction after recovery is divided into two minor sections— satisfaction about recovery process, and satisfaction about overall service process. The division helps further investigate customer behavioral intentions. Then, we for the first time in relative fields, have studied the comparisons between the types of service failure, and the types of recovery (service failure type—recovery expectation type; recovery expectation type—obtained compensation type). According to "matching hypothesis" (e. g. Smith et al., 1999), customers want to have compensations that are "matched" with service failures that they encountered. As an expansion, we look into the extent of matching between customer recovery expectation type and obtained recovery type in Chinese market. The sole purpose of this argument is to define whether the "mismatch" of types (failure type, recovery expectation type, recovery received type) have caused customers to exit even after recovery process. That is, customers receive undesired compensations or hotels give inappropriate compensations.

In sum, as an attempt to answer the research question, that is, in the hospitality industry of China, to which extent satisfaction recovery can be explained by customer attributions and expectation (dis)confirmation? Why do customers who accept service recovery still leave the service provider or do something that is not good for the service provider? Based on the Weiner's attribution theory, expectation-disconfirmation paradigm, "hypothesis matching" and justice theory, in the background of Chinese hospitality industry, we display five hypotheses in three sets of relationships: (1) the influences of service failure on customer attribution, the influences of customer attribution on recovery expectation and the influences of service failure on recovery expectation; (2) the influences of the difference between customer recovery expectation and obtained recovery on customer satisfaction after recovery; (3) the influences of customer satisfaction after recovery on behavioral intention. And then, according to "matching hypothesis", we explore the relationship between the type of service failure and the type of customer recovery expectation, and find out some mismatch between recovery expectations and obtained recovery.

To achieve research objectives, we targeted customers who claimed to have had unpleasant experiences with hotels in the past six months. By means of an online questionnaire, we have collected 318 valid responses and analyzed the data with SPSS 25.0. The results show that (1) customer attribution statistically significantly mediates the effects of service failure on recovery expectation; (2) the difference between recovery expectation and obtained recovery affects satisfaction after recovery; (3) customer satisfaction after recovery affects behavioral intentions; (4) types of recovery expectation are influenced by types of service failure; (5) obtained recovery differs from recovery expectation to some extent, mainly because "hotels not giving appropriate compensations" or "customers receiving undesired compensations"—such "mismatch" or "difference" affects the effectiveness of failure recovery (in terms of satisfying customers) and customer satisfaction after recovery.

The findings are helpful for the understanding of customer behaviors from service failure and recovery to satisfaction and behavioral intention, and practical implications for organizations within the industry.

1.1   Contribution of the study

Firstly, seeking responsible party is a natural reaction after experiencing service failure. Yet attribution theory is not as popular as justice theory when dealing with topics of service failure and recovery, not even in the studies of hospitality research. This research extends the body of knowledge on service failure and recovery. It introduces customer attribution as an important mediating variable between service failure and recovery expectation. It also proves that the types and severity of failure would influence customer attribution. For example, when there is core service failure, such as the room not clean, the food not safe, customers tend to blame hotels (external causes) instead of themselves (internal causes).

Secondly, it is also a natural reaction to anticipate recovery according to personal preference. Some customers take actions based upon that expectation. For instance, if the expectation is high, they might actively complain to the managerial team or third parties; otherwise, they might just walk away and switch providers. However, in the existing literature, customer recovery expectation is not well elaborated. Thus, in the second place, empirical studies usually have considered failure recovery as a unique variable whereas in the book, it is divided into customer recovery expectation and obtained recovery. The reason for adding obtained recovery is to verify the effectiveness of recovery policies. The results indicate that disconfirmation between customer recovery expectation and obtained recovery positively influences customer satisfaction after recovery.

Thirdly, to what extent do service failure and recovery expectation match each other requires attention? Only few theorists have shown interests like Roschk and Gelbrich (2014) based on the existing literature. Our contribution is to advance Roschk and Gelbrich's (2014) research on matching types of service failure and types of recovery expectation by adopting Bittner's (1990) detailed classification of service failures. The classification covers various angles including failures caused by individualized customer needs, requests and preference, not all attributed to hotels or environments.

Fourthly, after receiving recovery, customers would automatically compare it with primary expectation and disconfirmation during such process. This gap exists in two aspects: one is that little literature has considered recovery expectation and obtained recovery as separated ideas and thus ignored possible mediating variables (recovery expectation); the other is the "diconfirmation paradox"—if it is a positive disconfirmation, is it more satisfying with a massive surplus or perfect match (zero gap)? Some argue that valuable recovery is not equal to good recovery. For example, a thirsty customer given a fine cake is certainly not satisfied with the compensation. The divergence needs to be testified in more details. In this study, we for the first time look into the expected recovery type and obtained recovery type, and find out the disconfirmation lies in between. This could explain why customers choose to exit and why their loyalty remains low even after being provided with recoveries. Because there is usually a standard procedure for recovery in hotel, and it is designed for general circumstances.

Fifthly, it is a common practice to understand satisfaction after recovery as recovery satisfaction, yet we consider it as a combination of recovery satisfaction and overall satisfaction, and have proven it fruitful. It is found that customer's recovery satisfaction would strongly affect customer's overall satisfaction.

Sixthly, the researches about service failure and recovery and customer behavior are done mostly in Western context where the culture and market are greatly differentiated from in China. To conduct relative research in China with reference to those materials can be difficult but helpful in producing comprehensive understanding by applying theories in different scenarios. Chinese customers dislike direct conflict so they do not complain much when dissatisfied but switch service provider next time without hesitation. The difference in culture and the behavior is insightful.

All in all, the study has both theoretical and practical significance. In terms of market practice, a better understanding in the mechanism of customer behavior after experiencing service failure could honestly help organizations enact more appropriate and matching recovery policies. In current intense market, while earning profits, avoiding meaningless and ineffective spending is also vital for hotels. The common practice in recovery is to give customers exceeding valuable compensations but such policy ignores the individual preference of customers and is ineffective. With the research findings of this study, hotels can perform better customized recovery policies and contain customer loyalty in a more economic-efficient way.

Furthermore, to conduct such research in the context of Chinese market is meaningful. The market has a late start (after the 1980s), but is blooming over the last two decades. The business grows so fast that theoretical support is left rather behind, especially with the impact of new technology, conception and pattern of service. So far, the empirical literature addresses very little in the Chinese market in specific. Therefore, an investigation into the customer behavior of Chinese hospitality, can help hotel managers to better understand the characteristics of customer, prevent failures from happening, and design better recovery strategies accordingly. Also, the cultural difference is one of the drives for researching. In a tendency of outbound tourism, international organizations in hospitality can be inspired about the particular group of customers.

In academic area, this study for the first time has attempted to consider attribution as a mediator in researching the pathway from service failure to recovery. It is also the first time to involve customer recovery expectation and obtained recovery simultaneously in one theoretical framework, in order to the study the degree of matches (between service failure and recovery expectation, recovery expectation and obtained recovery). All may have a contribution to the relative literature.

1.2 Methodology

A survey encompasses all aspects of the research process, including research design, survey construction, sampling method, data collection, and response analysis. Surveys are based on participants' knowledge, experience, information, and opinions. Commonly, respondents answer a survey based on their memory.

The objective of using a survey in this study is to collect data and test the model from service failure to future behavioral intention. The variables used for this research include service failure, customer attribution, recovery expectation and obtained recovery, customer satisfaction after recovery, and behavioral intention.

Firstly, the survey instrument was designed based on the literature review. The instrument was first developed in English language and then translated into Chinese using a combination of parallel blind translation and modified direct translation as described by Guthery and Lowe (1995). The instrument was first translated by two bilinguals simultaneously and the two target versions of the instrument were compared and the consensus was reached. The translated instrument was then reviewed by five experts and some revisions have been made. After that, we did a pre-test on a sample of 55 respondents. We adjusted the text expression to ensure that no ambiguity in their understandings remains.

Secondly, the survey was conducted in a three-month period from April 2018 to June 2018. A total of 318 completed questionnaires were collected through the online distribution channel "Wenjuanxing", which is commonly acknowledged in the Chinese marketing academics (https://www. wjx. cn). The research subject selected are Chinese real hotel customers who have encountered hotel service failures and complained to service provider or manager in the past six months. The survey subject are distributed geographically in over 25 cities across China, as is designed to be a representative sample of Chinese hotel industry customers.

In this study, we mainly used two analytic methods—descriptive statistics which simply aims to testify the validity of the data, and multiple linear regression analysis which deal with more detailed information. SPSS 25.0 is employed for testing the hypothesis and analyzing the data.

1.3 Structure of the book

This book consists of nine well-organized chapters as is shown in Figure 1-1. It covers full and accurate contents, ranging from research objectives to relevant empirical studies.

The first chapter provides a general introduction to the topic and the book itself. It begins with research questions and objectives. It goes to explain significance of study, the chosen methodology and the structure of the book.

The next three chapters review the relevant literature existing in the field. Chapter 2 covers topics about service failure and customer attribution. Chapter 3 reviews literature on recovery expectation and obtained recovery, and satisfaction

CHAPTER 1   INTRODUCTION

· Research background of the book   · Set research questions and objects
· Significance of the study   · Propose methodology and testing techniques

CHAPTER 2 LITERATURE REVIEW ON SERVICE FAIURE AND CUSTOMER ATTRIBUTION

· Define the concept of service failure
· Introduce theories of attribution, general model of attribution field
· Find the relationship between service failure and customer attribution

CHAPTER 3   LITERATURE REVIEW ON RECOVERY EXPECTATION, OBTAINED RECOVERY AND SATISFACTION AFTER RECOVERY

· Define the concept of service recovery, satisfaction after recovery
· Introduce the justice theory, disconfirmation paradigm, and matching hypotheses
· Find the relationship among recovery expectation, obtained recovery and satisfaction after recovery
· Induce the limitations and gaps

CHAPTER 4   LITERATURE REVIEW ON CUSTOMER BEHAVIORAL INTENTION AFTER RECOVERY

· Introduce customer behavioral intention
· Find the relationship between satisfaction after recovery and behavioral intention
· Induce the limitations and gaps

CHAPTER 5   CONCEPTUAL MODEL AND HYPOTHESIS

· Identify research structure   · Propose hypotheses and research model

CHAPTER 6   RESEARCH METHODOLOGY

· Questionnaire design and data collecting
· Survey instrument
· Variable definition and measurement
· Reliability and validity
· Statistical analysis

CHAPTER 7   RESULTS

· Descriptive analysis of sample
· Test of hypothesis by SPSS 25.0

CHAPTER 8   DISCUSSION

· Discussion of sample
· Discussion of the results

CHAPTER 9   GENERAL CONCLUSION

· Theoretical contributions
· Managerial implications
· Limitations and future research avenues

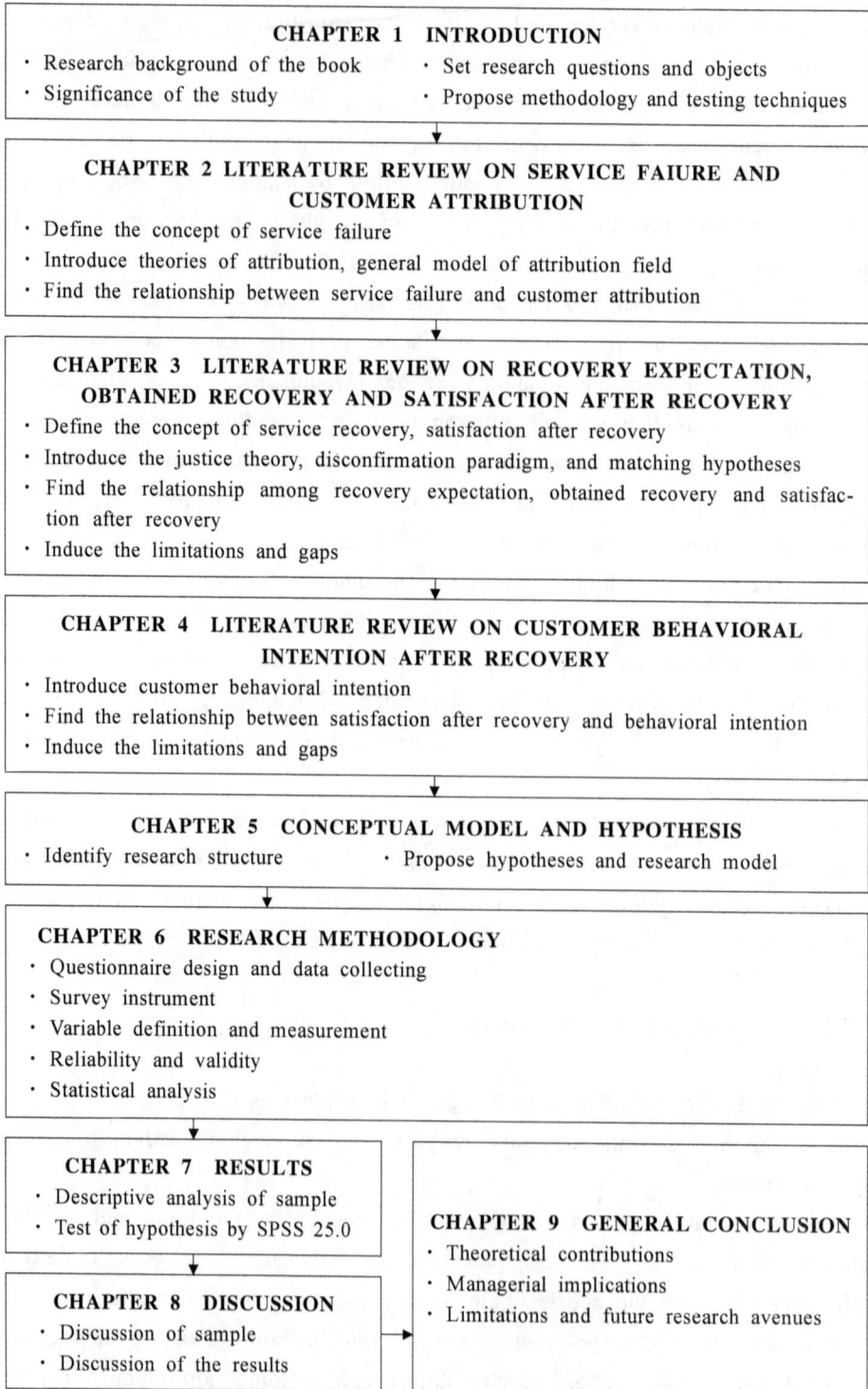

Figure 1-1   Illustration of the structure and content of the book

after recovery. Chapter 4 is mainly about theories of customer behavioral intention. This section introduces the concepts of complaint, repurchase, multiple responses simultaneously, and no action. It also establishes the relationships between satisfaction after recovery and behavioral intentions.

Chapter 5 moves on to the theoretical framework and research model. It comes up with a conceptual model that helps study the relationships among service failure, customer attribution, customer recovery expectation and obtained recovery, and satisfaction after recovery and behavioral intention. Moreover, five hypotheses concerning service failure, attribution, recovery and behavioral intention are proposed.

Chapter 6 describes the research methodology. It explains (1) data collection and sampling; (2) survey instruments; (3) definition of the variables and their measurement; (4) analysis of reliability and validity; (5) statistical analysis.

Chapter 7 displays descriptive analysis and tests the hypotheses of the study.

Chapter 8 provides a conclusive discussion. It describes the demographic characteristics of Chinese hospitality customers and their behavioral characteristics in the process of service and failure recovery. There are three main aspects: (1) the relationships among service failure, customer attribution and customer recovery expectation; (2) the relationships among customer recovery expectation, obtained recovery, and the difference (disconfirmation) between these two variables; (3) the relationship between customer satisfaction and behavioral intentions.

Chapter 9 is the general conclusion. It talks about the contributions and outlines the theoretical contributions, managerial implications, limitations of research, and future directions.

CHAPTER 2

LITERATURE REVIEW ON SERVICE FAILURE AND CUSTOMER ATTRIBUTION

Service failure and recovery is an important research subject in service marketing literature (Matos et al., 2012). Researchers have primarily used expectation-disconfirmation theory, attribution theory, and justice theory to study service failure and recovery. In this chapter, previous achievement regarding this study will be reviewed.

This chapter starts with a discussion on service failure literature. After that, it turns to the attribution theories and the first question of this study, that is, the relationship between service failure and customer attribution.

2.1   Service failure

As the global marketing is becoming increasingly competitive, service providers focus on delivering superior quality to their customers and aim to offer "zero defects" service. However, the perfect, error-free service provider that never slips up or encounters problems that impact on customers is unimaginable (Hibbert et al., 2012). Almost anything could result in service failures (Bitner et al., 1990), and mistakes are inevitable in service encounters (Bitner et al., 1990; Karatepe, 2006, Ennew et al., 2003; McColl-Kennedy et al., 2003).

Although service failures are common in the service industry (McColl-Kennedy et al., 2003), it is difficult to avoid them completely (Choi and Mattila, 2008; DeWitt and Brady, 2003; Hart et al., 1990), it does not make them any more acceptable to customers. Service failure leads to customer dissatisfaction, and jeopardizes the relationship between a service provider and its customers, threatening repeat patronage and loyalty (Webster and Sundaram, 1998), and generating negative WOM (Hibbert et al., 2012). These customer reactions have considerable economic implications for service provider (Hart et al., 1990), and thus much of research attention has been devoted to service failure (Grönroos, 1988; Sharma, 2008).

2.1.1 Definition of service failure

Service failure can occur at any time during the customer's relationship with a service provider (Kelley and Davis, 1994; Carlzon, 1987). Zeithaml et al. (1985) suggest that the unique characteristics of service are the reasons why service provider cannot truly offer a foolproof experience, and the unique characteristics also separate service from tangible goods. Those unique characteristics are intangibility, inseparability of production and consumption, heterogeneity, and perishability (Wolak et al., 1998).

Commonly, according to the nature of service, service failure is defined as a mistake, problem or error that occurs in the delivery of service (Bitner et al., 1990; Hoffman et al., 1995; Colgate and Norris, 2001). Similarly, Maxham (2001) defines service failures as any service-related accidents or problems (real and/or perceived) that may occur during a customer's experience with the service provider. Duffy et al. (2006) define service failures as the real or perceived breakdown of the service in terms of either outcome or process. It means service failure may be truly occurring and perceived by customer, or not really occurring but resulting in only the perception of customer.

Nyquist et al. (1985) suggest that a difference in the perception of the importance of service failures between employees and customers in the hotel industry might play an important role in tackling such failures. Parasuraman et al.'s research (1985) suggests the same result. They conducted interviews with firm executives and customer groups and identified significant gaps or discrepancies between executive perceptions about what customers expect and the actual customers' expectations (Kuenzel et al., 2011). Thus, a source of service failures might be a difference in the perception of quality held by customers and management (Kuenzel et al., 2011).

Consequently, a number of cases have identified that the customer' personality type is the main rationale for their perception of the failure, meaning that the customers themselves are the source of their own dissatisfaction (Bitner et al., 1994; Kuenzel et al., 2011). A subsequent study includes a typology of problematic customers from the employees' viewpoint (Bitner et al., 1994). Lovelock (1994) determines six types of customers as "wrong customers" and suggests that they should be avoided because they could easily confront a service provider with service failures. Identifying these types of customers as early as possible, could prevent potential service failure events which would then do harm to both sides (Lovelock, 1994).

The notion of "wrong customers" can manifest itself in situations where: product and customers fit poorly; customers' personality and style are very different comparing to that of the company; the mutual value produced by the bond between provider and customer is not sufficient; the customer lacks resources; the customer's demand is not met by the product; or the customer lacks the appropriate skills and technological efficiency needed for evaluating the consumption of the product (Lovelock, 1994).

Yet, all of the above definitions are based on the nature of service failure or the differentiated individual perceptions. On the other hand, based on the expectancy-disconfirmation paradigm, researchers' views on the definition of a "service failure" are more consistent. Hess et al. (2003) define service failure as service performance that falls below customer expectations. Chang et al. (2012) suggest that service failure refers to the disconfirmation of what customers perceive would be the product or service performed during the service delivery process. In other words, customers get something different from what they expected (Mueller et al., 2003). When customer requests are not satisfactorily fulfilled, services are not well-delivered, or delivered services are lower than minimum expectations, then service failures occur (Bitner et al., 1990, 1994). Thus, the majority of researchers define service failures as the situation "where customers feel there is a statistically significant gap between their expectations and the actual service standards as a result of the service provider's failure to provide services or products that meet customers' recognized standards or service behaviors regarded as unsatisfactory by customers" (Binter et al., 1990; Kelly and Davis, 1994).

According to this definition, we propose that the service failures in the hotel are the situations that customers believe that the level of service or product they obtained is lower than their original expectations, hence a significant negative gap between their expectation and what is obtained. Furthermore, the size of the gap is related to the serving time, severity of the service failure, frequency of service failures, service attitude and subsequent recovery strategies (Binter et al., 1990; Kelly and Davis, 1994).

2.1.2 Types of service failure

Relevant literature indicates that customers' evaluation of a particular type of recovery effort is based on the type of service failure they experience (Lewis and Spyrakopoulos, 2001, Chuang et al., 2012). Therefore, classifying service failures is beneficial for understanding customers' reactions and identifying potential recovery strategies (Siddiqui, 2010; Hoffman, 1995).

In the initial stages of service failure studies, researchers proposed a variety of detailed typologies of service failures or dissatisfying incidences (Bell and Zemke, 1987; Bitner et al., 1990; Hoffman et al., 1995; Smith et al., 1999). Bitner et al. (1990) first applied the critical incident technique (CIT) and collected the data from hotel, restaurants, and airlines as the representative of high-contact service to identify a service failure classification model (Chase, 1978). Service failures classified by Bitner et al. (1990) include three major groups, and a total of twelve categories (See Table 2-1):

Table 2-1 Twelve categories of service failure (Bitner et al., 1990)

Groups		Categories
Group 1	Employee response to service delivery system failure	(i) Unavailable service
		(ii) Unreasonably slow service
		(iii) Other core service failures
Group 2	Employee response to customer needs and requests	(i) Customer's special need
		(ii) Customer preference
		(iii) Admitted customer error
		(iv) Potentially disruptive others
Group 3	Unprompted and unsolicited employee action	(i) Attention paid to customer
		(ii) Truly out-of-the-ordinary employee behavior
		(iii) Employee behavior in the context of cultural norms
		(iv) Gestalt evaluation (societal/cultural insult)
		(v) Exemplary performance under adverse circumstances

Group 1: employees response to service delivery system failure. It consists of three categories, which are (i) unavailable service; (ii) unreasonably slow service; and (iii) other core service failures. Unavailable service refers to services normally available that are lacking or absent, such as an unavailable room in the hotel booked by customer.

Group 2: employee response to (implicit/explicit) customer needs and requests. There are four categories, including (i) customer's special need; (ii) customer preference; (iii) admitted customer error; and (iv) potentially disruptive others.

Group 3: unprompted and unsolicited employee action. The group comprises five categories, which are (i) attention paid to customer; (ii) truly out-of-the-ordinary employee behavior; this unusual action subcategory includes employee behaviors such as rudeness, abusiveness and inappropriate touching (Siddiqui, 2010); (iii) employee behavior in the context of cultural norms; (iv) gestalt evaluation (societal/cultural insult); (v) exemplary performance under adverse circumstances. That is, Service failure arises from employee behaviors that are totally unexpected by customers. These actions are not initiated by the customer, nor are they part of the service delivery system (Siddiqui, 2010).

Based on it, Hoffman et al. (1995) adopted the critical incident technique in the study of restaurant service failures, categorizing service failure into three types: (i) employee response to service delivery system failures such as product defects, slow/unavailable service, facility problems, unclear policy, out of stock menu items; (ii) employee response to implicit/explicit customer requests such as not cooked to order, seating problems; and (iii) unprompted and unsolicited employee actions like inappropriate employee behavior, wrong order, lost order, mischarged order. Furthermore, Armistead et al. (1995) presented three types of service failure according to error sources: service provider, customer or associated organization (Chang, Khan and Tsai, 2012).

Keaveney (1995) divided service failures into two types: core service failures and service encounter failures. A core service failure is a mistake, such as an error in billing, or a more dramatic service deficiency, whereas a service encounter failure is a deficiency in service delivery, for example, a staff member who appears uncaring, impolite, unresponsive, or unknowledgeable (Chuang et al., 2012).

Underlying all those typologies, there is a more generalized and parsimonious outcome-process classification (Gronroos, 1988; Zeithaml et al., 1991). Subsequently, Smith et al. (1999) identified two types of service failure: outcome-related failure and process-related failure. Outcome-related failure refers to what actually occurs during the service encounter, whereas process-related failure involves the manner in which the service is delivered. The former involves a firm failing to satisfy a basic need or perform a core service, for example, wrong bill for hotel guest or rotting food offered by a restaurant. The latter involves the flawed or deficient delivery of the core service, such as a hotel employee being rude to a customer (Zhu et al., 2004).

In addition, given "critical incidents are specific encounters between customers and service employees that are especially dissatisfying or satisfying for one or both parties" (Lovelock, 1998), CIT was then widely used by researchers within types of service failure and classification of incidents studies (Kelley et. al., 1993; Hoffman et al., 1995; Keaveney, 1995). It is originally proposed by Flanagan in 1954, and then introduced into the service marketing literature by Bitner et al. in 1990. Many studies afterwards on service marketing have been conducted on the basis of this technique (e.g. Flanagan 1954; Bitner, 1990; Coverly, Holme, Keller, Thompson and Toyoki, 2002; Carvalho and Brito, 2012).

Apart from the classification discussed above, Roschk and Gelbrich (2014) define failure type by the form of a company's flaw when delivering a product or service, and come up with the resource-based failure type classification. They distinguish between monetary failure, flawed goods, failed service, and lack of attention. In particular, Roschk and Gelbrich (2014) suggest that current failure type classifications are outcome versus process failure (Smith, Bolton, and Wagner, 1999; Zhu, Sivakumar, and Parasuraman, 2004), monetary versus non-monetary failure (Gelbrich and Roschk, 2011a; Gilly and Gelb, 1982), and irreversible versus non-repairable failures (Smith, Bolton, and Wagner, 1999). Drawing on the resource exchange theory, they provide new, resource-based classifications of compensation type and failure type and test them as moderators on the recovery effect of compensation.

This classification method is a great advance to study the matching degree of failure type and recovery type, but it also has obvious limitations. One is that the research will limit the failure type to the mistakes made by the company, but in fact there are many other causes of customer perceived service and product failures, and even customers themselves may be the cause of the failure. In the next section, we will describe the relevant contents (See 2.2). Yet because of the limitations, this study still go for the relatively most comprehensive classification by Bitner et al. (1990).

2.1.3 Severity of failure

Failure severity is the customer's perceived magnitude of the problem (Smith and Bolton, 1998). Hirschman (1970) is the first to conclude that customers would be more likely to voice their complaints when dissatisfied with an "important" product. After that, many researchers have made attempts to analyze the effects of the magnitude of the failure (also called severity of the failure / dissatisfaction problem) in a service failure / recovery encounter context (Hess et al., 2003; Smith and Bolton, 2002; Smith et al., 1999).

Firstly, there is considerable evidence to indicate that the magnitude of service failure (Harris et al., 2006; Hoffman et al., 1995) plays an important role in customer perceptions (Chuang et al., 2012). Therefore, many investigators have used the magnitude of service failure to measure a customer's evaluation of the perceived intensity of the service problem (Blodgett et al., 1997; Blodgett et al., 1995; Tax et al., 1998).

Secondly, Hoffman et al. (1995) suggest correctly understanding or identifying the severity of service failure is one of the antecedents to recovery expectations. They examined service failures occurred in restaurants and the results demonstrated that high scores on a failure rating variable (scale of minor to major) are associated with lower scores on a recovery rating (poor to good scale) and a retention percentage variable (Craighead et al., 2004). Their results indicate how severe the failure could have been in terms of money, time and inconvenience. The three highly correlated pre-recovery process severity variables were averaged to determine the pre-recovery severity and the three post-recovery process severity variables were averaged to determine the post-recovery severity (Hoffman et al., 1995).

Thirdly, severity of failure has increasingly been recognized as a key variable in determining how failure incidents will be reconciled (Smith et al., 1999; Levesque and Mc-Dougall, 2000) via the development of an appropriate recovery strategy (Hart et al., 1990). Several studies of service recovery effectiveness have demonstrated that the magnitude of the service failure is one of the factors determining customer satisfaction and has a statistically significant influence on customer responses to service recovery (Smith and Bolton, 2002; Weun et al., 2004). Chuang et al. (2012) also claim that the magnitude of a service failure can affect customer evaluations of recovery strategies. Furthermore,

Zeithaml et al. (1993) suggest that customer tolerance of service failures depends on the situation. Hence, the magnitude of service failure plays a key role in customer assessment of service recovery strategy. The extent to which customers are willing to accept this inconsistency is defined as the zones of tolerance (ZeithamI et al., 1993; Rust et al., 1996; Cronin and Taylor, 1992; Oliver, 1993; ZeithamI and Bitner 1996; Kotler, 1997).

Fourthly, previous researching indicates that complaining (to the seller and/ or to friends and relatives) and switching behavior would increase when the severity of problem increases (Richins, 1985). Chuang et al. (2012) draw on mental accounting theory to examine the effect of the relationship between service failure and service recovery on customer satisfaction. The results confirm the magnitude of service failure influences the effectiveness of service recovery efforts. The study finds that even the type of failure service perfectly matches the customer's mental account of the recovery effort when a serious service failure occurs, customers may remain dissatisfied because the perceived loss greatly outweighs the gain (Smith et al., 1999; Thaler, 1985). For example, an apology and compensation may create satisfaction following a 10-min wait for a clean room in a hotel, but they cannot tolerate the delayed or forgot morning call that may cause them to miss a flight. It appears that no realistic recovery efforts can easily erase an extreme loss (Magnini et al., 2007). Looking at the severity of service failure, Harris et al. (2006) report that greater perceived severity of loss not only leads to a lower satisfaction rate but also makes it more difficult to recover from service failure (Mattila, 1999).

2.1.4 Summary

Service failure and recovery is an important research subject in service marketing literature (Matos et al., 2012). Regardless of the types of service they provide, service providers sooner or later experience some degree of service failure (Wang et al., 2010). Service failures are likely to result in customers' dissatisfaction (Chang et al., 2012) and impact their relevant behavioral responses, such as complaining intentions, repurchase intentions, and WOM (Chang and Hsiao, 2008; Lin, 2010; Matos et al., 2012). As such, researchers investigate the relationship between the type of service failure and the type of service recovery. They argue that an effective service recovery strategy is contingent on the type of service failure (Beugre and Viswanathan, 2006).

On the other hand, the majority of the studies focus on explaining the connections between the causes of a service failure and the types of recovery strategies taken from different angles (Lin, 2006). Oliver and Swan (1989) explore the issue from the "disconfirmation" perspective, explaining that service failure is a concrete representation of the gap between customers' expectations and their actual experiences. Service failure classified by Bitner et al. (1990) includes three major groups, and a total of twelve categories. Afterwards numerous researchers have simply classified service failure into two different forms: outcome and process (Binter et al., 1990; Smith et al., 1999; Hoffman et al., 2003), core service failures and service encounter failures (Keaveney, 1995). They also explore the types of service failure and possible causes, which in general, can be identified from two facets—"objective" and "subjective" (Lin, 2006).

In this study, in order to more clearly understand the degree of the matching of the types of service failure, customer recovery expectation, and obtained recovery, we decide to adopt Bitner's (1990) classification which divides failure into three groups and twelve sub-units.

2.2   Attribution theory

Massive literature in consumer psychology has revealed a fact that customers seek reasons for service failures and this attribution of blame moderates the effects of failure on the level of customer satisfaction (Folkes, 1984; Folkes et al., 1987; Oliver and DeSarbo, 1988; Anderson, Scott Baggett and Widener, 2009). Not only that, but it is confirmed by many theorists that attributions of responsibility for failures would affect many aspects like consumer communication (Richins, 1983; Curren and Folkes, 1987; Folkes et al., 1987), preferred recovery strategies (Folkes, 1984; 1988), and future repurchase intentions (Folkes et al., 1987; Swanson and Kelley, 2001).

That is, attribution theory is considered as a theoretical basis that could provide additional insights into factors which determine the consumer perceptions of an organization's recovery efforts in response to a service failure (Swanson and Kelley, 2001). It may also provide insights in studying consumer perceptions and behavioral intentions related to service recovery experiences (Swanson and Kelley, 2001). Hence, attribution theory is perceived highly valuable in this study and will be reviewed in detail.

2.2.1 Heider's naive psychology (1958)

Attribution literally means a grant of responsibility (Akpoyomare Oghojafor et al., 2012). The earliest attribution theory is "naive psychology" observed in the works of Heider (Heider, 1944, 1958; Robertson et al., 1974). According to Heider's theory, most people, who are new to psychologists, are trying to understand the behavior of others to make the world more predictable (Mirsadeghi, 2013). Attribution theory could help people to explain the behaviors of others by describing ways in which people make causal explanations for their behaviors (Borkowski and Allen, 2003). Heider (1958) suggested that it is a theory of perception which takes the point of view of the lay observer, as he classes and explains incoming information and infers causality, rather than the analytic framework of the scientific observer (Robertson et al., 1974).

From then on, numerous researchers have tried to understand and explain why people do what they do (e.g. Heider, 1944; Heider, 1958; Jones and Davis, 1965; Kelly, 1967; Ross and Fletcher, 1985; Borkowski and Allen, 2003).

Specifically, according to Heider's "naive analysis of action", researchers' hypothesis is that individuals draw conclusions, namely, people's performance like amateur or naive scientist in that they try to determine why things happen to themselves or to others (Dubinsky, Skinner and Whittler, 1989). Heider deems that people have two behavioral motives, the need to understand the world around them, and the need to control their environment (Borkowski and Allen, 2003). Then, people generally explain behavior in two ways: they attribute the behavior either to themselves (internal) or to a situation (external) (Oghojafor et al., 2012). Therefore, in his theory, Heider (1958) divides the behavior attributes into two parts: external factors or internal factors. That is, when an internal attribution is made, the cause of the given behavior is within the person (e. g. attitude, aptitude, character and personality), whereas in occasions when an external attribution is made, the cause of the given behavior is assigned to the situation (e.g. environment or weather) in which the behavior was observed (Oghojafor et al., 2012).

Furthermore, Heider proposed that people act based on their beliefs, no matter these beliefs are valid or not (Borkowski and Allen, 2003). As described by Robertson and Rossiter (1974), attribution theory regards the processes by which individuals explain events in their subjective environment. Its value is its concentration on subjectively operative causal processes—the "real" factors from the actor's vantage point—which determine his perception, thoughts, and actions.

Based on Heider's idea, several models have been developed, attempting to interpret the process by which these attributions are made regarding self-attribution (e. g. Weiner, 1974; Abramson, Seligman and Teasdale, 1978) and social attributions made in the case of the behaviors and outcomes of others (e.g. Kelley, 1973; Huning, and Thomson, 2011). Dubinsky et al. (1989) believe that an observer may look at causes within or outside that person in seeking to explain why someone does something, and in order to make assumptions about events, some kind of "inference" about either the person or the environment is made.

2.2.2 Jones et al.'s correspondent inference theory (1965, 1976)

The discussion concerning attribution theory often begins with Heider's work, then briefly visits Jones and Davis's contribution, and moves on to Harold Kelley's theoretical model (Malle, 2011).

Jones and Davis (1965) revealed that the causal attribution to explain a person's behavior toward an object can be made based on the informational cues generated from the behavior. Since the informational cues are generated from a single behavior in a given situation, researchers believe that information on the generalizability of the person, the object, or the situation can be indirectly inferred from the behavior (Wang, 2008). The research of Jones et al. (1965, 1976) is called the "correspondent inference theory".

In brief, individuals, in their efforts to understand the causes of a behavior; they determine whether to attribute behaviors to a dispositional (the person who performed it) or to a situational (the surrounding environment) cause. Furthermore, the more an action departs from one's expectation, the more confidence one will have in attributing a personal disposition to this behavior (Jones and McGillis, 1976; Naveh and Katz-Navon, 2014).

And then, according to Jones and Davis's (1965) theory of correspondent inference, researchers believe that people do inference based on three factors. The first factor is freedom of choice, that is, the degree of one's freedom of choice. Researchers suggest that behaviors which are freely chosen are better to show private attribution from the behaviors which may be imposed. The second factor is social desirability / expectancy, which refers to the degree of expected behavior that leads people to the understanding of social trend. Behaviors that are away from the social norms, tell us something more about the person from the normal behaviors that are part of a social role or be expected under the circumstances. The third factor is the inferred orientation impacts or consequences of one's behavior. Several actions have the desired returns a person's inner motivations and actions clearly desirable to produce a single output or return are not acceptable (Mirsadeghi, 2013).

On the other hand, Kelley and Michela (1980) believe that the antecedent of attribution is illustrated by Jones and Davis's theory of correspondent inference, and divided it into three classes. For example, motivation is raised by Jones and Davis's auxiliary hypothesis of hedonic relevance. The three antecedent of attribution concerns a naive perceiver's explanation for a target person's action (Kelley and Michela, 1980). Specifically, Kelley and Michela (1980) suggest that the attribution is affected by information, the perceiver's belief and motivation (See Table 2-2).

Table 2-2 The three antecedents of attribution

Classes	Interpretation
Information	In this situation, about the consequences of the action, which might be compared with the consequences of other action the actor might have taken. His intention is inferred according to the principle of non-common effects: the intention governing the action is indicated by those of its consequences not common to the alternative actions, and the fewer such non-common effects, the less ambiguous is.
Belief	In this case, about what other actors would do in the same situation (social desirability). If few persons would have acted as the actor did, his intention is revealing of his personal needs or attitudes.
Motivation	If the action affects the perceiver's welfare, there is greater likelihood that a disposition will be inferred from it. This occurs because the impact on the perceiver's welfare becomes a focal effect to which the other effects are assimilated, and thereby the number of irrespective (non-common) effects is reduced. Thus, the perceiver's motivation, elicited by the action's consequences for him, is thought to affect the processing of information about the action.

Source: Kelley and Michela (1980).

In their study, they proposed that correspondent inference theory limited the case in which the action is known to be intentional, so researchers put forward the hypothesis: "The fewer distinctive reasons an actor has for an action and the less these reasons are widely shared in the culture, the more informative is that action about the identifying dispositions of the actor." (Kelley and Michela,

1980). Then, there is the issue of whether the effects of someone's behavior were intended.

Researchers have suggested that "intent" or "intentionality" may be an additional dimension of attribution (Gordon and Bowlby, 1989; Thomas and Pondy, 1977; Weiner, 1985a; Justice Tillman et al., 2014). They believe that individuals are more likely to draw a correspondent inference if the behavior appears intentional than when it is unintentional. Tillman et al. (2014) suggest that people make inferences about behaviors by specifying the actor's intention, which is related to their underlying disposition. Then, peer perceptions of intent may influence their evaluation of the behaviors of peers such as performance of citizenship behaviors. Many researchers support that perceived intent influences individual perceptions and behaviors (Gordon and Bowlby, 1989; Cotte, Aoulter and Moore, 2005; Justice Tillman et al., 2014). In fact, intentional behavior is likely to be attributed to personality (internal causes), and accidental behavior is likely to be attributed to situation (external causes).

2.2.3   Kelley's classical attribution theory (1967, 1971, 1972, 1973)

Kelley's (1967, 1973) theory mainly extended Heider's (1958) assertion that individuals have an innate need to assign causality to events (Dubinsky et al., 1989), and defined attribution theory as the "process by which an individual interprets events as being caused by a particular part of an environment" (Kelly, 1967). The central idea of Kelley's attribution theory is that an individual is motivated "to attain a cognitive mastery of the causal structure of his environment". Researcher assumes that people can understand the why about others' behavior (Oghojafor, 2012).

According to Kelley's (1967, 1973) classical attribution research, individuals attempt to make sense out of his environment by the attribution of causal relationships (Robertson et al., 1974), they want to know if one's behavior occurs mainly because of their traits or motives (a person attribution), the task or situation (an entity attribution), or a combination of the two (a context attribution) (Dubinsky et al., 1989). That is, the categories of causal attribution that people generate in response to information include: stimulus, person, circumstance, or a combination of these three (Laczniak et al., 2001). Researchers proposed that for many problems in social psychology, the relevant causal factors are persons, stimuli, times, and modalities of interaction with stimuli (Kelley, 1967; Kelley and Michela, 1980).

Kelly tried to explain the way people perceive internal and external attribution, and postulate the model of covariation (Oghojafor, 2012). In his model, Kelley focused on how individuals determine the cause of a behavior or event by considering information regarding the consensus, consistency, and distinctiveness of the behavior or event (Eberly et al., 2011). Covariation theory (Kelley, 1967, 1972) argues that the causal attribution to explain a person's behavior towards an object can be made based on a priori beliefs in the generalizability of the object, the situation, and the person. It means that distinctiveness, consistency and consensus can be used to measure the priori beliefs in the generalizability of the object, the situation, and the person, respectively (Wang, 2008).

In addition, Bemmels (1991) illustrated the three variables with examples, and interpreted as "distinctiveness is the extent to which the behavior in question is unique to a specific entity, it relates to variation in behavior across entities for the same individual", "consistency is the extent to which the behavior in question has been exhibited by the individual on this entity in the past, it relates to variation in behavior over time for the same individual and the same entity", and "consensus is the extent to which other individuals in the same environment exhibit the same behavior, it relates to variation in behavior across individuals, all else held constant" (Bemmels, 1991).

The theoretical argument of Kelley (1967) also goes into further detail about three types of information that observers use in evaluating the covariance of behavior with potential situational causes: distinctiveness, consistency and consensus (Sjovall et al., 2004).

The first variable is distinctiveness, it refers to the degree to which the behavior occurs only within a particular situation, or is repeated by the actor in other situations (Sjovall et al., 2004). The impression is attributed to the thing if it uniquely occurs when the thing is present and does not occur in its absence (Settle, 1972). Namely, distinctiveness was explained as the extent to which the person performs the behavior toward only the object in all situations (Wang, 2008). Sparkman and Locander (1980) consider that distinctiveness decreases with an increase in the number of other stimuli that elicit the same behavior. It means the behavior is attributed to the stimulus if it occurs only when the stimulus is present and not in its absence (maximum distinctiveness) (Sparkman and Locander, 1980).

The second variable is consistency. Consistency refers to the degree to which an action is repeated across time in a given situation. Kelley (1967) also discusses consistency across modality, or method of interaction, with a potential external cause (Sjovall et al., 2004). The basic principle of the Kelley's covariation model states that the effect is attributed to one of the causes which covarie over time. It also means that the behavior at various occasions varies (Oghojafor et al., 2012). That is, consistency includes both consistency over time and consistency over modality.

Consistency over time means that each time the thing is presented, the individual's reactions must be the same or nearly so. Consistency increases with the number of occasions on which the stimulus elicits the same behavior. It is minimized if each time the stimulus is in present, the reaction of the individual whose behavior is being analyzed is the same or nearly so (Sparkman and Locander, 1980). Consistency over modality means that his reaction must be consistent even though his mode of interaction with the thing varies (Settle, 1972). Consistency increases with the number of situations in which the stimulus elicits the same behavior. A person's behavior is most consistent if his / her reaction is consistent even though the mode of interaction with the stimulus varies (Sparkman and Locander, 1980). In sum, consistency means the extent to which the person performs the behavior toward the object in other situations (Wang, 2008).

The third one is consensus. Consensus refers to the degree to which others, besides the actor, take a particular action in a situation (Sjovall et al., 2004). Consensus increases with the number of other persons displaying the same behavior toward the same stimulus (Sparkman and Locander, 1980); that is, consensus concerns whether others react in the same manner to some stimulus or situation as the person being considered, for example, does the effect vary across different persons? (Dubinsky et al., 1989). For high consensus, the stimulus must cause similar behavior by other actors (Sparkman and Locander, 1980).

Further, Kelley's theory suggests that people use three types of information when evaluating potential internal or external causes for a particular observed behavior (Sjovall et al., 2004) (See Table 2-3).

Table 2-3 Kelley's covariation theory regarding three types of information

Consensus	Distinctiveness	Consistency	Resulting attribution
High	High	High	External influences
Low	Low	High	Internal disposition
Either (high or low)	Either (high or low)	Low	External influences

Source: Kelley (1967), Sjovall et al. (2004), Dubinsky et al. (1989).

As indicated in Table 2-3, Kelley argues that an attribution can be clearly made either to a specific cause within the external situation or to the disposition of the actor when one of two patterns emerge from the available information.

Specifically, individuals are most likely to attribute another person's behavior to external causes (i.e. stimulus attribution; situational factors) under conditions of high consensus, high consistency, and high distinctiveness. Conversely, Behavior is attributed to internal causes (i.e. person attribution, dispositional factors) when it exhibits low distinctiveness, high consistency, and low consensus (e.g. Kelley, 1967; Dubinsky et al, 1989; Knouse, 1989; Sjovall et al., 2004; Akpoyomare Oghojafor et al., 2012). Moreover, when there is low consistency across time or modality, Kelley argues that no clear dispositional or specific situational cause can be derived and the action is attributed to some undefined aspect of the particular situation (Sjovall and Talk, 2004).

In conclusion, Kelley's model explores the dimensions that people use to locate the causality of a behavior or event, which can involve oneself or others (Eberly et al., 2011). The formation of causal attributions is governed primarily by information relating to three variables: distinctiveness, consistency, and consensus (Bemmels, 1991). As we know, Kelly's attribution theory is often referred to as classical attribution theory and is widely used by researchers, but some researchers suggest that Kelly's covariation model has some limitations. The most prominent is that it fails to distinguish the intentional from unintentional behaviors (Oghojafor, 2012).

2.2.4 Weiner's attribution theory (1980, 1985a, 1985b)

Like other attribution theorists, Weiner et al. (1972, 1974, 1986) also derived their work from Heider (1958). Weiner's research focused on achievement, he identified ability, effort, task difficulty, and luck as the most important factors affecting attributions, and their theoretical framework has become a major research paradigm (Oghojafor et al, 2012). In his opinion, effort and ability are considered as internal causes and conform to Kelley's "person" attribution, whereas luck and task difficulty are perceived as external causes and conform to Kelley's "entity" and "context" attributions (Dubinsky et al, 1989).

Moreover, Weiner (1974, 1986) raise a three-stage process that underlies an attribution: (1) the person must perceive or observe the behavior, (2) then the person must believe that the behavior was intentionally performed, and (3) then the person must decide if they believe the other person was forced to carry out the behavior (the cause is attributed to the situation) or not (the cause is attributed to the other person) (Oghojafor et al, 2012).

Furthermore, Weiner (1985a, 1986) proposed three dimensions as the basis of consumer causal attribution inferences. Researchers believe that consumers ascribe responsibility only after attributing causality (Anderson et al., 2009). It means that causal attribution theory support that consumers make inferences about the causes of failures in the delivery of services (Heider, 1958). And these inferences are made according to locus of causality, controllability and stability (Weiner, 1985a, 1986; Vázquez-Casielles et al., 2007).

Locus of control implies the identification of the responsible party (Anderson et al., 2009). According to Weiner (1979), Borkowski et al. (2003) proposed that when one tries to describe the processes of explaining events and the relating behavior, external or internal attributions can be given. To protect their ego, consumers tend to perceive that they are not responsible for failures (Hui and Toffoli, 2002) and they often attribute bad results to situational (or external causes), while attribution good results to their own abilities (or internal causes) (Ye, 2005; Vázquez-Casielles et al., 2007). That is, an external attribution assigns causality to an outside agent or force and claims that some outside force motivated the event. By contrast, an internal attribution assigns causality to factors within the person and claims that the person was directly responsible for the event (Borkowski et al., 2003).

The second factor is controllability, which refers to whether the person had the power to exert control over the events of the situation (Borkowski et al., 2003). Researchers believe that control attribution involves the consumers' beliefs about whether the firm could avoid a failure from occurring, or alternatively it is the situation that forces the firm to follow a certain course of action (Weiner, 1985a, 2000; Hui et al., 2006; Vázquez-Casielles et al., 2007). Therefore, controllability is the influence the various parties have over the incident and its resolution (Anderson et al., 2009). The greater the perception of service quality from the past is, the more likely consumers will attribute to the service organization who has high levels of competence and effort to avoid service failures (Narayandas 1998; Vázquez-Casielles et al., 2007). Namely, controllability contrast causes one can control, such as skill, efficacy, and from causes one cannot control, such as aptitude, mood, others' actions, and luck (Akpoyomare Oghojafor, 2012). When a service failure occurs in the context of high-quality past service performance, consumers tend to infer that the organization is highly competent and had little control over the failure, which otherwise would have been avoided (Hess et al., 2003; Vázquez-Casielles et al., 2007).

The third dimension is stability, meaning the extent to which a cause is viewed as temporary or predictable and permanent (Vázquez-Casielles et al., 2007). In brief, the stability dimension captures whether causes change over time or not (Akpoyomare Oghojafor, 2012), or whether the incident is likely to be repeated (Anderson et al, 2009). Moreover, Heider (1958) argued that consumers often use consistency principles to form attributions (Vázquez-Casielles et al., 2007). Stability of the cause is concerning with whether the behavior is consistent over time because of the individual's values and beliefs or because of outside elements such as rules or laws that would determine a person's behavior in the various situations (Borkowski et al., 2003). Specifically, Weiner (2000) consider that consumers are likely to attribute a current failure to unstable, rather than stable, causes when past experiences of service quality have been positive. Consumers who have experienced high-quality past service performance are less likely to make stable attributions when a failure occurs. It means that positive attitudes make consumers less tendency to attribute failures to stable causes, and they can be very beneficial for the organization (Hess et al. 2003; Bagozzi et al. 2002; Vázquez-Casielles et al., 2007). Oliver (1999) also states that consumers having cumulative quality of service experiences are likely to develop positive attitudes towards the service provider. However, an excellent service organization should have less tolerance for stable failures (Vázquez-Casielles et al., 2007). The reason is that customers will experience lower satisfaction when the cause of the service failure is perceived as stable (Casado and Mas 2002; Tsiros and Mittal 2000; Tsiros et al. 2004; O'Neill and Mattila 2004) and controllable (Oliver and DeSarbo, 1988; Vázquez-Casielles et al., 2007).

Based on the three dimensions, Weiner suggested that individuals explain their performance decisions by cognitively constructing their reality in terms of internal-external, controllable-uncontrollable, and stable-unstable factors (Borkowski et al., 2003). Generally, ability is considered a stable and uncontrollable cause; effort, an unstable and controllable cause. Task difficulty is generally regarded as a stable and controllable cause; luck, an unstable and uncontrollable cause (Dubinsky et al., 1989).

As noted, attribution theory is more concerned with the individual's cognitive perceptions than the underlying reality of events (Daley, 1996; Borkowski et al., 2003). Attribution theory is closely associated with the concept of motivation (Oghojafor et al., 2012). Outcome attribution theory proposed by Weiner et al. (1972) argue that, in a particular situation in which the observer is involved, the causal attribution to interpret an observer's own behavior toward an object can be made based on the priori beliefs in the generalizability of the object, the situation, and the person. People's behavioral consequences are used to measure the priori beliefs in the generalizability (Wang, 2008).

Kelley (1967, 1973) and Weiner et al.'s (1972) work in attribution theory have received empirical supports from several investigations (e. g. Deaux 1976; Harvey and Weary 1984; McArthur 1972; Pruitt and Insko 1980; Weiner, Russell, and Lerman 1979) and so provide the conceptual framework for other studies (Dubinsky et al., 1989). Such as Bem's Self-perception Theory and Shaver's Hybrid Attribution Theory (Mirsadeghi, 2013), these theories are skipped here because the contents are beside the cover of our study.

2.2.5　General model of the attribution field

It is well known that attribution theories are conducted and enjoy their greatest popularity (Johnson, 2006) primarily within social psychology (Kelley and Michela, 1980), and the focus has been the perceived causes of other persons' behavior. A parallel analysis has been made of the perceived causes of one's own behavior, and the third topic has concerned differences between other-perception and self-perception (Kelley and Michela, 1980). However, recognition of attribution theories in marketing and consumer research is great extent due to comprehensive reviews by Mizerski, Golden, and Kernan (1979) and Folkes (1988).

Attributions are the causal explanations that individuals use to interpret the world around them and adopt to their environment, especially when reacting to events viewed as important, novel, unexpected, and negative (Weiner, 1990; Martinko, Harvey, and Douglas, 2007; Eberly et al., 2011). Researchers believe that the term "attribution" has two primary meanings. The first one refers to explanations of behavior, such as answers to "why" questions; the second refers to inferences or ascriptions, such as inferring traits from behavior, ascribing blame to a person (Malle, 2011). What the two meanings have in common is a process of assigning: in attribution as explanation, a behavior is assigned to its cause; in attribution as inference, a quality or attribute is assigned to the agent based on an observed behavior (Malle, 2011). Kelley and Michela (1980) identified the study of perceived causation by the term "attribution theory", and defined attribution as the perception or inference of cause.

Despite the connection between these phenomena, they have distinct psychological characteristics (Hamilton, 1998; Hilton, Smith, and Kin, 1995; Malle, 2011). Kelley and Michela (1980) proposed a general model of attribution field as the basis of later researches.

As illustrated in Figure 2-1, attribution can be regarded as the mediating variable lying between its antecedents (e.g. information, beliefs, motivation) and consequences (e.g. behavior, affect, expectancy) (Bierhoff, 1989; Wang, 2008). Kelley and Michela (1980) consider that causal attributions are assumed to play a central role in human behavior in both cases. They constitute the person's understanding of the causal structure of the world and, therefore, are important determinants of his interaction with that world (Kelley and Michela, 1980).

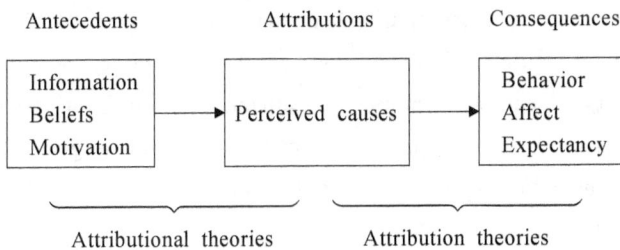

Figure 2-1 General model of the attribution field

Within this broad field, those investigators interested in cognitive processes have focused primarily on the antecedents-attributions link and those interested in the dynamics of behavior, on the attributions-consequences link. Thus, it is possible to draw a rough distinction between what might be called "attribution" and "attributional" research (Kelley and Michela, 1980).

Based on the general model of attribution field by Kelley and Michela (1980), Wang (2008) differentiate "attribution" and "attributional" research. Attribution theories can be used to investigate "what are the cause(s) of an event perceived by an individual?" In other words, the independent variables are the information, beliefs, and motivation while the dependent variables are the perceived causes. However, "attributional" theories aim to answer another type of question, like "what will an individual imply from the cause(s)?" Attributional theories involve with the attributional process, which is the effects of causal attribution on behaviors, affects, and expectancies (Bierhoff, 1989). In his opinion, the investigation on attribution and behavioral outcomes should follow such as route: observed event → attribution process (using attribution theories) → attribution of causality → attributional process (using attributional theories) → behavioral outcomes (Weiner, 2000; Wang, 2008).

Wang (2008) also suggests that attribution theories and attributional theories need to be properly applied in their corresponding stages to render sufficient and robust theoretical foundations to marketing research. Nevertheless, it should be recognized that attribution theories and attributional theories, by their names, are artificially divided. Some attribution theories, such as self-perception theory and outcome attribution theory, span over both attribution process and attributional process.

Moreover, Feldman (1981) proposed that there are two fundamental principles for attribution theory. The first one, covariation, states that the perceived cause of an event is found among the conditions varying with the occurrence of the event rather than among those that are unchanging (Shaver, 1975). Kelley (1967, 1971, 1972) made a detailed discussion of this principle. More detail can be found in 3.1. The second principle of attribution, discounting, states that an observer will discount any single causal explanation for a given behavior when more than one plausible cause is available (e. g. Kruglanski, 1970; Strickland, 1958; Feldman, 1981).

However, regarding the general model of attribution, Kelley and Michela (1980) pointed out the limitation of present research—they suggest that the present reviewers may be too close to the field to be objective enough in their evaluations and predictions. In most respects, the problems of the field are those of psychology in general, reflecting too few researchers spread too thinly over too many problems. Each question has received far less attention, in terms of number of paradigms and replications, than definitive and undoubtedly complex answer requires. Conceptually, on both attribution and attributional side in Figure 2-1, the theories are piecemeal and greatly in need of synthesis. Here again the problems are those of psychology in general, which lacks conceptual frameworks for meshing cognitive, motivational, and behavioral factors.

2.2.6 Summary

According to previous literature, attribution theories have their roots in Heider's description of the "naive psychologist", and enjoyed their greatest popularity in social psychology (Johnson, 2006). Attribution theories have also been widely used by marketing researchers (e. g. Folkes, 1984; Curren and Folkes, 1987; Wofford and Goodwin, 1990; Gooding andKinicki, 1995; Swanson, and Kelley, 2001).

The main attribution theories include: Heider's naive psychology (1958), Jones and associates' correspondence of inference work (Jones and Davis, 1965; Jones and McGillis, 1976), Kelley's theory of external attribution (1967, 1971, 1972, 1973), and the attribution research of Weiner (1980, 1985a, 1985b). However, following Heider's initial work, the most influential lines of attribution research is originated from Kelley and Weiner (Eberly et al., 2011). As a result, the theory itself is no longer a single-dimensional argument, but a collection of many attribution "theories" (Swanson and Kelley, 2001; Kelley and Michela, 1980).

Researchers attempt to find causal explanations for events and human behaviors based on these attribution theories (Huning, and Thomson, 2011). They define the term "attribution" as perceiving the causes of behavior (Weiner, 2000), it has two primary meanings: the first one refers to explanations of behavior, for example, answers to "why" questions; the second refers to inferences or ascriptions, for example, inferring traits from behavior, and ascribing blame to a person (Malle, 2011). Nevertheless, there is still consensus in these theories. As Kelley and Michela (1980) point out, it is commonly believed that people often explain behaviors in terms of its causes and the consequent interpretations would play an important role in the determination of reactions. Swanson and Kelley (2001) describe the collective attribution theories as concerning with the task of causal inferences and how the perception influences evaluations and behaviors.

These theories are beneficial to the study of consumer satisfaction because attributions intervene and exert influences on consumers after they have experienced a product-related outcome and prior to their re-purchase decision.

Kim et al. (2014) indicate that consumers create attributions when they compare their level of aspiration regarding a specific product / service and the initial performance of that product/service, and then question the basis of the result.

It is assumed that customers would proactively seek reasons for product and service failures (Weiner, 1985a, 2000; Anderson, Baggett and Widener, 2009). According to one of the mainstream attribution theories by Weiner (1992), individuals will interpret failure and success in a way that will enable them to retain a positive self-image. More exactly, individuals will explain their causes of failure and success in terms of three dimensions: locus of control (internal or external), stability (stable or unstable), and controllability (controllable or uncontrollable) (Oghojafor, 2012).

Locus of control is proposed originally by Rotter (1966). It refers to whether the cause of failure or success has something to do with the consumer or if it is about the production or distribution of the product (Folkes, 1984; Weiner, 1992). Stability refers to causes of failure or success that are either temporary (fluctuating over time) or permanent (remaining stable over time), and controllability describes if the cause of failure or success is controllable (choice is involved) or uncontrollable (constraints force a product outcome) (Kim et al., 2014).

Based on service failure and customer attribution literature, causal attribution is the "spontaneous" behavior by customers after they experience negative events. Thus, we propose the first hypotheses as:

H1: Service failure that customer experienced in hotel influences customer attribution.

H1a: Type of service failure that customer experienced in hotel influences customer attribution (to hotel, customer andenvironment).

H1b: Severity of service failure that customer experienced in hotel influences customer attribution (to hotel, customer and environment).

H1c: Stability and controllability of service failure influence customer attribution (to hotel, customer, and environment).

CHAPTER 3

LITERATURE REVIEW ON RECOVERY EXPECTATION, OBTAINED RECOVERY AND SATISFACTION AFTER RECOVERY

In almost all service markets, organizations strive to delight customers by providing products and services in good quality. Unfortunately, despite such efforts, organizations are not always able to delight customers (Beugre and Viswanathan, 2006). Sometimes mistakes would happen or things would go wrong (Yeop Yunus et al., 2012). Fisk et al. (1993) argue that it is impossible to secure 100% error-free service (Dong et al., 2008). Zero-defect service (Reichheld and Sasser, 1990) might be an unattainable goal beyond reach, no matter how rigorous the organization's service procedures and employee training or how advanced its technology (Hart, Heskett, and Sasser, 1990; Mattila, 1999).

Service failure represents a negative experience, both for the customer and the service provider. To decrease the negative impact of service failure, recovery strategies are often developed and implemented by organizations (Beugre and Viswanathan, 2006; Brady, 2000; Metz, 2000; Quick, 2000; Zhu et al., 2004). Service failures and recovery strategies also have long been the topics of keen interests to service researchers (e.g. Gronroos, 1988; McCollough, Berry, andYadav, 2000; Tax, Brown, and Chandrashekaran, 1998).

In this section, we introduce the concept of service recovery, antecedents of customer recovery expectation, recovery strategies that is provided by service provider (customer obtained from hotel), and some basic theories that are often used in service recovery research, including the justice theory, expectation-disconfirmation paradigm, matching theory, and attribution theories (See 2.2).

3.1 The concept of service recovery

Although service failures have clear negative impact, research would suggest that effective application of service recovery techniques may enable a company to maintain customer loyalty (Hoffman, Kelly, and Rotalsky 1995; Craighead et al., 2004).

Regarding the concept of service recovery, Grönroos (1988) define it as the actions taken by an organization in response to a service failure (Dong et al., 2008, Nikbin et al., 2010, Kelley et al., 1994). That is, all actions that an organization may take to correct a service failure are considered as service recovery efforts (Andreassen, 2001; Valenzuela et al., 2005).

Other researchers have similar definition concerning service recovery, for instance, Johnson and Hewa (1997) suggest that service recovery refers to actions of a service provider to mitigate and/or repair the damage to a customer that result from the provider's failure to deliver a service as is designed (Beugre and Viswanathan., 2006). Miller, et al. (2000) define service recovery as actions designed to resolve problems, change negative attitudes of dissatisfied consumers and ultimately keep these consumers. Wang et al. (2010) and Boshoff (2007) describe service recovery as the actions by a service firm to restore a customer to a state of satisfaction after a service failure and is an effective strategy to solve service failure and change customer attitudes from dissatisfied to satisfied (Craighead, Karwan and Miller, 2004; Hoffman, Kellyand Rotalsky, 1995; Fan et al., 2013). More specifically, Zemke (1993) define planned service recovery as: "... a thought-out, preplanned process for returning aggrieved customers to a state of satisfaction with the company or institution after a service ... has failed to live up to expectations or promised performance."

In brief, service recovery is composed by all activities and efforts the service provider may take to rectify, amend, compensate, and restore the loss(es) incurred after the failure (Dong et al., 2008) and restore a customer from a state of dissatisfaction to a state of satisfaction as much as possible (Hocutt et al., 1997).

According to these definitions by researchers, the goal of service recovery is to ensure customer satisfaction, maintain loyalty and avoid the harmful impact of service failure (Keaveney, 1995; Valenzuela et al., 2005; Craighead et al., 2004), as well as to appease dissatisfied customers and reduce potential damage to customer relationships through service recovery (Ha and Jang, 2009; Zemke, 1993; Nikbin et al., 2010). Normally, service providers have many generic options (recovery strategies) available to ameliorate service failure incidents (Craighead et al., 2004). Grönroos (1988) specify two dimensions to follow service recovery, namely outcome and process. The outcome, or technical dimension means what is done (tangible compensation), whereas the process, or functional dimension concerns how it is done (employee interaction with the customer). Both will impact customer perceptions of service recovery (Dong et al., 2008).

3.2   Theoretical foundation of service failure and recovery

According to previous literature, there are some dominant theoretical frameworks which have been widely used in service failure, recovery effort and satisfaction after recovery research. These are justice theory (e.g. Blodgett et al., 1997; Bowen et al., 1999; Conlon and Murray, 1996; Davidow, 2000, 2003; Karatepe, 2006, Liao, 2007; Miller et al., 2000 Smith et al., 1999; Tax et al., 1998; Wirtz and Mattila, 2004; Chan and Ngai, 2010), expectation-disconfirmation paradigm (e.g. Bearden and Teel 1983; Oliver 1980, 1981, 1989, 1993; Oliver and Bearden, 1985; Oliver and Burke, 1999; Swan and Trawick, 1981; Singh and Widing, 1991; McCollough et al., 2000) and attribution theory (see 2.2) (e.g. Folkes, 1984, 1988; Folkes et al., 1987; Oliver and DeSarbo, 1988; Anderson et al., 2009; Swanson and Kelley, 2001).

In addition, the "matching hypothesis" (Smith et al., 1999; Smith, Bolton and Wagner, 1999; Worsfold et al., 2007) is very important for the understanding of the relationship between service failures that customer experienced, customer recovery expectations and recovery strategies that customer obtained. It will be discussed in this section as well.

3.2.1   Justice theory
Justice theory has been used widely in service failure, customer satisfaction and recovery strategy researches (Goodwin and Ross 1992; Hocutt et al., 1997; Tax et al., 1998; McCollough and Berry, 2000; Boshoff, 2012). It is developed based on the classical equity theory (Adams, 1963, 1965).

3.2.1.1   Equity theory
Equity theory, proposed by Adams (1965), takes the position that individuals

in relational exchanges will seek out equity (balance). Based on the work of Adams (1963), a distinction has been made between negative inequity (under-benefitting), equity and positive inequity (over-benefitting). That is, both negative inequity (under-benefitting) and positive inequity (over-benefitting) will lead to some kind of distress (Boshoff, 2012; Kim et al., 2014).

In service failure and recovery literature, the equity theory has been widely used to explain consumer formation of satisfaction perceptions (Fisk, 1985; Oliver and Swan, 1989; Sanchez-Gutierrez et al., 2011; Lii et al., 2013), and understanding customer reactions to service failures and subsequent recovery management (Blodgett et al., 1997; Hoffman and Kelley, 2000; Miller et al., 2000; Tax et al., 1998; Robbinsand and Miller, 2004).

Specifically, researchers have found a relationship between equity and consumer satisfaction (Oliver and Swan, 1989). Andreassen (2000) proposes that equity or inequity affect the satisfaction or dissatisfaction of those who are sensitive to this phenomenon. Satisfaction or dissatisfaction judgment is believed to be formed as a summary of equity/inequity of one's own outcome relative to the other party's outcome, given input (Andreassen, 2000). It means that equity judgment is based on two steps: (1) the consumer compares his outcome to input; (2) he performs a relative comparison of this to the other exchange party.

Thus, researchers believe that consumer satisfaction is positively related to consumers' perceived fairness (Clemmer and Schneider, 1996; Oliver and Swan, 1989; Wang et al., 2010). However, an interesting finding is that consumers prefer to be differentiated from others in service. The degree to which the outcome is seen to be a result of unbiased policy versus a special favor had an impact on customer satisfaction. It is possible that consumer perceive an outcome more favorably so far as the ratio of inputs to outputs is in their favor. That is, individuals are more likely to accept, even prefer inequity when the result is to their advantages (Sparks and McColl-Kennedy, 1998).

The limitation of the equity theory is that only focuses on the outcome, but ignores procedural and interactional. Yet consumers clearly have more than sole focus on results. Due to this shortcoming, the justice theory has replaced the concept of equity theory.

3.2.1.2 Justice theory

Justice theory adopts the foundations of equity theory. In this theory, researchers have suggested customers' perceived justice is a multi-dimensional concept (Greenberg, 1996), and plays a statistically significant role in shaping customer satisfaction after service failure and recovery (Sabharwal et al., 2010).

Colquitt (2001) proposes that there are four distinct dimensions of justice being generally evaluated in a service recovery context: procedural, the process used to resolve the problem; the result of the recovery process; the manner and the interaction between the operator and complainant in dealing with the problem; and the candid communication with the complainant (Chan and Ngai, 2010).

However, most researchers suggest that when failure happens, customers are looking for perceived justice consisting of three components—distributive justice, procedural justice, and interactional justice (e.g. Adams, 1963; Greenburg, 1990; Tax and Brown, 1998; Gonzalez et al., 2010). Obviously, they classify the informational dimension into the interactive dimension.

More specifically, it means that customer evaluate fairness with the service failure and service recovery by three dimensions: distributive, procedural, and interactional justice (Nikbin et al., 2010).

Distributive justice, proposed by Adams (1965), focuses on the perceived fairness of the outcome of the service encounter (Homans, 1961). Distributive justice means the consumer's perception of what he or she receives as the outcome of the service recovery process (McColl-Kennedy and Sparks, 2003), such as a free drink voucher for a slow meal service in a restaurant (Wang et al., 2010).

Procedural justice, proposed by Lind and Tyler (1988), refers to the perceived fairness of the process, which is used to rectify the service failure. In the service context, procedural justice which is the actual process that is applied by the service provider to resolve the problem. Therefore, it emphasizes on the process more than the outcome (Smith, et al., 1999).

Interactional justice, proposed by Bies and Moag (1986), concentrates on the perceived fairness of the means the customer is treated throughout the service encounter. Interactional justice, is defined as the ways used to deal with service failure by and between consumer and service provider. Examples of interactional justice could be whether the service provider shows sensitivity, empathy, compassion, dignity, and respect to customers in the service failure or not (Sparks and Mccoll-Kennedy, 2001; Wang et al., 2010). Tax et al. (1998) believe that justice theory has been applied to understand service recovery from the consumer perspective in the interpersonal service context (Robertson et al., 2012).

Previous research has regarded service failures and recovery efforts as losses and gains, assuming that consumer satisfaction will be improved if perceived justice is restored during the recovery process (e. g. McColl-Kennedy and Sparks, 2003; Smith, Bolton, and Wagner, 1999; Li, Fock, and Mattila, 2012). According to justice theory, a systematic assessment of effective recovery actions would involve active knowledge of the customer's satisfaction with the recovery option itself, the recovery process (e. g. complaint procedures, time), and interpersonal issues (e.g. empathy, courtesy, and professionalism), throughout the recovery process (Maxham and Netemeyer 2002; Tax and Brown 1998; Gonzalez et al., 2010). Researchers believe that deploying recovery efforts that meet distributive justice standard without the consideration of customer procedural and interactional justice needs may still result in customer defections (Blodgett, Hill, and Tax, 1997; Tax and Brown, 1998).

Overall, justice theory has been mainly adopted in explaining how customers evaluate service providers' reactions to service failure/recovery (Nikbin et al., 2010).

On one hand, recent researches in the marketing literature have identified perceived justice as a crucial concept in explaining how customer evaluate the response of an organization in dealing with a service failure (e.g. De Matos et al., 2009; Hoffman and Kelley, 2000; Mattila, 2001; Mattila and Cranage, 2005; Shapiro and NiemanGonder, 2006; Lii, Pant and Lee, 2012). Konovsky (2000) also argues that justice theory is a useful framework for situations characterized by conflict (Hibbert et al., 2012).

On the other hand, justice theory has been widely adopted in the study of the effectiveness of service recovery strategies (activities) and post-recovery behavior (consequences) (e. g. Chan and Ngai, 2010; Wirtz and Mattila, 2004; Wang et al., 2010), to explain why consumers consider particular service recovery strategies more or less favorably (Hibbert et al., 2012). It is argued that recovery efforts (e.g. compensation, promptness) enhance awareness of fairness, post-complaint satisfaction, and favorable customer behavior (Davidow 2003; Smith et al. 1999; Gelbrich, 2010). Most of these studies reach an agreement that customers are more likely to continue doing business with a company if they are satisfied with the service recovery (Andreassen, 2001; Smith and Bolton, 1998; Beugre and Viswanathan, 2006). Similarly, Tax et al. (1998) report positive influences of customers' justice evaluations on satisfaction, trust, and commitment after a service complaint experience (Dong et al., 2008).

In brief, justice theory framework has prevailed due to its explanation on the way that customers evaluate service providers' reactions to service failure / recovery (e.g. Nikbin et al., 2010; Clemmer, 1993; Tyler, 1994; Sparks et al., 1998). The service failure and recovery literature focuses on justice theory as a statistically significant way to explain consumers' perceptions of service failures and subsequent recovery efforts as well as the connection between the service recovery and post-recovery satisfaction (Holloway et al., 2005). Researchers have examined the impact of service failure and recovery on perceptions of justice and customer satisfaction (Andreassen, 2001; Maxham and Netemeyer, 2003; Smith and Bolton, 1998).

The drawbacks of the justice theory lie in the standards that customers use to judge. Different from the expectation-disconfirmation paradigm which compares expectation with perceived outcome, equity is a relative dimension (Andreassen, 2000). The consumers compare their outcome to input and compare their outcome to the outcome of other exchange parties. Obviously, it is only related to the subjective judgment of the individual. Whether it is the investment and compensation of oneself or others is a personal feeling, and people always overestimate their own input and underestimate the input of others.

Commonly, even if the results are fair, the process is fair, and the interaction is fair; if it does not meet customer expectation, customers are still not satisfied. For example, due to weather delays, even if all customers have the same result, the process and communication, and it is still impossible to satisfy the guests. The next time they take a flight, they will naturally try to avoid the airlines with high delay rate.

Since the justice theory ignores the differences between individuals, and it is difficult to explain some questions like the same recovery strategies and effort, for example, why some customers are satisfied, and some customers are unlikely to accept, such questions may be related to the customer's original expectations and attribution. Thus, the expectation-disconfirmation paradigm will be introduced in the following sections to sort this confusion.

3.2.2   Disconfirmation paradigm

The expectation-disconfirmation paradigm is one of the widely used and accepted theory in the consumer behavior literature (Johnston, 1995; Kim et al., 2012). The expectancy-disconfirmation model consists of three constructs: expectations, service performance, and disconfirmation (Churchill and Surprenant, 1982).

Hereon, expectations are most typically defined as the predicted level of performance, or what a consumer anticipates will occur (Oliver, 1993; Parasuraman et al., 1994; Bolton and Drew, 1991; Zeithaml et al., 1993). A review of the literature indicates that many expectation categories have been suggested, including experience-based norms (Woodruff et al., 1983), ideal, minimum tolerable, and deserved expectations (Miller, 1997), normative expectations and desired expectations (Swan et al., 1982; Spreng and Olshavsky, 1992; Yeop-Yunus, 2012). Kim et al. (2014) suggest that consumer expectations include two broad categories: ideal product performance and expected product performance. Ideal product performance pertains to optimal product performance; it can also refer to what consumers believe performance "can be" in the future (Tse and Wilton, 1988). Expected product performance refers to the most likely performance of a product; it is the most frequently employed pre-consumption comparison standard in consumer satisfaction research (Kim et al., 2014).

According to this model, confirmation (leaving the consumer in a neutral state) occurs when the service or recovery is performed as expected. Disconfirmation (including positive disconfirmation and negative disconfirmation) occurs when the service or recovery performance does not meet prior expectations. Specifically, the concept of disconfirmation arises from discrepancies between prior expectations and actual performance (Churchill and Surprenant, 1982; Oliver, 1997). Positive disconfirmation occurs when performance surpasses expectations, which usually promotes the level of customer satisfaction. Negative disconfirmation (e. g. service failure, recovery failure) occurs when performance is below expectations (Binter et al., 1990; Kelly and Davis, 1994), such a result usually leads to dissatisfaction (Oliver, 1997).

Generally, the more negative the disconfirmation is, the stronger the dissatisfaction is, whereas the more positive the disconfirmation is, the stronger the satisfaction is (McCollough et al., 2000). It means that customer satisfaction is directly influenced by expectations, performance, and disconfirmation (Oliver, 1980; Oliver and Bearden, 1983). Thus, the higher the initial expectation is, the more difficult it becomes to satisfy a customer (Yeop-Yunus, 2012).

In brief, the expectation-disconfirmation model (Oliver, 1980, 1997) lies in the proposition that customer (dis)satisfaction is formed through (dis)confirmation, for instance, the gap between expectations and performance. Based on this model, one can assume that when a customer's perceived service/recovery performance is roughly matched by their expectations, the customer would be satisfied. In contrast, when the perceived service / recovery performance is far "better or worse" than expectations, the customer could possibly be delighted or dissatisfied (Kim et al., 2012) (See Figure 3-1).

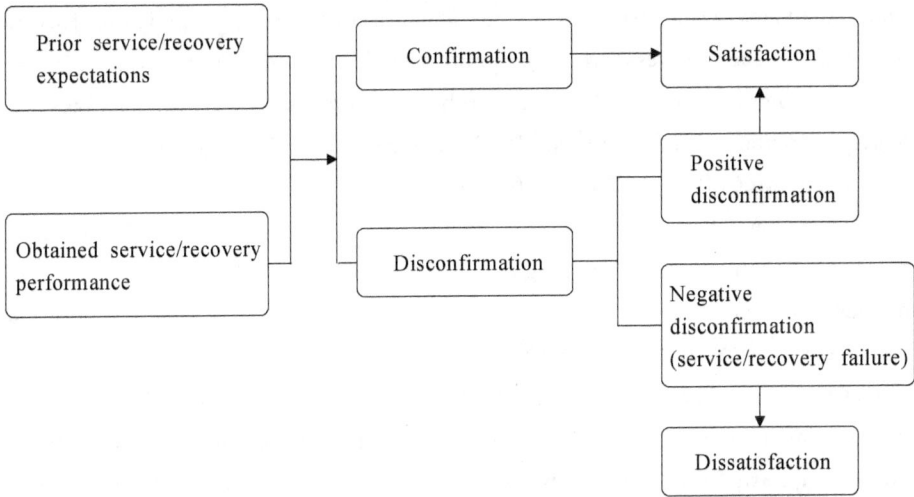

Figure 3-1   The expectation-disconfirmation model (Oliver, 1980, 1997, etc.)

In addition, Vázquez-Casielles et al. (2012) propose that researchers need to pay attention to the application of the expectancy-disconfirmation paradigm. There are two sets of disconfirmations in failure / recovery encounters. Service encounter satisfaction is decided not only by the disconfirmation of service performance, but also by the disconfirmation of recovery performance (Smith and Bolton, 1998).

In the first phase of service delivery, consumers keep pre-consumption expectations of service performance, and compare the perceived performance with their expectations. In the recovery phase of service encounters, recovery expectations have been held to be the standard against the evaluation of recovery performance (e. g. Kelly and Davis, 1994; Oliver, 1981; Singh and Widing, 1991).

Singh and Widing (1991) suggest that service encounter satisfaction should be decided by consumers' perception of recovery efforts and their recovery expectations. It means, consumers assess recovery actions against their expectations of appropriate recovery efforts, which results in a second disconfirmation judgment (Oliver, 1981). This is termed as "secondary satisfaction" and is combined with the original dissatisfaction in order to determine customers' overall satisfaction toward a service encounter (Ma, 2012).

In this case, recovery expectations are quite important from a motivational perspective (McCollough et al., 2000) and should be modeled as a separate factor for service encounter satisfaction (Ma, 2012). For instance, many customers do not complain to the service provider about a dissatisfying experience. However, those who do seek redress are often motivated by recovery expectations (referred to in the complaining literature as probability or likelihood of success) (e. g. Blodgett, Granbois, and Walters, 1993; Hirschman, 1970; Richins 1983, 1987; Singh, 1990; McCollough et al., 2000).

In addition, there are several theories that are closely related to the expectation-disconfirmation paradigm, which are helpful for us to better understand the model.

3.2.2.1 Comparison level theory

LaTour and Peat (1979) suggest that the expectancy-disconfirmation model puts too much emphasis on the impact of service provider claims and not enough emphasis on other key sources of expectations, such as previous consumption experiences, interactions with other consumers. Therefore, they attempt to conceptualize consumer satisfaction through Thibaut and Kelly's comparison level theory (1959).

According to comparison level theory, consumer satisfaction with service or product performance is determined by the gap between the outcome and an identified standard of comparison. Outcomes above the comparison level reflect satisfaction whereas outcomes below the comparison level reflect dissatisfaction. The basic notion of this theory is that comparison level itself is determined by "the average of salient outcomes for the same or similar interactions that one has experienced or is aware of" (LaTour and Peat, 1979). There are three determinants of comparison level: (1) outcomes a consumer has directly experienced, (2) outcomes other consumers experienced with similar products or services, and (3) outcomes promised by the service provider (Kim et al., 2014).

This study is considered as a supplement of expectation-disconfirmation paradigm. Performance is determined by service provider, and expectation is determined by customer's experience and knowledge. Especially in service recovery process, the customer recovery expectation largely decides the recovery effectiveness.

3.2.2.2 The experience–based–norm framework

According to this theory, the standard of comparison based on consumers' experiences expands to similar situation, service and product, not just the same thing. Researchers consider that under the expectancy-disconfirmation model, expectations are based on consumers' experiences with the focal brand. However, turning to norms as a standard of comparison, it expands the base of experience to include other brands (Cadotte et al., 1987). Kim et al. (2014) interpret this view as consumers' experiences may not be isolated to focal brand, instead, these experiences may include a brand unit, other units of the same brand, other similar brands, or a whole collection of products competing for the same need.

For example, if a consumer books a room in a Sheraton hotel, the expectancy-disconfirmation framework would assume the consumer's expectation is created from previous consumption experiences with the same hotel product and service. In contrast, with the experience-based-norm framework, it would be assumed that consumer expectations are established from the cumulative total of previous consumption experiences with all similarly luxury hotel stayed by the consumer. Such purchases might include Hilton, Hyatt, and Marriot hotel, and other luxury brands. Thus, the consumer's expectation prior to stay in Sheraton hotel will be based on the average performance of all previous luxury hotel brands booked and stayed by the consumer.

This framework is also a possible extension for the expectation-disconfirmation paradigm. It indicates that customer expectation is influencesd by their knowledge of a specific service industry. Previous literature has suggested that customer expectation is influencesd by various dimensions, and customers tend not to identify it one by one. Therefore, comparison level theory and experience-based-norm framework as parts of expectation-disconfirmation paradigm, are more appropriate in applying on this study. In brief, expectation-disconfirmation paradigm is the basic theory of these frameworks.

3.2.2.3 Value–percept disparity theory

The value-percept disparity model developed by Westbrook and Reilly (1983) is considered to be a special type of norm-based theory. This theoretical perspective suggests that consumer satisfaction is an emotional response generated by a cognitive-evaluative process in which the perceptions of an object are compared to a consumer's values, needs, wants, or desires (Kim et al., 2014).

Although expectations under the expectancy-disconfirmation framework indicate beliefs about what will happen in the future, what is expected in a product may not correspond to what is wanted or desired in that product (Spreng et al., 1996). Essentially, "the greater the disparity between perceptions of the product and values, the greater the dissatisfaction predicted by this theory, conversely, the smaller the value-percept disparity, the greater the satisfaction" (Yi, 1989). Furthermore, Westbrook and Reilly propose that consumer satisfaction do not directly come from a logical comparison of product performance to a specified evaluation standard, instead, it can also be viewed as an emotional response (1983).

The connection between perceived value and customer satisfaction has been discussed in the service literature. It is contended that value has a direct impact on how satisfied customers are with a supplier and that satisfaction depends on value (Ravald and Grönroos, 1996). Zeithaml (1988) suggests that customers who perceive that they received "value for money" are more satisfied than customers who do not think so. Other researchers also agree with the positive influences of perceived value on customer satisfaction (e.g. Fornell et al., 1996). They suggest that consumer satisfaction is generally explained to be a post-consumption evaluation dependent on perceived quality and value (Hu et al., 2009).

It is assumed that value-percept disparity influences customer satisfaction. This argument will be tested in the context of Chinese customer in this study. And the motive for targeting the Chinese market is that there may be some difference compared with western customers.

To summarize, the limitation of value-percept disparity theory is the disability to form a constant and clear view on the determinants of customer expectation. And in the study of service failure and recovery, researchers tend to have differentiated focus on the three constructive elements in the model, which are performance, expectation, and disparity. Clearly, performance has gained more attention in hoping to achieve a surplus of customer expectation by employing different service and recovery strategies and efforts. Also, they perceive customer expectation as standards and try to increase satisfaction level by all means. However, the research attention dispatched to customer expectation on the recovery process is relatively minimal. And within the limited amount of researches, there is only an interest in the expectation prior to failure; whereas the expectation prior to service recovery is too little and scattered. Hence, the determinants of customer expectation are too complex to have a universal agreement. The preconditions of service recovery expectation will be elaborated in 3.3.1.

3.2.3 Matching hypothesis

Research by Smith et al. (1999) indicates that customers who have experienced service failure and recovery encounters are more willing to receive those resources that match the type of loss that they suffered. In other words, they choose to receive recovery resources that "match" the type of failure they experience in "amounts" that are commensurate with the magnitude of the failure. Smith et al. (1999) propose this as the "matching hypothesis" (Smith et al., 1999; Smith, Bolton and Wagner, 1999; Worsfold et al., 2007). Worsfold et al. (2007) describe the hypothesis in a more specific way. That is, if customers experience loss in finance, they hope they will be compensated financially. If service failure takes social resources from the customers (e. g. customer is inconvenienced), customers prefer to receive psychological, social, or symbolic recognition as the compensation (Worsfold et al., 2007). To sum up, the recovery resources received by the customers should "match" the "type of failure" they experienced. Roschk and Gelbrich (2014) also examine this hypothesis by proposing a new classification for both compensation and failure type and they have found three major results. One is that the strongest recovery effect is generally observed when compensation represents a resource similar to the failure it is supposed to offset. It is consistent with "matching hypothesis".

On the other hand, the recovery resources they received should "match" the magnitude of service recovery (i. e. the extent of tangibles provided). In this case, it could bring higher consumer satisfaction because the consumer believes that the service provider should go "extra mile" to provide fair restitution for them (Wang et al., 2010). However, if the consumer perceives that the compensation from the service provider is lower or less than what they expect (based on the magnitude of service failure), consumers will be dissatisfied and "double deviation" occurs. This is in line with the basic notion of expectation disconfirmation theory, defining satisfaction as exceeding customers' expectation (Andreassen, 2000; Oliver and Swan, 1989; Wang et al., 2010).

Consequently, "the matching hypothesis" directly affects the expectation of service recovery. Service provider can produce substantial damage to customers' satisfaction, loyalty, and retention when their responses to service failures do not match what customers expect after unpleasant experiences (Craighead et al., 2004). Furthermore, just as Craighead et al. (2004) postulated in their study, responding the "needs" of a maltreated customer with the correct service recovery activities is not only an inseparable part in current service management practice, but it is also in accordance with conceptual models of strategic fit.

However, Craighead et al. (2004) also questioned the result by others since the authors believed that the matching of recovery efforts has led to conflicting outcomes. For example, many of the studies have tried to explain the effectiveness of the "how" of service recovery (for example, emphasizing apologies and empathy), yet many of these studies have explicitly emphasized on the need for more tangible compensation and immediate assistance provided by the organization (e.g. Bitner, Booms, and Tetreault 1990; Smith, Bolton, and Wagner 1999; Craighead et al., 2004). Some studies (e. g. Levesque and McDougall, 2000) propose that there may be a general ineffectiveness of "a standard assistance and compensation strategy", but Craighead et al. (2004) have noted such circumstances only exist in the cases of the loyal customers and only on certain dimensions. Miller et al. (2000) find that the fair fix may be the vital element, irrespective of what else is in the recovery portfolio, and so on. Therefore, in the study of service failure and recovery, the "matching hypothesis" needs to be further tested.

3.3   Customer recovery expectation and obtained recovery from service provider

According to the expectation-disconfirmation paradigm and matching hypothesis, the effects of failure recovery is determined by the gap between customer expectation and actual performance. A high level of "matching" would usually lead to better effects but it is noted that customers expect exceeding compensation. So, the service provider needs to know the real standard of customer expectation to gain real satisfaction on recovery.

In a word, there are two elements for practitioners to consider for raising the level of satisfaction after recovery: customer expectation and recovery efforts (the recovery strategy, which is also the actual compensation gained by customer).

3.3.1 Customer recovery expectation

Service recovery involves activities that are performed when customers find initial service delivery behaviors falling short of the customer's tolerance (e.g. Zeithaml, Berry and Parasuraman, 1993; Kelley et al., 1994). The period from the start of service failure to the awareness of service failure by the service provider is called the pre-recovery phase and may last from a few seconds to several weeks or even months. It is during this time that customers create their expectations on service recovery based on several key variables that are in place prior to service recovery efforts (Craighead et al., 2004).

Craighead et al. suggest that these key variables are antecedents to recovery efforts and, therefore, have an important impact on post-event satisfaction and loyalty. These antecedents revolve around customer loyalty, customer expectations, and situational factors. Other researchers also suggest that the antecedents of service recovery activities such as the degree of consumer's loyalty, perceived service quality and severity of failure all have an impact on the success of recovery activities and consumer satisfaction (Bitner, 1990; Kelley and Davis, 1994; Miller, Craighead and Karwan, 2000; Wang et al., 2010).

Moreover, in addition to consumer-perceived service quality, customer organizational commitment, severity of failure and service guarantee are identified as antecedents of service recovery expectations (Craighead et al., 2004; Miller et al., 2000), Hess et al. (2003) also find that attribution of service failure affects consumer recovery expectations (Ma, 2012).

The following paragraphs provide details on the specific antecedents focused upon the literature.

3.3.1.1 Severity and type of failure

Service failure is likely to be a key factor determining customer's perceptions of the company and satisfaction levels (Bitner, Booms and Tetreault 1990; Sparks et al., 1998). Service failure severity refers to the customer's perceived intensity of a service problem (Weun et al., 2004; Matos, Vieira and Veiga, 2012), namely, the magnitude of a service failure. Kelley et al. (1994) and Hoffman et al. (1995) have proposed that the magnitude or gravity of the service failure may directly influence the customer's satisfaction (Mirsadeghi, 2013). Furthermore, they suggest that the consequences of service recovery efforts may also be subject to the customer's perception of the criticality of the consumption experience (Ostrom and Iacobucci, 1995; Sundaram, Jurowski and Webster, 1997; Webster and Sundram, 1998; Mirsadeghi, 2013).

The study by Smith and Bolton (1998) indicates that service failure can become a means for customers to update their level of cumulative satisfaction. Cumulative satisfaction is the primary antecedent of customer loyalty (Gelbrich and Roschk, 2011). Negative experience caused by service failure might, for instance, impacts future assessments of satisfaction by customers (Matos, Vieira and Veiga, 2012). In line with this, Kelley and Davis' (1994) study focuses on predictive service recovery expectations because previous research demonstrates that expectations are subject to updating after each service encounter (Boulding et al. 1993; Kelley et al., 1994). Consequently, service failure experiences should have an impact on the subsequent predictive expectations associated with the corresponding service recovery (Kelley et al., 1994). In addition, researchers also find that the magnitude of a service failure can vary (KelleyandDavis, 1994) depending on individual and situational factors, and understanding the seriousness of a failure is critical in determining an appropriate recovery strategy (Hart et al., 1990; Mattila, 1999).

Generally, researchers suggest that the more intense or severe the service failure is, the greater the customer's perceived loss is. Research shows that failure severity has a negative impact on customer satisfaction and re-patronage intentions (Smith and Bolton, 1998; Matos, Vieira and Veiga, 2012). The results from Smith and Bolton's (1998) experimental study also indicate that it might be more difficult for service organizations to make an effective recovery when the failure is perceived as serious rather than minor by the consumer (Mattila, 1999). Therefore, researchers propose that the more serious the failure is, the more difficult it would be to raise the customer's level of post-recovery satisfaction to that of no failure (Mattila, 1999). Furthermore, Hoffman, Kelley and Rotalsky (1995) examine service failures occurring in restaurants and confirm a linear correlation between service failure ratings and service recovery ratings (Mattila, 1999). Their results demonstrate that high scores on a failure rating variable (scale of minor to major) are associated with lower scores on a recovery rating (poor to good scale) and a retention percentage variable (Craighead et al., 2004).

Therefore, magnitude of failure correlates negatively with post-recovery satisfaction. Through recovery efforts, customers may be willing to forgive minor mistakes but not serious ones. When a customer considers a service failure to be serious, it might be extremely difficult to regain his confidence. In these instances, prevention might be better than cure (Mattila, 1999).

As discussed, researchers tend to believe the severity of service failure affects customer expectation of recovery. On the other side, it can be predicted that the type of failure would also have an influence on recovery expectation. According to equity theory and matching hypothesis, customers would like to have compensation that matches their losses, and feel fairly treated. Thus, if it is a monetary loss, they would expect financial compensations; if it is related to emotion or esteem, they would naturally expect a decent apology, explaination and respect. Roschk and Gelbrich (2014) have researched a lot regarding this subject, suggesting a match between the type of service failure and recovery strategy would result in favorable outcomes. This is because customers have expectation for recovery in accordance with the type of failure, and such recovery expectation usually matches the failure type, perfectly conforming to the "matching hypothesis" (See 3.2.3).

Smith and Bolton (1998) also believe that the serious, core-attributed, systematic failure would give customers high recovery expectations which is more difficult to recover losses. They did not take the severity of failure and its type apart into separate constructs, claiming the two factors are both vital in service recovery. Thus, the study believes the severity of failure and its type are both important preconditions to service recovery.

3.3.1.2   Quality image (e.g. brand, hotel star-rating)

Increased customer expectations about service indicates that the service provider should not only serve the customer in the service process but is also expected to solve customers' service relevant problems (e.g. Brown et al., 1994; Pitt and Jeantrout, 1994; Sparks et al., 1998). Kelley and Davis (1994) reveal that those customers who valued service quality highly also owned the highest expectations with regard to service recovery. Their reason is that organizations that provide a high level of quality would also deliver a high level of recovery (Craighead et al., 2004). Specifically, Craighead et al. (2004) divide service quality into high quality and lower quality. Research requires the respondents to answer how they had chosen their specific provider in a certain fixed scenario. If the response is related to reputation, personal experience, or recommendation, the company is regarded as high quality company; if they responded sale, convenience or "no other choices available", the company is perceived as lower quality company (Craighead et al., 2004).

Therefore, brand, hotel star-rating, and the cumulative experiences of staying would affect the customer's recovery expectations. For example, the higher the star-rating a hotel possesses, the higher the customer's expectation of recovery would be or the better the brand is, the higher the customer's recovery expectations would be. Thus, we define this effect as "quality image", such as brand image, the image from industry recognition (star-rating).

3.3.1.3   Provider–customer relationship

Generally, recovery has been defined as an organization's response when it encounters service failure (Grönroos, 1988). Obviously, the customer's role is less valued in the recovery process (Dong et al., 2008). Given the important role service recovery plays in securing customer satisfaction, lacking the research on customer participation in service recovery results in a major gap in the field of marketing literature (Dong et al., 2008). Thus, some researchers such as Kim et al. (2012) attempted to verify the moderating roles of the customer-firm relationship with respect to customers' responses to service failure and recovery. The findings indicate that in general, high relational customers tend to have high recovery expectations, at the same time, respond more favorably to recovery efforts than those of low relational customers in both low and high recovery situations (Kim et al., 2012). They suggest that high APR (a priori relationship between customer and provider) customers who have been highly satisfied and held high revisit intentions are likely to have high recovery expectations.

Similarly, many of potential positive outcomes resulting from effective service recovery have been identified by previous researches (e.g. Fisk et al., 1993; Tax et al., 1998; Zeithaml and Bitner, 2003). According to these literature, the "customer's role" or provider-customer relationship is often presented as customer loyalty, customer organizational commitment, customer participation, and so on.

Many studies agree that customer loyalty is a factor affecting consumer recovery expectations (e.g. Kelley and Davis, 1994; Hess et al., 2003; Miller et al., 2000; Craighead et al., 2004). That is, the higher degree of loyalty customers possess, the higher expectations for service recovery they would have (Craighead et al., 2004).

Customer organizational commitment is defined as customers' identification with and involvement in an organization (Kelley and Davis, 1994; Ma, 2012). Commonly, researchers agree that customer organizational commitment is a factor that affects customer recovery expectations (Craighead et al., 2004; Hess et al., 2003; Kelley and Davis, 1994; Miller et al., 2000). Some customers have a strong commitment to an organization and they will expect to maintain the relationship. They are more inclined to regard the organizations' impressive responses to service failures as a manner to maintain the equity of relationship between customers and organization (Ma, 2012).

Dong et al. (2008) provide the concept of co-created service recovery, defining customer participation in service recovery as "the degree to which the consumer is involved in taking actions to respond to a service failure". Dong et al. (2008) believe that service recovery is an interactional process in which consumers can actively contribute to achieving service recovery outcomes. These evidences suggest that consumer participation in recovery does influences service recovery outcomes. Being consistent with this, researchers propose that consumer participation in service recovery will exert influences on customers' satisfaction with service recovery (Hibbert et al., 2012).

Consequently, customers who are involved in the service recovery process are more likely to have high levels of satisfaction when it comes to the service recovery (Dong et al., 2008). Higher cumulative satisfaction would lead customers to have higher recovery expectations. High expectations are more preferable than low expectations for service firms to attract customers (Kim et al., 2012). It is because a high expectation on recovery would make customers feel safe even when service failure occurs, that hotels are able to repay the losses. Therefore, out of this consideration, customers would choose hotels with sound guarantees. For example, Guests will choose hotels that often offer very generous compensation when a service failure occurs. Because they expect that they will get such compensation if there is a similar service failure during the stay. In terms of a priori revisit intention, more committed customers tend to have higher expectations for service recovery (Kelley and Davis, 1994) due to their higher expectations of relationship continuity (Hess et al., 2003).

Service recovery research has given valuable insights that can be applied to service recovery when service provider-consumer relations have been disrupted because of problematic consumer contributions. Various types of expectations have been highlighted in the literature (Ojasalo, 2001). Nevertheless, previous researches have rarely examined the role of this key factor in customer attribution and obtained recovery (Hibbert et al., 2012).

3.3.1.4 Service guarantee

Service guarantees have been identified as one of the antecedents of service recovery expectations in the studies of Craighead et al. (2004) and Miller et al. (2000). Although developing and implementing a guarantee will lead to high costs, it has been suggested that the benefits gained outweigh the costs in the long-term (Hart, 1988; Wirtz and Kum, 2001; Wong, Tsaur and Wang, 2009). Service guarantees comprise a promise to a customer (marketing), the delivery of a service to the customer (operations), and actions taken to appease the customer for the service failures (recovery) (Baker and Collier, 2005). In other words, a service guarantee is defined as an extension of a product warranty in the background of service settings (Wong, Tsaur and Wang, 2009). It provides what the consumers can expect (the promise or coverage) and the actions the company will take when it fails to deliver what is promised before (the payout) (Hart, Schlesinger and Maher, 1992; McDougall et al., 1998; Wong, Tsaur and Wang, 2009).

In addition, although customers would expect to be compensated, consistent with the advertised guarantee payout, it is likely that they would also expect the organization to correct the service failure. Callan and Moore (1998) propose that the guarantee offered by the organization will give consumers an expectation of a certain level of service, and when the service fails, the promise of a payout and / or that the service will strengthen their beliefs that their complaints will bring about a positive outcome for them (Robertson et al. 2012). Commonly, the organization will commit resources to fulfill the promise they have guaranteed (Herbig and Milewicz, 1996).

Service guarantees have won considerable support and recognition from practitioners and academics for it is regarded as a unique strategy to reduce consumer-perceived risk effectively, both service failure and its negative consequences (McDougall, Levesque and VanderPlaat, 1998; Wirtz and Kum, 2001; Wirtz, Kum and Lee, 2000; Wong, Tsaur and Wang, 2009).

Specifically, two main types of service guarantee are attribute-specific and full-satisfaction guarantees (Kashyap, 2001; McDougall et al., 1998; Wirtz and Kum, 2001). The results of previous researches indicate that it does great benefit to a higher-price service to employ a full-satisfaction guarantee, given the consumers' higher expectation of service quality and willingness to buy, and the lower perceived performance risk. In contrast, for lower-price services, an attribute-specific guarantee is advisable due to consumers' higher expected service quality and willingness to buy, and the lower perceived financial risk (Wong, Tsaur and Wang, 2009).

Consumers are inclined to find salient information from the environment so that their risk perceptions can be reduced in these remote contexts. As such, service guarantees can make it tangible that recovery will be forthcoming (Robertson et al. 2012).

Moreover, Liden and Skalen (2003) cite many of companies who have claimed that they have successfully integrated guarantees into their service offerings, such as Radisson SAS, Domino's Pizza, and Lands End Hotels. The conditions for these endeavors are that well-understood service guarantees are designed to help to create a positive and reasoned expectation for the benefit of the customers (Craighead et al., 2004). Hart (1988) has shown with service guarantees of this type how companies can structure service processes, correct errors in service delivery, and build customer loyalty in a better way.

3.3.1.5 Attribution of service failure

Researchers find that consumer recovery expectations (Hess et al., 2003) and post-recovery behavior (Ma, 2012) would be impacted by consumer attribution of service failure.

According to previous literature, attribution theory is a collection of several theories that are relevant with the assignment of causal inferences and how these interpretations impact evaluation and behavior (Swanson and Kelley, 2001). Thus, researchers hold that attribution theories can provide additional insight into the factors that decide customer perceptions of an organization's recovery efforts in response to a service failure with a theoretical basis (Swanson and Kelley, 2001). Furthermore, it is proposed that the perceived causes of a recovery can have a statistically significant impact on post-service recovery evaluations and behaviors. It means, attribution theory may also provide more understanding on consumer perceptions and intentions relative to service recovery experiences (Swanson and Kelley, 2001).

More specifically, researchers believe that consumers attribute causality before ascribing responsibility (Anderson et al, 2009). Weiner (1985a, 1986) propose three dimensions (locus of causality, stability and controllability) as the basis of customer causal attribution inferences (Vázquez-Casielles et al., 2007). Weiner's classification of causal attributions has been widely applied in marketing research (e.g. Folkes, 1984; Curren and Folkes, 1987; Wofford and Goodwin, 1990; Gooding and Kinicki, 1995; Swanson and Kelley, 2001) particularly in service failure and recovery studies because each of the three dimensions is linked to behavioral consequences.

First, locus of causality refers to whether the service failure is caused by service provider (include service employee), customers, or environmental situations (Heider, 1958; Lewis and Daltroy, 1990; Kelley, Hoffman, and Davis, 1993; Swanson and Kelley, 2001). On the basis of Heider's theory, consumer and marketing research (e.g. Richins, 1983; Folkes, 1984; Curren and Folkes, 1987;

Oliver and DeSarbo, 1988) have investigated internal and external customer locus of attributions (Swanson and Kelley, 2001).

According to these researches, consumer expectations of recovery may vary by the causal attributions they infer after a failure occurs. It means that the degree to which customer puts blame on the service provider for a failure would influences their expectation of recovery on the organization and evaluations of the service encounter. Folkes (1988) describe the situation as "problems arising from consumer actions should be solved by consumers, whereas problems arising from firms' actions should be solved by firms". Research by Smith et al. (1999) shows that customers who experience service-failure and recovery encounters prefer to receive resources matching the type of loss that they experienced. However, if the customer attributes the service failure to a cause outside the provider's control, customers may be less critical, even if service failures are in high-magnitude (Folkes, 1984). Thus, causal attributions customer infer after a failure occurs can indeed influences the customer expectation of recovery.

Second, controllability refers to whether the causal agent could have control over the cause or not. Some failures can be avoided or prevented by the actor, while other failures are constrained to human capability. The relation between controllability and recovery expectations also has been set up by previous studies. For example, Hess et al. (2003) argue that when the cause of failure is considered as controllable, recovery expectations will be higher than when the cause of failure is considered as uncontrollable. The study of Folkes (1984) implicitly indicates the positive relationship between the controllability and recovery expectations. Folkes (1984) and Weiner (1980) confirm that controllability influences consumer affects or emotions toward the causal agent.

Third, stability refers to the extent to which a cause is regarded as temporary or predictable and permanent. Hess et al. (2003) describe the relationship between stability and recovery expectation in detail. When the cause of a failure is perceived as stable, consumers would "expect the organization to be aware of the recurrence of such failures and have policies and procedures in place to compensate affected customers". Hess et al. (2003) further argue, "Customers are less likely to expect the organization to give high priority to failures that are temporary". Therefore, following the discussion made by Hess et al. (2003), the positive relationship between stability and customer recovery expectations is also expected. In addition, based on research from the attribution theory and service literature, Swanson and Kelley (2001) suggest that recovery perceived as stable should lead to more favorable customer evaluations and behaviors intentions than unstable service recovery attributions.

Consequently, causal attributions relevant with service recovery are predicted to influences customer expectation and perceptions of service recovery, even when the service recovery outcome is held constant (Swanson and Kelley, 2001).

Overall, service recovery expectations are based on the type and severity of service failure that customer experienced, quality image in customer mind (It is a comprehensive impression of factors such as group brand, hotel star-rating, word of mouth, etc.), provider-customer relationship, service guarantee by provider, and attribution of service failure (See Figure 3-2), and other possible factors. These factors that affect recovery expectations should also help service providers to make recovery decisions for service failures (Ma, 2012).

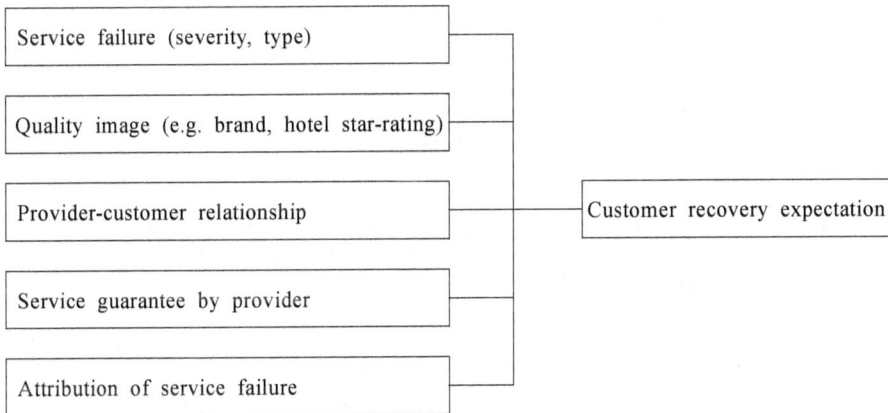

Figure 3-2 Antecedents of service recovery expectation

Source: Bitner, 1990; Kelley and Davis, 1994; Miller, Craighead and Karwan, 2000; Hess et al., 2003; Craighead et al., 2004; Wang et al., 2010, etc.

According to the above literature review part, there are many factors influencing customer's recovery expectation (See Figure 3-2). We only focus on the key factors of service failure that customer experienced and customer attribution (See Figure 3-3), and propose the following assumptions:

H2: Customer attribution (locus, stability, controllability) influences customer recovery expectation (recovery magnitude of expectation, recovery type of expectation).

H2a: Locus of attribution influences customer expectation (recovery magnitude of expectation, recovery type of expectation).

H2b: Stability of service failure influences customer expectation (recovery magnitude of expectation, recovery type of expectation).

H2c: Controllability of service failure influences customer expectation (recovery magnitude of expectation, recovery type of expectation).

H3: Service failure (type, severity) that customer experienced in a hotel influences customer recovery expectation (recovery magnitude of expectation, recovery type of expectation).

H3a: Type of service failure that customer experienced in hotel influences customer recovery expectation (recovery magnitude of expectation, recovery type of expectation).

H3b: Severity of service failure that customer experienced in hotel influences customer recovery expectation (recovery magnitude of expectation, recovery type of expectation).

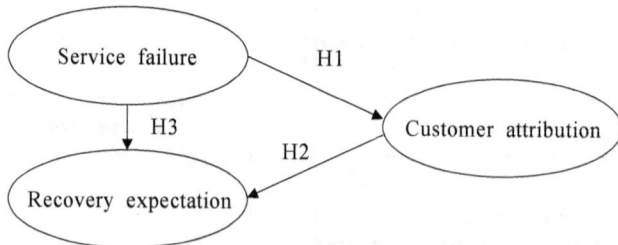

Figure 3-3   The relationship between service failure, customer attribution and recovery expectation

3.3.2 Recovery obtained by customer

The challenge facing service providers is about how to recognize the variety of potential failure situations and the specific, effective ways to respond to each of them (Craighead et al., 2004). Typically, employees are forced to protect themselves when facing customers who are dissatisfied with the service. Organizations may choose to discuss with employees and customers about acceptable recovery options to formalize the recovery process and then provide specific and effective recovery strategies to resolve specific types of failures (Gonzalez et al., 2010). Thus, it might be reasonable to study the recovery strategies in two dimensions—the options that providers could offer and the recovery strategies that customers have obtained.

Commonly, when it comes to the study of service recovery strategies, researchers are exploring the types and efforts of recovery strategies that an organization is prepared to offer. As is defined by many theorists, service recovery strategies refer to the methods applied by an organization and its employees in the process of putting the customer in the place of satisfaction (Danaher and Mattsson, 1994; Sparks and McColl-Kennedy, 2001; Nikbin et al., 2010).

Researchers propose that strategies designed to mitigate the effects of service failure can be classified into two categories: proactive and reactive, which are both trying to moderate the negative consequences of service failure (DeWitt and Brady, 2003). Proactive strategies are enacted prior to an error in service, whereas reactive strategies operate after service failure occurs. Examples of the former can be providing service-quality guarantees, offering choice to customers before service delivery, and attempting to develop harmonious relationship between service providers and customers. Examples of the second strategies include providing post-failure apologies, explaination, and offering compensation to the customers (Worsfold et al., 2007).

By looking into the empirical evidence, it is possible to conclude that proactive strategies aiming to prevent mistakes from happening barely exist in reality. In line with this, most researches focus on recovery strategies after service failure occurs (reactive strategies) rather than before service failure occurs (proactive strategies). Researchers have classified service recovery strategies after failure occurs into different categories.

Firstly, numerous researchers differentiate two types of service recovery efforts from each other: psychological and tangible. A large amount of literature has proved that successful service recovery activities require both psychological and tangible compensations (Bell and Ridge, 1992; Clark, Kaminiski and Rink, 1992), such as monetary compensation (Roschk and Gelbrich, 2014, 2015, 2018), promptness and fairness (Wang et al., 2010).

Schweikart et al. (1993) and Miller et al. (2000) possess a different opinion about categorizing recovery activities, which also refer to psychological and tangible forms of recovery (Craighead et al., 2004). In the former recovery, an apology for a failure is needed, and the firms will show empathy towards the customer (Johnston and Fern, 1999; Miller et al., 2000; Zemke, 1994); in the latter recovery, the organization should re-perform the service, exchange the product, or provide a refund or in-kind compensation (Lewis and McCann, 2004;

Miller et al., 2000; Zemke, 1994; Chuang et al., 2012, Fan et al., 2013).

Similarly, Bitner et al. (1990) and Tax et al. (1998) provide some service recovery strategies as refunds, replacements, apologies, and upgrades (Hibbert, et al., 2012). Sparks et al. (1998) propose that service recovery strategies may contain explaining the reasons for service failure to customer, apologizing, empowering staff to address the failure on the spot, or making efforts to compensate the customers (e.g. Bitner, 1990; Goodwin and Ross, 1990; Sparks and Callan, 1996; Sparks et al., 1998). Davidow (2003) has divided the companies' responses to service failure (or recovery strategies) into six separated dimensions: timeliness, facilitation, redress, apology, credibility, and attentiveness (Casado-Díaz and Nicolau-Gonzálbez, 2009). Research by Gonzalez et al. (2010) divides the recovery strategies into five categories—apologetic, compensatory, reimbursement, restoration, and unresponsiveness (Gonzalez, Hoffman, and Ingram, 2005; Hoffman and Kelley, 1996; Gonzalez et al., 2010).

Roschk and Gelbrich (2014) also based on the tangible-psychological classification and propose a new resource-based compensation type classification. They distinguish concepts like monetary compensation, new / exchanged goods, new/re-performed service, and psychological compensation (See Table 3-1).

Table 3-1   Resource-based compensation type classification (Roschk and Gelbrich, 2014)

Resource-based compensation type classification		
Monetary compensation	Delayed monetary compensation	Voucher
		Store credit
	Immediate monetary compensation	Discount
		Money back
New/exchanged goods		
New/re-performed service		
Psychological compensation		Apology

Roschk and Gelbrich (2014) propose that four compensation forms fall into monetary compensation: voucher (coupon for a price reduction on the next purchase), store credit (a loan disbursed with the next purchase), discount (a price reduction < 100% of the purchase price), and money back (100% price reduction). Among them, voucher and store credit represent delayed monetary compensation. They are tied to a future purchase and can only be redeemed, when the consumer repurchases from the same service provider. In contrast, discount and money back are immediate monetary compensation. They are tied to the present purchase and offset a failure immediately when it occurred (Kim and Ulgado, 2012). Psychological compensation comes in forms of an apology. It means that the company expresses regret and empathy for the customer's distress (Liao, 2007). They also subsume "status" under this category because an apology re-establishes self-esteem, which may have suffered through a company's failure (Roschk, and Kaiser, 2013; Roschk and Gelbrich, 2014).

Secondly, in the views of Binter et al. (1990), Kelly et al. (1993) and Spreng et al. (1995), recovery strategies can be divided into active strategies and passive recovery strategies. The active strategies include apology, timely responses, while the passive recovery strategies include providing the explanation of the failure or providing compensation in some ways such as provision of free services or products, making a refund or providing customers sales discounts or discount vouchers.

To further analyze, when the causes of a service failure are internal, or when a service failure is very severe, service providers will take active recovery strategies in order to show that they are responsible and they can be trusted (Lin, 2006). From previous studies in relevant fields, the organizations are inclined to take active recovery strategies following a service failure so that a better reputation and interactive relationship with customers would likely be maintained (Spector, 1982; Anderson et al., 1992; Hoffman et al., 1995; Churchill et al., 1997; Smith et al., 1999; Boone et al., 2000; Bono and Judge, 2001). In contrast, Lin (2006) indicates if the causes of a service failure are external, or when a service failure is less severe, they might choose to take passive recovery strategies. Therefore, researchers believe that the causal locus of attribution have effects on the recovery strategies provided by organization, that is, recovery strategies obtained by customers.

Thirdly, Beugre et al. (2006) apply two types of recovery in their research which are distributive recovery and interactional recovery. Beugre et al. state that distributive failure can be compensated by distributive recovery. The form of service recovery corresponding to interactional failure is interactional recovery. Obviously, this view is based on justice theory and consistent with matching theory.

Although there are many approaches, it has been realized that these are not equally effective when they are applied to handling customer complaints in different situations (Blodgett, Hill, and Tax 1997; Hoffman and Kelley 1996; Tax and Brown 1998; Gonzalez et al., 2010). Hence, the "matching hypothesis" (Smith et al., 1999) becomes a very important principle when selecting proper service strategies for certain situations.

In summary, the mainstream of academic research in relevant studies focuses on the organization, of its actions and consequences; whereas there is, amazingly, an ignorance of the attitudes that customers have towards recovery strategies. Therefore, in this study, we consider, in customers' perspective, the recovery obtained by customers—that is, the recovery process received from service provider after a service failure.

3.4   Customer satisfaction after recovery

Many studies have shown that a successful service recovery following a service failure can have a positive effect on consumers' attitudes and exert a positive impact on customer satisfaction (e.g. Conlon and Murray, 1996; McColl-Kennedy et al., 2003; Chuang et al., 2012; Mattila, 2001; Gruber et al., 2011). Spreng et al. (1995) find that proper and effective service recovery efforts have the potential to convert a service failure into a favorable service encounter and thereby the realization of secondary satisfaction.

Based on expectation-disconfirmation paradigm, McCollough (2000) suggested the three consequences of recovery efforts: superior recovery, adequate recovery, and inferior recovery. Superior recovery refers to recovery efforts exceeding the customer's expectations, so the outcome is positively disconfirmed, and customer feels satisfaction and surprise; adequate recovery refers to recovery performance that reach the consumer recovery expectations, so the outcome is confirmed, and customer is satisfied; and inferior recovery refers to recovery efforts that do not meet the consumer recovery expectations, so the result is disconfirmed, and customer feels dissatisfaction.

Indeed, good service recovery could help a company to turn a potentially negative situation into a positive one (Gustafsson, 2009; Lii et al., 2012). There is some evidence for "service recovery paradox" in which customer satisfaction and patronage intentions would even increase above pre-failure levels in occasions when they are very satisfied with the recovery efforts (Hart et al., 1990; Liao, 2007).

However, poor service recovery would go further to reinforce the negative effects of service failures, such as negative word-of-mouth (WOM) and switching behavior (Blodgett, Hill, and Tax, 1997; Gruber et al., 2011). These poor service recoveries would deteriorate the already low customer evaluations following a failure, leading to a "double deviation" effect (Bitner et al., 1990; Hart et al., 1990; Johnston and Fern, 1999; Mattila, 2001; Casado-Díaz, 2009).

Therefore, in order to achieve effective recovery consequence and avoid double deviation, service recovery research has sought to examine the service recovery strategies of organizations (Davidow, 2003) and the consumer outcomes following organizations' service recovery attempts (Smith et al., 1999; Hibbert et al., 2012).

In the context of hospitality, Chang and Hsiao (2010) suggest that successful service recovery will improve perceived justice and reduce perceived risk so that customer-perceived value will be enhanced. Further, exceptional service recovery may result in a paradoxical situation where a customer who experienced a service failure might become more satisfied and loyal with the organization than one who did not encounter a problem (Ok et al., 2007). However, in fact, empirical researches reveal that more than 50% of service provider's recovery responses to customer complaints will strengthen customers' negative evaluations of a service (Hart et al., 1990; Kim et al., 2012) and double deviation situation would take place.

3.4.1 Double deviation

Bitner et al. (1990) define a "double deviation" situation as an inappropriate and/or inadequate response to failures in the service delivery system (Casado-Díaz and Nicolau-Gonzálbez, 2009). In such situations, the firms fail to deliver an appropriate or adequate customer service after an initial failure (Bunker and Bradley, 2007; Wu and Lo, 2012), implying that customers are doubly faced with a service failure, the primary service failure and the following failed service recovery (Casado-Díaz and Nicolau-Gonzálbez, 2009).

Accordingly, successful service recovery can help organizations produce more effective service delivery process to handle the following potential service failure (Tax et al., 1998). In contrast, poor service recoveries (ineffective service recovery efforts), would not only exacerbate customer dissatisfaction but also weaken customer trust, exerting a "double deviation" effect (Bitner et al., 1990). It is believed that doing it right timely with proper recovery strategies plays a key role in maintaining customer satisfaction and loyalty (Liao, 2007).

Generally, double deviation scenarios will drive customers to take more harmful actions to the firm, such as complaint, switch and exit. However, it is surprising to find that the consequences of these double deviation effects, which seem to be rather common, have gained little attention in field of marketing literature (Davidow, 2003). For instance, in Hoffman et al.'s (1995) study, it is revealed that the cases in which restaurant personnel failed to take actions to execute a recovery when responding to service failure take up to 20% in the critical incidents (Mattila, 1999). Keaveney's (1995) work finds that service failure and almost 60% of the critical behaviors by service providers in response to failed recoveries led directly to customer dissatisfaction and switch. These findings have also provided convincing evidence for the potentially negative impact caused by service failures followed by ineffective or even non-existent service recoveries strategies (Casado-Díaz and Nicolau-Gonzálbez, 2009).

Further, Casado-Díaz et al. (2009) argue that the key point is what happens following these critical encounters, which makes the behavior of customers inclined to follow and how customers perceive the firm's recovery efforts and how these efforts will influences customers' behaviors. To analyze "how" customers choose the proper type of response (no action, complaint, exit, and complaint and exit), Casado-Díaz et al. estimate ordered probit models. The results suggest that the magnitude of service failure, recovery strategies the firms take, distributive and procedural justice, recovery-related emotions and satisfaction with the service recovery all contribute heavily to customers' choice in terms of the response type.

3.4.2 Service recovery paradox

Hart et al. (1990) state this situation earlier: "A good recovery can turn angry, frustrated customers into loyal ones. They believe that good recovery will produce more goodwill than if things had gone smoothly at the beginning." McCullough and Bharadwaj (1992) introduce the term "service recovery paradox", which implies that, followed by a highly timely and effective service recovery strategy, a failure can help the company to win higher satisfaction ratings from customers than if the failure had never occurred (namely, the service had been correctly performed initially) (Krishna et al., 2011; Mattila, 1999). From this perspective, an effective service recovery effort can bring more customer satisfaction to the firm, making "recovery paradox" possible—a situation where the overall customers satisfaction levels are higher after recovery than they are prior to the service failure (Smith and Bolton, 1998; Maxham and Netemeyer, 2002; Vázquez-Casielles et al., 2010). In brief, these researchers reveal the fact that highly effective recovery efforts can make a "service recovery paradox" possible in which secondary satisfaction exceeds pre-failure levels (Dong et al., 2008).

Based on the principle of "service recovery paradox", recovery efforts exert an impact on satisfaction (Johnston and Fern, 1999; Magnini et al., 2007; De Matos et al., 2007; Michel and Meuter, 2008; Ok et al., 2007; Priluck and Lala, 2009). This satisfaction increases on the condition that the customer's favorable assessment of the service recovery strategies is carried out by the company to handle the service failure (Vázquez-Casielles et al., 2012). With historical experiences and new information integrated, customers will re-evaluate and update their overall satisfaction levels, for example, customers' satisfaction with service recovery, affective commitment, or trust (Vázquez-Casielles et al., 2012).

As such, by taking right recovery activities, companies may utilize the service recovery paradox phenomenon to obtain satisfaction, trust, and loyalty from their consumers (Krishna et al., 2011). On the basis of the customers' retention, companies may also acquire more benefits. For example, recovered customers will be more satisfied with the service provided by the company and in turn they will provide the company with a long-term value that would compensate for the recovery costs (Vázquez-Casielles et al., 2012).

However, some researchers have challenged the "service recovery paradox", such as McCullough, Berry and Yadav (2000), Weun et al. (2004), Mattila (1999), O'Donohoe and Turley (2007). Although researches have established the positive image of service recovery in post-failure consumer satisfaction (Bitner et al., 1990; Hoffman et al., 1995; Kelley et al., 1993; McCollough and Bharadwaj, 1992; Spreng et al., 1995), some still claim that a serious service failure (like failure to honor a reservation in hotel) might render the following service recovery ineffective. Mattila (1999) finds that "For high-magnitude failure, post-recovery satisfaction levels are not brought to a level comparable to the no-failure service situation. For low-magnitude failure (like serving the wrong dish in restaurant), a satisfaction level comparable to no-failure satisfaction is reached, but post-recovery satisfaction ratings would not exceed the no-failure ratings".

Thus, these findings are used to prove that the service recovery paradox may not be supported by empirical evidence (Boshoff, 1997; Boshoff and Leong,

1998). The phenomenon of service recovery paradox might indeed be limited to some highly exceptional service recovery efforts (Smith and Bolton, 1998; Mattila, 1999).

3.4.3   Expectation-disconfirmation and satisfaction after recovery

Service recovery refers to "putting right what has gone wrong" (Bailey, 1994). McCollough (2000) suggests three consequences resulting from different service recovery efforts: recovery satisfaction, recovery paradox and double deviation. Recovery satisfaction refers to situations in which recovery performance meets the customer recovery expectations by adequate recovery strategies. Service recovery paradox refers to situations in which recovery performance exceeds the customer expectations by superior recovery strategies, namely "little extra" (Clark et al., 1992; Mattila, 1999), in which satisfaction after a failure and recovery effort exceeds pre-failure levels (Dong et al., 2008); double deviation effect (Bitner et al., 1990; Liao, 2007) refers to situations in which recovery performance does not reach (lower or less) the consumer recovery expectations as a result of inferior recovery, namely, a secondary service failure (Wu and Lo, 2012) (See Figure 3-2).

However, previous researches prove that the phenomenon of service recovery paradox might indeed be limited to highly exceptional service recovery efforts and may not be supported by empirical evidence (Boshoff, 1997; Boshoff and Leong, 1998). While the consequences of these seemingly common double deviation effects will motivate the customers to respond to the firm in the most harmful way, such as complaint and exit (Casado-Díaz et al., 2009). Therefore, taking timely and effective tactics are recommended as strategies for compensating for service failure and for the sound results from an adequate service recovery (Chang et al., 2012).

To conclude, service recovery should not be viewed as an effective tool for all service failures, nor can it be an effective cure for chronic unreliability (Berry and Parasuraman, 1991; Mattila, 1999). A recovery strategy will be effective when the service provider exhibits high reliability in the process of service delivery. Management must be clear about that only when these recoveries can enhance the effect of the product/service offering and the entire operation of the service and recoveries can become a competitive tool (Mattila, 1999).

In addition, according to previous literature, there are two sets of disconfirmations between expectation and actual performance in service failure and recovery encounter. In the first phase of service delivery, customers hold expectations from pre-consumption, and compare the perceived performance with their expectations. In the recovery phase, customers evaluate recovery efforts against their expectations, which results in a secondary disconfirmation judgment (Oliver, 1981). This is termed "secondary satisfaction"(Etzel and Silverman, 1981; Gilly, 1987; Westbrook, 1987). Thus, customer overall satisfaction after recovery is determined not only by the disconfirmation of service performance (failure), but also by the disconfirmation of service recovery (Smith and Bolton, 1998). Namely, recovery satisfaction is combined with the original dissatisfaction in order to determine the customer overall satisfaction towards a service encounter.

Therefore, some researchers propose that customer satisfaction after recovery should include recovery satisfaction and overall satisfaction (Mattila, 2001; Gruber et al., 2011). Overall satisfaction is the accumulation of satisfaction from pre-failure to post-recovery (See Figure 3-4).

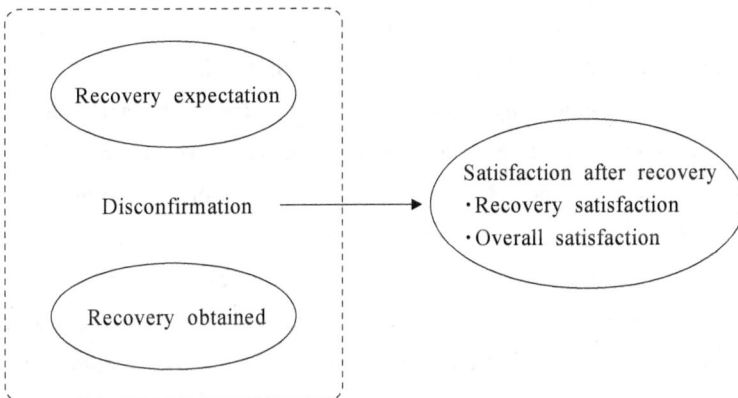

Figure 3-4 The relationship between recovery expectation, obtained recovery and recovery satisfaction

Thus, we come up with the following hypotheses:

H4: The disconfirmation (discrepency between customer recovery expectation and obtained recovery) has effects on customer satisfaction after recovery (include recovery satisfaction and overall satisfaction).

H4a: The disconfirmation (discrepency between customer recovery expectation and obtained recovery) influences customer recovery satisfaction.

H4b: The disconfirmation (discrepency between customer recovery expectation and obtained recovery) influences customer overall satisfaction.

3.5   Literature limitation

In the research of service recovery and customer satisfaction on recovery, the following arguments are debatable and worth noting. First of all, it is now commonly agreed that when customers encounter service failure, they tend to use "matching" to decide if the recovery strategy is satisfying or not. However, based on different theories, the standards used for "matching" is then much varied.

Justice theory believes the customer satisfaction depends on the comparison between three dimensions, which are distributive justice, procedural justice, and interactional justice. Expectation-disconfirmation paradigm, however, compares the customer expectation on recovery and recovery obtained. Obviously, the higher the expectation is, the harder it is for the provider to meet satisfaction. Hence, researchers engage to further determine factors that influences expectations. Yet, there still lacks a general consensus. Possible suggestions are being self-experience, experience from others, branding reputation, or even some emotional elements, like cognitive values, personal wills would have a decent impact on expectations.

The current literature (Chapter 2) shows that when service failure occurs, customers would automatically look for causal attribution, and such attribution may influence customer's expectation on recovery, or even affect the next consumption of service and choices. Evidently, the causal attribution is also an important factor, which is mostly missed by existing researches—only few has taken it into account for studying customer recovery expectations.

In addition, there are three typical researches when it comes to service recovery and customer satisfaction. The first one is to use methods like CIT to study service failure and influences its recovery has over customer satisfaction, which is from the customer perspective. The second is to study the effectiveness of the recovery strategies that an organization offers, which is based on the stakes of organizations. The third is to study the matching between the types of failure and recovery strategies, which is beneficial for both practitioners and manifesting the "matching hypothesis". The third one is rare, but with typical examples like the Roschk and Gelbrich (2014), who verify some theoretical arguments and bring a new classification on failure types called resource-based compensation classification.

What's more, according to attribution theory, justice theory, matching hypothesis, and expectation-disconfirmation paradigm, researchers find that customers would make their own thinking about recovery expectation based on types of failure, severity, attribution (locus, controllability, stability). Recovery expectation here includes expectation on severity and types. Meanwhile, factors (types of failure, severity, attribution—locus, controllability, stability) could have matching problems.

Finally, the magnitude and types of recovery expectation also have matching problems with the magnitude and types of recovery that customers obtained. There are two phases of failure recovery. In phase one, the expectation is formed prior to recovery process; then in phase two, it gets to compensations that customers obtained from the organization. So, occasions that organizations do not come up with exactly matching recovery strategies may exist. Such disconfirmation has two possibilities: one is that customers are having exceedingly well compensations in both types and amounts (positive disconfirmation); the other is that customers are having inadequate compensation (negative disconfirmation), which is a secondary failure on recovery and will bring secondary harms to customers hence even higher dissatisfaction. We find that usually, most researchers only make a distinction between types of failure and recovery, and make analysis on the matching hypothesis; instead, the customer expectation and obtained compensation are not much differentiated, and their matching hypothesis is not further analyzed.

In all, the four dimensions will be testified to certain extends in this study.

3.6 Conclusion

This chapter focuses on the relationship between customer recovery expectation, recovery obtained from service provider and customer satisfaction after recovery. Firstly, it introduces the concept of service recovery. All actions that a service organization may take to correct a service failure, amend, compensate, and restore the losses, and change customer attitudes from dissatisfied to satisfied are considered as service recovery (Hoffman et al., 1995; Andreassen, 2001; Craighead et al., 2004; Valenzuela et al., 2005; Dong et al., 2008; Fan et al., 2013).

Commonly, researchers distinguish service recovery efforts by two types: psychological and tangible. Roschk and Gelbrich (2014) propose new resource-based compensation type classification based on this type of classification. They are monetary compensation, new/exchanged goods, new/re-performed service, and psychological compensation.

Secondly, some basic theories often used in service recovery researches are viewed, including the justice theory, expectation-disconfirmation paradigm, matching hypotheses, and attribution theories. According to these literature review, we propose that service failure (type, severity) and customer attribution (locus, controllability, stability) have effect on customer's recovery expectation.

Thirdly, based on expectation-disconfirmation paradigm, disconfirmation between customer recovery expectation and the obtained recovery leads to the difference of customer recovery satisfaction. Thus, researchers present three consequences of service recovery efforts: recovery satisfaction, recovery paradox and double deviation. Recovery satisfaction refers to recovery performance that meets the customer recovery expectations with the utilization of adequate recovery strategies; service recovery paradox refers to the situation when recovery performance exceeds the customer's expectations by superior recovery strategies; double deviation effect happens when recovery performance does not meet the consumer recovery expectations as a result of inferior recovery, namely, a second service failure (Wu and Lo, 2012).

With successful performance, a service recovery action may convert the customer's dissatisfaction into satisfaction, and making recovery paradox possible. If the service provider fails to address the attempted service recovery in a satisfying way, the outcome will be disappointing (Hart et al., 1990). When the service provider makes no efforts to compensate for the service failure, the customer's negative evaluation is magnified to a double deviation from that customer's primary service expectation (Bitner et al., 1990; Mattila, 1999). According to this paradigm, we believe that the positive disconfirmation influences customer satisfaction after recovery (include recovery satisfaction and overall satisfaction) when recovery obtained is meet or higher than recovery expectation in a positive way, and negative disconfirmation decreases customer's recovery satisfaction when customer obtained is lower than recovery expectation.

Fourthly, according to matching hypothesis (Smith et al., 1999; Worsfold et al., 2007), it reveals that customers tend to accept situations when the type of recovery strategies "match" the type of loss they have experienced, and the magnitude of recovery effort "match" the severity of the failure they encounter (Smith et al., 1999; Smith et al., 1999). Thus, matching hypothesis needs to be considered in severer recovery process and it will influence the effectiveness of recovery strategies.

Researches have also indicated that there are various approaches to service recovery but these approaches are not equally effective when applied to address customer complaints in specific situations (Blodgett et al., 1997; Hoffman and Kelley 1996; Tax and Brown, 1998; Gonzalez et al., 2010). Therefore, matching hypothesis is a very important principle in selecting service strategies in a certain case.

Fifthly, most of the recovery researches focus on recovery expectation, recovery strategy and recovery satisfaction, while only a few attempts to link service failure with recovery based on attribution theories, and most of them believe the matching hypothesis. However, few researchers have differentiated customer's recovery expectation and obtained recovery. Thus, it is difficult to find appropriate recovery strategy to delight customer.

Finally, the more negative the disconfirmation is, the greater the dissatisfaction would be; whereas the more positive the disconfirmation is, the greater the satisfaction would be (McCollough et al., 2000). Further, Smith and Bolton (1998) propose that service encounter satisfaction is determined not only by the disconfirmation of service performance (failure), but also by the disconfirmation of service recovery performance (Smith and Bolton, 1998; Ma, 2012). It is termed as "overall satisfaction".

Accordingly, most service recovery articles share a common theme, that is, customers must be satisfied with the firm's recovery efforts (Tax et al., 1998). Otherwise, many negative outcomes will happen, including lost sales, negative word-of-mouth and defections (Andreassen, 1999; McCollough et al., 2000; Boshoff, 2005). Clearly, the process of failure and recovery efforts should be improved so that customer satisfaction can be enhanced and the customers can gain benefit from it. (Tax and Brown, 1998). Customer satisfaction is related to customer retention, positive referrals and increased purchase frequency, which in turn can produce the positive organizational outcomes such as revenue growth and increased profitability (Heskett et al. 1994; Maxham 2001; Gonzalez et al., 2010). In the next chapter, we will introduce customers' behavioral intentions after service recovery.

CHAPTER 4

LITERATURE REVIEW ON CUSTOMER
BEHAVIORAL INTENTION AFTER RECOVERY

According to the previous literature, customers who are satisfied are more likely to establish loyalty, repurchases and favorable word of mouth (Fornell, 1992; Hu et al., 2009; Matzler et al., 2006). Furthermore, some empirical studies indicate a positive relationship between customer satisfaction and customer loyalty (Kandampully and Suhartanto, 2000; Dimitriades, 2006; Chi and Qu, 2008; Faullant et al., 2008), as well as the relationship between customer satisfaction and positive word of mouth (Söderlund, 1998). In contrast, when dissatisfied, consumers can respond in a variety of ways (Bearden and Teel 1983; Richins 1983; Singh, 1988), such as taking legal actions or walking away from the purchase (Huang et al., 1996). In this study, we only focus on customer dissatisfaction. Customer dissatisfaction is not the symmetric of satisfaction, which justifies the focus on the peculiar literature dealing with dissatisfaction.

Some researchers have differentiated the consequences of customer dissatisfaction. For example, Hirschman (1970) classifies responses to dissatisfaction as exit (switch provider), voice (complaints to friends, sellers, consumer organizations) or loyalty (do nothing). Day and Landon's (1977) hierarchical typology distinguishes between taking some action and taking no action at the first level and between public actions (for instance, seek redress directly from business, take legal actions, complain to public or private agencies) and private actions (for instance, boycott sellers or manufacturer, warn friends and relatives) at the second level. On the other hand, Day and Landon's generalize six behaviors: no action, word of mouth, boycott, complaining to the seller, seeking redress and taking third party action. Later, the classification proposed by Singh (1988), categorizes the consequences as complaint to the seller, negative word of mouth, switching provider, and taking legal actions. In addition, Singh (1988) develops a three-dimensional typology that discriminates among Customer Complaint Behavior (CCB) responses based on the object towards where the response is directed (for instance, family/friends, third parties, and sellers/ manufacturers).

Based on the above literature (Hirschman, 1970; Day and Landon, 1977; Singh, 1988), Tax et al. (1998) adopt four post-purchase options in their study, including exit, complaint to firm, third-party action and continued patronage. Bonifield and Cole (2008) classify the post-purchase behavioral intentions as exiting, engaging in negative word of mouth, and participating in two different types of voice (to management and to third parties). Casado-Díaz et al. (2009) consider four possible responses in their work, which are no action, complaint behavior (to the company and/or to relatives and friends), exit behavior (switching provider), and complaint and exit behavior (both simultaneously). More specifically, a dissatisfied customer may engage in nine multiple forms of complaint behavior, including: no action, boycotting the product class, boycotting the brand, boycotting the seller, spreading negative word of mouth, seeking redress from the seller, seeking redress from the manufacturer, seeking redress from a third party, or complaining publicly (Day et al., 1981; Levesque and McDougall, 1993; Morel et al., 1997; Mattsson et al., 2004).

Therefore, customer responses to dissatisfaction could be classified as: (1) no action (doing nothing)—it means that customer do not complain to firms; (2) complaint behavior—customer voice the dissatisfaction experience to the firms, third parties, and relatives and friends (negative word of mouth); (3) exit—customer switch provider or exit consumption; (4) multiple responses simultaneously (See Figure 4-1).

Researchers suggest that these types of responses have different level of harmful consequences for company (or service provider), therefore, they should be analyzed separately (Casado-Díaz et al., 2009) (See Figure 4-2).

In sum, we posit the following hypotheses:

H5: Customer satisfaction after recovery influences customer behavioral intention.

H5a: Customer satisfaction after recovery (include recovery satisfaction and overall satisfaction) positively influences the likelihood of repurchasing the services of this hotel in the future.

H5b: Customer satisfaction after recovery (include recovery satisfaction and overall satisfaction) positively influences the likelihood of recommending this hotel to other people.

H5c: Customer satisfaction after recovery (include recovery satisfaction and overall satisfaction) negatively influences the likelihood of discouraging other people to use the hotel service.

H5d: Customer satisfaction after recovery (include recovery satisfaction and overall satisfaction) negatively influences the likelihood of complaining to the hotel and manager.

H5e: Customer satisfaction after recovery (include recovery satisfaction and overall satisfaction) negatively influences the likelihood of complaining to third parties.

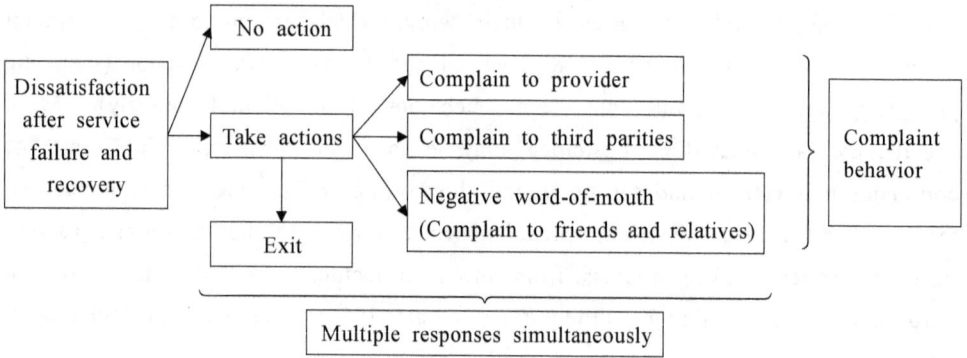

Source: Tax et al, 1998; Casado-Díaz et al., 2009, and so on.

Figure 4-1 Customer responses to dissatisfaction experience

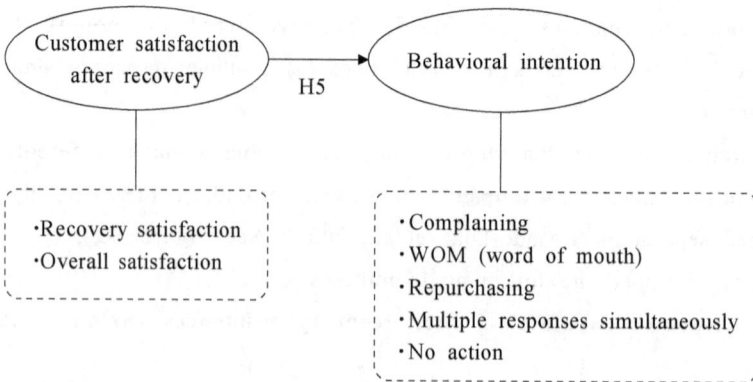

Figure 4-2 Satisfaction after recovery and behavioral intention

4.1   Complaint behavioral intention

According to the previous literature, researchers believe that less than half of the problems experienced by consumers are directly voiced, so complaint behavior is "the tip-of-the-iceberg" (Best and Andreasen, 1977; Wall et al., 1977). Companies are normally aware only of a small percentage of breakdowns and most of the problems stay hidden (Butelli, 2007). However, researchers and practitioners also believe that a complaint behavior allows service provider to obtain customer feedback that is useful in making improvements to customer satisfaction, loyalty, long-term sales and therefore profits (Fornell and Wernefelt, 1987; Kelley et al., 1993; Reichheld, 1993; Reichheld and Sasser, 1990; Tronvoll, 2008).

For this reason, researchers suggest that the small amount of complaints is a valid indicator for customer dissatisfaction, but complaining reduction should not be considered as a valuable and desirable purpose for firms (Butelli, 2007). Furthermore, they propose that a company may have a better chance of retaining a customer by encouraging that customer to complain, and then addressing that complaint, than it does by assuming non-complaining customers are satisfied (Spreng et al., 1995; Davidow, 2000). It is suggested that toll-free lines (Strahle et al., 1992), service guarantees (Bolfing, 1989; Callan and Moore, 1998), and hassle-free complaint procedures (Kendall and Russ, 1975), are several ways an organization have to encourage complaints (Davidow, 2000).

4.1.1   Conceptualization of customer complaint behavior

The most common definition of customer complaint behavior, however, is proposed by Singh (1988), based on the version of Singh and Howell (1985), which defines CCB as "a set of multiple (behavioral and non-behavioral) responses, some or all of which are triggered by perceived dissatisfaction with a purchase episode".

However, the scope of this concept is limited, focusing on voice behavior only, which refers to customers' expression of their dissatisfaction to the responsible party when the service or product failure occur (Butelli, 2007). Based on Oh (2003, 2004), it is possible to make an important distinction between direct complaint (to product/service provider) and indirect complaint (to third parties, such as consumer association or a body hierarchically superior). Indirect complaint is one of the less chosen (Best and Andreasen, 1977) and normally it is not the first-choice option.

Focusing on voice behavior, there are different descriptions of customer complaint behavior. Landon (1980) defines CCB as "an expression of dissatisfaction by individual consumers (or on a consumer's behalf) to a responsible party in either the distribution channel or a complaint handling agency". Day (1980) extends this definition by excluding false claims and emphasizes those claims that should be honest and reasonable. Oliver (1980) notes that CCB is a dissatisfaction in nature, and it is caused by the negative disconfirmation of purchase expectations. Then, Jacoby and Jaccard (1981) define complaint behavior as an action taken by consumers that involves communicating something negative regarding a product or service, either the firm manufacturing or marketing that product or service, or to some third-party like organizational entity (Tronvoll, 2008). Day et al. (1981) demonstrate that consumer complaining is a "specific consumption experience ... in which a consumer has recognized a highly unsatisfactory experience of sufficient impact that is neither assimilated nor otherwise quickly forgotten". Grönroos (1988) defines CCB as a post-incident reaction by customers left dissatisfied after a service failure. In addition, Mowen (1993) points that complaint behavior is any one of the actions that is triggered by perceived dissatisfaction with a purchase episode. Stephens (2000) indicates that "complaining is a post purchase process that may or may not occur when customers are disappointed". Some scholars have even identified complaint behavior in terms of action-taking (Heung and Lam, 2003).

According to these definitions, it is found that there are some discussions in the study of the CCB researchers. First, most of them suggest customer complaint behavior is a complex construction, which includes the complaining customer's state of mind, a behavioral, and/or a communicational act (Tronvoll, 2008). Therefore, the researchers are not only concerned about the complaint behavior itself, but also concerned with the emotions related to complaints. For example, many studies argue that customer satisfaction, loyalty, and future behavioral intentions are influencesd by a customer's emotions during the service encounter (Oliver, 1997; Cronin et al., 2000; Barsky and Nash, 2002). Other studies have investigated the influences of customers' affective state on their service evaluations (Taylor, 1994; Dube and Maute, 1996; Hui and Tse, 1996; Andreassen, 2000) and on satisfaction processes (Westbrook and Oliver, 1991; Mano and Oliver, 1993; Oliver, 1993; Wirtz and Bateson, 1999).

In addition, Zeelenberg and Pieters (2004) investigate the impact of emotions on dissatisfaction and subsequent customer behavior responses, such as complaining and word of mouth. They find that emotions have a direct impact on behavior, over and above the effects of dissatisfaction. Tronvoll (2011) also finds frustration to be a predictor of complain behavior. Bonifield and Cole (2007) predict that two negative valence of emotions (anger and regret), underling or mediating the effects of consumers' appraisals about service failure on post-purchase behaviors. Smith and Bolton (2002) specifically address how customers' emotional responses to service failures influence their evaluations of various types of recovery efforts and their satisfaction with the service encounter. Past consumer researching finds consumption emotions are statistically significant predictors of complaining and both positive and negative word of mouth (Nyer, 1997; Westbrook, 1987).

Second, it is believed that complaint behavior could be triggered by perceived dissatisfaction. They argue that dissatisfaction serves as the motivation for complaint behavior (Oliver, 1977; Day, 1984). It means that the satisfaction level influences the intentions to complain (Andreassen, 1999; Teel, 1983; Fernandes and Dos Santos, 2007; Voorhees and Brady, 2006). Therefore, some researchers investigate the relationship between customer dissatisfaction and complaint behavior. These studies indicate that dissatisfied customers may express their dissatisfaction behaviorally (Zeelenberg and Pieters, 2004); dissatisfaction and complaints have a stable long-term equilibrium relationship, which permits them to influences each other positively (Onyeaso, 2007; Sharma et al., 2010).

However, there are some different ideas regarding this relationship. Singh (1990) suggests that customer dissatisfaction can act as a trigger that may results in complaint behavior, but customer dissatisfaction itself does not play a major role in determining complaint behaviors. Furthermore, Sharma et al. (2010) consider that customer dissatisfaction with the product or service often triggers the process of complaining, although the strength of this relevance appears to be low to moderate because of the presence of several mediating or moderating variables (Jacoby and Jaccard, 1981; Keng et al., 1995; Singh and Pandya, 1991).

Finally, there are different viewpoints concerning customer's possible choice for expressing dissatisfaction. With a wide range of perspectives, researchers suggest that customers have three options, including complaining to the product and/or service provider, to third parties, and to their friends and relatives (Day, 1984; Richins, 1983; Singh, 1988). De Matos et al. (2012) define CCB as factors causing consumers to express dissatisfaction, either formally to the service provider/consumer agency, or informally via negative recommendations to friends and relatives. They believe that voice is the only type of customer complaining behavior that benefits organizations because it gives them the opportunity to recover and retain consumers effectively (Tax et al., 1998). Therefore, voice should be encouraged (Robertson et al., 2012).

Yet, some researchers narrow the scope of complaints into public actions, excluding private behavior. According to the two-level hierarchical classification schema proposed by Day and Landon (1977), the second level represents the distinction between public and private action. Public actions include seeking redress or refund from the provider, complain to a consumer organization, and legal action. Private actions include word-of-mouth communication to friends and relatives and performing exit behavior (Singh, 1988). Some researchers believe that public and private behaviors have different motivations (Brown and Beltramini, 1989). When consumers feel that their actions may result in rectifying dissatisfaction, they are likely to bring their complaints to the seller but when they do not feel that sense of control to limit their complaints to family and friends (Brown and Beltramini, 1990). Therefore, they limit the complaint behavior to public actions.

For these reasons, customers' complaint behaviors are researched from different point of views by different researchers (Chang et al., 2012). Some investigate the motives for complaining, including: seeking redress, seeking apology, seeking compensation, requesting corrective action and expressing emotional anger (Heung and Lam, 2003; Nimako and Mensah, 2012). In this study, we classify complaint behaviors as complaint to service providers, complaint to third parties, and complaint to friends and family (negative word of mouth).

4.1.2   Complaint to service providers

Once the service delivery does not meet the customers' predictive expectations, some customers take an action to resolve the conflict, and they often choose to complain to managers or employees (Ok et al., 2007; Ekiz and Arasli, 2007). Compared to other responses, voice to the manager/supervisor is a direct, confrontational approach to relieving dissatisfaction (Chan and Wan, 2008). By voicing their discontent to a responsible party, consumers may vent their frustration and, perhaps more important, get redress for their dissatisfaction (East, 2000; Jaccard, 1981). On the other hand, literature indicates that one motivation for complaining is to help the provider to improve service quality (Bark et al., 1994; Lovelock and Wirtz, 2007), sustain a valued relationship (Bowlby, 1979), and get corrective actions from the provider (Krishna et al., 2011). It shows that the customers still have faith in the provider, and this is a great signal to support the view of "complaining customers are the best customers" (Eccles and Durand, 1998).

Researchers believe that while some dissatisfied customers remain loyal, others might switch all or part of their business elsewhere (Mattsson et al., 2004). In any cases, when a customer complains to a service provider, the company has an opportunity to recover the situation (McColl et al., 2005). In fact, most of the service providers engage in service recovery in an attempt to rectify a customer complaint regarding a perceived service failure (Spreng et al., 1995; Pranic and Roehl, 2012).

In sum, researchers believe that it is important to encourage customers to complain to service provider. Numerous investigations focus on the factors that influence customers' complaint to the provider or other concerned parties.

Firstly, situation variables influence customers' responses to service problems (Richins, 1983, 1987; Kelley and Davis, 1994; Keaveney, 1995; Singh and Wilkes, 1996; Levesque and McDougall, 2000), such as levels of dissatisfaction (Chiu et al., 1988; Mittal et al., 2008; Cheng and Lam, 2008; Ashraf et al., 2013). Levesque and McDougall (2000) suggest that customers are more likely to complain to the service provider as problem severity increases. Different criticality levels, Ostrom and Iacobucci (1995) consider that customers are more likely to complain when problems are encountered in high criticality situations (Richins, 1983, 1987; Webster and Sundaram, 1998; Levesque and McDougall, 2000). Chang and Tsai (2012) also raise that in front of other customers or when dining on a special social occasion, the reaction to service failures may be very different when compared to other dining occasions. Moreover, the likelihood of service recovery (Blodget and Granbois, 1992), the ease of process of complaining (Blodget and Anderson, 2000), the perception that whether company will respond back (Huppertz, 2007; Ashraf et al., 2013) also influences the complaint action of dissatisfaction customer.

Secondly, most researchers believe that customers' complaint behaviors are influenced by affective and cognitive factors. Customer satisfaction is influenced by both cognitive and affective factors, such as specific product or service features, customers' perceptions of quality, their attributions for service success or failure, and their perceptions of fairness, customers' emotional responses

(Liljander et al., 1997; Zeithaml et al., 2000; Pranic et al., 2012), and consumer's attitude towards complaining (Kim et al., 2003; Ashraf et al., 2013).

Specifically, the emotional features such as helplessness may determine whether angry (frustrated) customers would complain to the provider (which may initiate problem resolution) and/or engage in negative WOM to others (which may not initiate problem resolution) (Gelbrich, 2010). Choraria (2013) defines the major categories of negative emotions that influences customer's intention to complain as anger, unhappiness and sadness.

On the other hand, researchers believe that cognitive factors influence customer complain behavior. For example, justice theory, which is one of the most popular foundations predicts that in such a situation an aggrieved consumer would try to restore equity by complaining to the service provider and expecting some forms of remedial action. The evaluation of this remedial action may be considered on three dimensions: procedural justice, interactional justice and distributive justice (Sparks and McColl-Kennedy, 2001; Schoefer and Diamantopolous, 2008; Gustafson, 2009; Boshoff, 2012). According to attribution theory, the perceived cause of a service failure will influences the dissatisfied consumer's response. Customers prefer that the offending firm accepts the blame instead of attributes blame to the customer or a third party (Chan and Ngai, 2010).

Thirdly, customer personality and cultural value influence their response to service failure. Customers from different cultures show different complaining behavior of service failure (Yuksel et al., 2006). Reasons of cultural influences include: culture decides patterns of consumption, and what is acceptable in society (Steenkamp et al., 1999).

According to psychological and communicative literature, researchers reveal that "face" concerns are more important to study in conflict management (Cocroft and Ting-Toomi, 1994). It is because that being socially accepted is the fundamental need of every person (Hwang et al., 2003). In contrast to Western people, Asian people, in the cases of service failure, normally do not complain and are more likely to switch provider and spread negative word of mouth (Chan and Wan, 2008; Ashraf et al., 2013). American visitors are more likely to take personal actions and make complains to management, as compared to the Chinese group. On the other hand, the Chinese group is more likely to use bad-mouthing behaviors than the Americans (Chang et al., 2012).

In addition, the customer's background and their social or business status may also impact their complaint behavior. These factors contribute to the probability of customer complaints (Lau and Ng, 2001).

Moreover, Vázquez-Casielles et al. (2012) suggest that the financial compensation increases the customer's predisposition towards complaining to the company. McColl et al. (2005) propose that a service guarantee will encourage dissatisfied customers to complain to the service provider after a negative service encounter. Cheng and Lam (2008) investigate the role of the customer-seller relationship in the intention of complaints, and results show that the complaining intention of Chinese consumers is influencesd by customer-seller relationships. Similar results come from Hui et al. (2011). Given that customers who have close relationships with sellers are more committed to the organization (Liljande and Stranvik, 1995), they are more likely to voice out their dissatisfaction for the goodness of the organization, in order to avoid the possibility of its occurring again (Cheng and Lam, 2008).

As can be seen in previous literature, the current researches are mainly dealing with customer's complaining behavior after service failure. Yet as for customers who have already received recovery, whether they might continue to complain to the server is less noticed in researches.

4.1.3 Complaint to third parties

When consumers encounter service failures, they are facing several options, including switching provider, a complaint aimed towards the provider, a complaint via a third party, negative word of mouth or simply doing nothing (Huppertz, 2003; Singh, 1989; Goetzinger et al., 2006). After ordering these options by the level of effort required to complain, a hierarchy emerges. Complaining to family and friends (termed "private complaint" or "negative word of mouth") sits at the bottom, complaining to the business (termed "voice complaint") is at the next level, and complaining to a third-party, which is the most effortful process, sits at the top (Hogarth et al., 2001; Russell-Bennett et al., 2015). On the other hand, De Matos and Leis (2013) suggest that a condition of low satisfaction would have a higher negative effect on the intention to complain to third parties like a consumer agency, followed by negative word of mouth and complaint to the company. Among these options, third party complaining behavior has been the least extensively researched (Goetzinger et al., 2006).

According to Singh (1988), third party complaining behavior centers on expressing dissatisfaction with a service encounter to individuals external to the consumer's social circle, such as newspapers and legal agencies (Ramirez et al.,

2008). It also includes online complaints via third parties at present (Goetzinger et al., 2006). Namely, the consumer complains to one or more agencies directly are not directly involved in the exchange relationship (Singh, 1989). Thus, a third-party in the complaint literature is an organization who can intervenes on behalf of the consumer (not family or friends) (Russell-Bennett et al., 2015).

Regarding the motivation of complaint to the third party, there are various factors such as the level of dissatisfaction, financial issues, negative emotions. For example, De Matos and Leis's (2013) results support the theory that customers with lower satisfaction are more likely to engage in complaint behaviors, such as third party, private and voice response (Singh, 1988). Bougie et al. (2003) demonstrate that third party complaining is likely to increase when customer satisfaction levels decrease following a service failure (Ramirez et al., 2008). On the other hand, Hogarth et al. (2001) suggest that people will only go to a third party when the amount at stake is high. Seeking redress from third parties rather than from service providers almost always increases costs to the focal industry and the society in general (Singh, 1989). However, Russell-Bennett et al. (2015) find that people will complain over small and non-financial issues. They offer an alternative explanation for complaining to a third party that incorporates emotions as well as cognitive responses. It means that consumers exhibit negative emotional responses when dissatisfied and this may lead to a complaint to a third party (Russell-Bennett et al., 2011). Vázquez-Casielles et al. (2012) also confirm that angry customers may increase their predisposition towards complaining to third parties instead of to the company.

Other researchers consider that the customers' complaint behavior that aims to modify the company's policies and practices and that is directed directly towards the company or towards the third party (Crié, 2001; Hirschman, 1970). Bonifield and Cole (2008) also propose that voice occurs when individuals try to change the practices and policies of the offending organization by complaining directly to the firm or to third parties such as consumer and government organizations. Moreover, they pose the explanations that social comparison reduces the tendency to complain to third parties.

Additionally, the results of Ramirez et al.'s (2008) investigation reveal that an interaction between the recovery attempt initiated by the firm and the consumer's relative level of authoritarianism impacts their tendencies to engage in third party complaining behaviors. More specifically, De Matos et al. (2011) suggest that the effect of procedural justice on satisfaction with service recovery is moderated by uncertainty avoidance orientation, and the effect of recovery satisfaction on the intention to complain to third parties was moderated by power distance orientation. De Matos and Leis (2013) consider that when customers perceived first dissatisfaction with service failure followed by dissatisfaction with service recovery, namely a double deviation, they are more likely to demand compensation from the firm or from third parties, like a consumer agency.

4.1.4 WOM behavioral intention

Complaint actions taken by a consumer are not just complaining to service providers, but also include actions like spreading negative WOM. The dissatisfied customer will even complain to third parties, such as a consumer council or write a letter of complaint to management (Heung and Lam, 2003; Huang and Chang, 2008). The great majority of dissatisfaction customers will participate in private word of mouth as opposed to either taking no action, or registering a formal complaint of some form (Richins, 1983; Swanson and Kelley, 2001). According to previous "no action" literature, not only the complainers but also most of the dissatisfaction customers who do not complain to company are also likely to exit, and engage in negative WOM, especially in the competitive industries (Etzel and Silverman, 1981; Fornell and Wernerfelt, 1987; Blodgett et. al., 1993; Spreng et.al., 1995; Buttle and Burton, 2002).

Negative word of mouth is the intentions wherein customers recommend others not to purchase the goods or services from a particular firm or service provider (Richins, 1983; Sabharwal et al., 2010). NWOM communication, is defined as interpersonal communication concerning a marketing organization or product that denigrates the object of the communication (Richins, 1987; Singh, 1988; Laczniak et al., 2001; Bonifield and Cole, 2008). It can also be conceptualized as the dissatisfied customers deciding to tell their friends and relatives about their unpleasant experience with a product or service (Butelli, 2007). Researchers comprehend it as an alternative complaint response, a private complaint response to friends and family relative to a public complaint to the firm (Ashley and Varki, 2009).

Several service marketing researchers have considered the word of mouth intentions associated with service encounters (Parasuraman et al., 1988, 1991; Boulding et al., 1993; Swansonand and Kelley, 2001). They establish the importance of satisfaction and dissatisfaction as antecedents of word of mouth behavior (Richins,

1983; Yi, 1990; Spreng et al., 1995; Holloway et al., 2005). Results of these studies indicate that a positive correlation between dissatisfaction and NWOM (Szymanski and Henard, 2001; Holloway, Wang, and Parish, 2005). Namely, less-satisfied customers are more likely to be pernickety and engage in NWOM (Oliver, 1997; Anderson, 1998; Roos et al., 2004; Yanamandram and White, 2006; De Matos et al., 2012).

Many other researches propose that WOM is an important post-purchase behavior (Day, 1980); the main reason is that consumers believe that WOM communication information is highly credible than others, such as advertising messages (Spreng et al., 1995; Ashley and Varki, 2009). People often trust information from friends and family, particularly when they do not have prior experience with the service provider (Brown and Reingen, 1987; Tax et al., 1993; Ashley and Varki, 2009). Therefore, the NWOM information can influences receiver's beliefs about a particular firm, and their intentions to purchase from that firm (Spreng et al., 1995). Namely, it can influence many potential consumers' daily product and service choices (Allsop et al., 2007; Lii et al., 2012).

On the other hand, previous studies show that consumers are more likely to engage in negative word of mouth than positive word of mouth (Arndt, 1967; Richins, 1983). For example, studies indicate that unhappy customers may tell 10—20 people about their bad experience with a service company (Mattila, 2001; Liao, 2007). Anderson (1998) finds that dissatisfied customers engage more in WOM than satisfied customers and negative communications may be delivered with greater force than positive ones (Sabharwal et al., 2010). Moreover, it is worth noting that as preliminary research indicates, negative word of mouth may be particularly detrimental in the internet environment, where "word of mouse spreads even faster than word of mouth" (Reichheld and Schefter, 2000; Holloway et al., 2005).

Corresponding to the communicator's behavior, regarding the receivers of NWOM information, there is evidence that consumers give negative information and non-marketer controlled sources of information greater weight in their purchase decisions (Lutz, 1975; Spreng et al., 1995). Herr et al. (1991) suggest that relative to positive word of mouth, negative word of mouth is more influential in determining the receiver's attitudes and purchase intentions (Herr et al., 1991; Holloway et al., 2005). Researchers often use "negativity effect" to explain this consumer behavior (Klein, 1991; Rozin and Royzman, 2001). That is why customer said to others and in worst cases may decrease sales and profits of the company (Anton et al., 2007; Ashraf et al, 2013) and negative word of mouth presents a formidable challenge for firms.

Moreover, researchers find that negative word of mouth can be particularly detrimental in service industries, where the intangibility of the service makes it difficult to evaluate the service in advance and people rely more on the opinions of others (Clark et al., 1992; Ashley and Varki, 2009).

Previous researches have indicated that service failure may cause loss of customer loyalty; the objectives that consumer pursuit through engage in NWOM is different, which are alerting their affiliation of a possible danger (Richins, 1983; Curren and Folkes, 1987; Swanson and Kelley, 2001), punishing the dissatisfying product or service provider, and simply expressing their negative emotion, such as anger and frustration (Butelli, 2007).

Formally, a desire for revenge is defined as customers' need to punish and cause harm to firms for the damages they have caused (Bechwati and Morrin 2003; Grégoire and Fisher, 2006). Customers hold a grudge against firms and fail to forgive (McCullough et al., 2003). It means that customers' inability to "let go" (Finkel et al., 2002; Grégoire et al., 2009). It is found that a frustrated and angry customer may find ways to punish the provider (Alexander, 2002).

Grégoire and Fisher (2006) define the customer retaliation as the customers' seeking avenge to the perceived inequality in the exchange between themselves and the firm (Ramirez et al., 2008). These authors propose that as a consequence of the failure, the customer may choose from a range of reactions including launching negative word of mouth campaigns and pursuing third party complaint options against the transgressing firm (Grégoire and Fisher, 2006; Aaker et al., 2004).

Spreading WOM indicates that consumers try to convince themselves of their decision by convincing others, which is one of the strategies most often employed by individuals for reducing post decision dissonance (Wangenheim, 2005; Sabharwal et al., 2010). They also propose that relationship quality is instrumental in determining customer reactions (Ramirez et al., 2008).

In addition, numerous researchers focus on service recovery context. Maxham (2001) suggested that firms may restore customers' propensity to spread positive communications by ensuring satisfactory problem handling. Most of them believe that if a firm handles complaint effectively, this not only tends to reduce the occurrence of NWOM, but also increases the likelihood that customers may recommend the service to friends, relatives, and others (Blodgett et al., 1993,

1997; Davidow, 2000; Maxham, 2001; Orsingher et al., 2009; Swanson and Hsu, 2011).

4.2   Repurchase behavioral intention

Goodman and Ward (1993) suggest that for every five customers who encounter a problem, one will be lost for good. According to the previous literature, the terms "switching", "defection" and "exit" are used interchangeable (Colgate and Hedge, 2001) for the description of the situation that customers who stop purchasing the company's product/service (Webster and Sundaram, 1998; Andreassen, 2000; Ok et al., 2007). Stewart (1998) identifies three dyadic descriptors of the customer exit: (1) revocable or irrevocable, (2) complete termination or reduction of patronage, and (3) mutual or unilateral exit.

In Singh's (1988) taxonomy, exit or switching is another major category of private responses other than negative word of mouth (Chan and Wan, 2008). Exit is often implemented if voice is not successful (Blodgett et al., 1993; Ok, Back, and Shanklin, 2007). Krishna et al. (2011) explain that consumers are sensitive, and they may switch provider rather to complain, just because of the fear that they may not be properly treated.

4.2.1   Definition: exit, defection and switch provider

As Hirschman (1970) mentioned, exit means that customers discontinue purchasing behavior from the seller (Sabharwal et al., 2010). It is an escape from an objectionable situation or an active effort by the customer to terminate relationship with the seller (Hirschman, 1970). In other words, exit means voluntary separation from service provider (Farrell, 1983) or voluntary termination of exchange relationship (Singh, 1990; Ok et al., 2007; Sabharwal et al., 2010). In most cases, exit means switch provider.

Same as the concept of exit, Colgate and Hedge (2001) define defection as the customer's decision to stop purchasing a particular service or patronizing the service firm completely, which is a gradual dissolution of relationships due to problems and failures encountered over time (Malhotra et al., 2008). Stewart (1998) in a study of customer defection in the banking industry defines defection as the ending of the relationship between customer and bank.

75% of the customer who have experienced service failure have told it to at least one other person, although only 7% have told it to the service provider and stayed, and 85% have switched (Buttle and Burton, 2002). Since the cost of gaining a new customer usually exceeds greatly the cost of retaining a customer, managers are increasingly concerned with minimizing customer defections (Spreng et al., 1995), and some of researchers want to know the reasons of switching behavior and creating what is called "a switching barrier" for retaining customers.

4.2.2   The reasons for customer to switch provider

Regarding the reasons of customer switching provider, researchers have considered several different perspectives. Some of them have consistently found a relationship between satisfaction and repurchase intentions (Yi, 1990; Spreng et al., 1995). The result contains two aspects. The first one is the connection between the initial service satisfaction and switch provider. They suggest that service failures create a negative impact on the customer's intention to repurchase from the service provider and they constitute a statistically significant factor in customers' switching from one service provider to another (McCollough et al., 2000; Browning et al., 2013). Therefore, one of the important consequences of satisfaction is increased repurchase intentions. The second is the connection between recovery satisfaction and switch provider. Halstead and Page (1992) find that satisfaction with the complaint response leads to higher repurchase intentions for dissatisfied consumers.

However, Keaveney's (1995) study confirms that even satisfied customers may switch service providers; the main drives are convenience, competitor action or price. Specifically, Keaveney (1995) explores the reasons for customers to switch service providers using a critical incident technique (CIT) and codes it into eight general categories: pricing, inconvenience, core service failure, failed service encounter, response to failed service, competition, ethical problems, and involuntary switching.

Moreover, Stewart (1998) suggests that boredom and satiation may be possible triggers to exit, but conversely habitual behaviors can reduce exit risk. She highlights the key determinants of switching: a perceived decline in service and thus satisfaction, the availability of alternatives, the cost of switching (barriers) and potential for, and potential of, alternative behaviors (Buttle and Burton, 2002).

4.2.3   The cost of switching (barrier)

Researches indicate that switching cost and alternative attractiveness statistically significantly influences on the customer defection or loyalty. Most of them focus on the cost of switching, and mention that firms might retain their customers by creating switching barriers that should add value to their services (Ranaweera and Prabhu, 2003; Valenzuela et al., 2005).

Jones et al. (2000) defines switching barrier as any factor that makes it difficult or costly for customers to change providers. Therefore, Ping (1993) classifies switching barriers in switching cost, alternative attractiveness, investment, and uniqueness of investment in this wholesaler. Jones et al. (2000) divide switching barriers in three types: (1) interpersonal relationship, (2) switching cost, and (3) attractiveness of alternatives. Julander and Soderberg (2003) propose that switching barriers can be regarded as positive or negative. Hirschman (1970) explains these two concepts by saying that positive switching barriers are related to "wanting to be in a relationship" while negative switching barriers are related to "having to be in a relationship". Relative to positive switching barriers, these refer to the strength of the interpersonal relationship between the customer and the supplier (Berry and Parasuraman, 1991; Tumball and Willson, 1989). Concerning negative switching barriers, these include switching cost and attractiveness of existing alternatives (Valenzuela et al., 2005).

Although switching cost is not the only factor that influences the exit decision, it is considered the most important. The results of researches indicate that consumers will judge the switching costs before any exit decision is made (Malhotra et al., 2008). It means that consumers judge the decision to stay or to defect from a relationship with current supplier according to the switching cost. Switching costs are defined as the costs of finding, evaluating, and adopting another solution (Hawkins et al., 2004). It is the cost of switching between different brands of products or services (Chen and Hitt, 2002).

However, for Lee et al. (2001), switching costs are costs incurred by changing providers, which would not incur if customers stay with their current provider. They suggest that the costs of switching depend on the levels of the information search cost, perceived risk, substitutability of the service provider and geographical proximity to the service provider (Malhotra et al., 2008). This definition is similar to switching barriers, also includes alternative attractiveness. Therefore, the term "switching barriers" and "switching costs" could be used interchangeably generally.

Chen and Hitt (2002) point out that switching cost could be explicit and implicit. Explicit switching costs include transaction cost, learning cost, and artificial cost, whereas implicit costs are associated with decision bias and risk aversion, as follows (See Table 4-1):

Table 4-1 Switching costs

Explicit costs	Transaction cost	Cost occurred to start a new relationship with a provider and/or costs necessary to terminate an existing relationship
	Learning cost	The effort required by the customer to reach the same level of comfort with a new product as they had for an old product
	Artificial cost	Cost created by deliberate actions of company
Implicit costs	Decision biase	like the "Status Quo Bias", the tendency for people to like things to stay relatively the same
	Risk aversion	When consumer exposed to uncertainty, they attempt to reduce that uncertainty. It is a preference for a sure outcome with higher or equal expected value

Source: Chen and Hitt, 2002; Kahneman and Tverksy, 1984.

Furthermore, Fornell (1992) establishes an idea that the connection between customer satisfaction and customer loyalty depends on factors such as market regulation, switching costs, brand equity, existence of loyalty programs, proprietary technology, and product differentiation at the industry level. Several authors have mentioned that these factors and others, such as number of attractive alternatives in the market, can be considered as switching barriers (Fornell, 1992; Jones et al., 2000; Julander and Soderberg, 2003; Valenzuela et al., 2005).

In addition, the researches regarding exit behaviors are explored in various perspectives. Day and Landon (1977) link "exit" to "boycott" as a more radical and active reaction to dissatisfaction (Butelli, 2007). Reill (1997) suggests that 14%—15% of switchers do so because their complaint is not handled satisfactorily. While many marketing activities are designed to gain new customers, concerning for repeat purchasing by current customers is designed to maintain existing customers by decreasing customer exit (Spreng et al., 1995). Providers should maintain trust and loyalty to give a platform for customers to feel comfortable and confident to complain without hesitation (Johnston 1998; Krishna et al., 2011). Exit should appeal more to collectivist because of its non-confrontational nature. Moreover, exit is non-instrumental, which would likely make it less attractive to the redress minded individualists (Chan and Wan, 2008).

4.3　Multiple responses simultaneously

Based on previous literature, the consumer reactions to dissatisfaction are composed by multiple responses (or behaviors), including complaint to the seller, negative word of mouth, switching provider, and taking legal actions (Singh, 1988). According to Singh (1990), these "response styles", imply a unique set of responses that one or more consumers utilize to deal with a particular dissatisfying situation (Schoefer and Diamantopoulos, 2009). Therefore, these options are not mutually exclusive and any dissatisfied customer may engage in multiple responses (Casado-Díaz and Nicolau-Gonzálbez, 2009). In other words, consumers are not restricted to one type of complaining behavior; rather, some consumers might choose to complain to the seller, at the same time, complain to friends, or complain (to the seller and / or to friends) and switch provider (Blodgett and Granbois, 1992).

However, our understanding of the structure of dissatisfaction responses and the factors that influences these responses is still quite limited (Casado-Díaz and Nicolau-Gonzálbez, 2009). There is a gap in the study of multiple responses simultaneously to dissatisfaction. Little to know why and when customer could or will take which action responses simultaneously to their dissatisfaction experience.

4.4　No action

Although some researchers have identified "no action" or the similar "non-behavioral, doing nothing" categories when classifying customer behavior after recovery, researchers from a different angle consider the conception fairly differently. Some researchers name this situation "loyalty", in which the customer decides not to complain, but to stay loyal instead to a service or to a product accepting silently and passively its decline. In this case, the word "loyal" has no moral or positive value (Butelli, 2007). Loyalty is one of those cognitive, non-behavioral reactions, which can affect consumers' perception of the problem up to deny that dissatisfaction exists (Olshavsky, 1977). The customer is loyal, despite the problem experienced and the consequent dissatisfaction, especially when there are no available alternatives.

Some other researchers perceive "no action" the same as "do not complain" and "non-complaint". They suggest that no action means that dissatisfied customers do not complain directly to firms, they just walkaway silently and switch provider, and sometimes spread negative word of mouth (Chebat et al., 2005; Voorhees et al., 2006; Makkonen, 2014).

Undoubtedly, comparing to complaints, non-complaint behaviors are harder to detect (Chebat et al., 2005). Besides, customers who make complaints are generally representatives of those "no action" customers, of their wills. So, in this study, the research subjects are mainly complainers who suffered recent service failures.

4.5 Literature limitations

First of all, in the prediction of customer future behaviors, the mainstream opinion is to consider the customer satisfaction level after recovery, suggesting a positive and linear relationship between them. Yet some voices disagree, arguing it is the accumulated "overall satisfaction level" which consists of satisfaction about recovery and after recovery that matters most. There is slight difference between the two measurements, meaning that customers who are satisfied with compensation (meets expectation) may not be satisfied with the whole product or service process. In that way, they would still be unlikely to repeat purchase behaviors in the future. In contrast, some might be unhappy with the recovery process, but the whole purchase is considered fair in mind. In this sense, they might continue to repeat purchase or even make recommendations to others out of value for money for example. The existing literature usually deals with satisfaction studies, but is lacking a cognition to separate the concept of "satisfaction" and link it to behavior analysis respectively.

Secondly, researchers believe that even though satisfaction level influences customer behavior like making complaints, there might be other factors (Singh, 1990; Sharma et al., 2010). According to literature previously discussed, the customer's attribution and service failure would impact the expectation, causing a disconfirmation between reality and expectation, and then affect satisfaction, hence future behaviors. However, researches that skip the mediating "disconfirmation" and study the relationship between attribution, service failure and customer behavior directly are rare. Such fact leads to a deficiency in knowledge about whether attribution would affect customer behaviors directly. For example, if the customer attributes to the hotel, and the cause is uncontrollable, would the possibility of re-purchase be affected? Neither could we know if the type of failure and severity would affect future intentions.

Thirdly, most studies on dissatisfied customers focus on the timeline at which service failure occurs, but little attention has been paid to where the recovery fails again. For instance, customers may complain when encounter a service failure, but they would hardly continue to complain if the recovery fails again; instead, they prefer to negative word of mouth or exit. That is, the consequence can be worse if an organization fails in the recovery process than the original service process. Thus, in this study, we would testify the impact the satisfaction level after recovery has over the customer behavior.

Finally, the current literature has noticed several behaviors that customers might take after recovery failure, but not in a systematic level—it usually looks into one sole behavior where in reality people might take several at the same time. For example, a customer could exit and spread negative word of mouth on internet on his way to another alternative. We shall make more attempts in this study on such themes.

4.6   Conclusion

Abundant literature indicates that there is some relationship between satisfaction after recovery and customer's behavioral intention. That is, successful service recovery can have a positive effect on consumers' recovery satisfaction and overall satisfaction. Then, satisfaction after recovery influences customer's behavioral intentions (Mattila, 2001; Gruber et al., 2011).

Researchers have systematically examined the relationship between customer satisfaction and its consequences, namely, why and how consumers respond to service failures and customer dissatisfaction (Oliver, 1980, 1997; Labarbera and Marzursky, 1983; Anderson, 1998; Szymanski and Henard, 2001; Crié, 2003; Ha, 2006). Then, they have classified the customer dissatisfaction responses as "no action" and "take some action" (Day and Landon, 1977). In general, no action means that the dissatisfied customers do no complain directly to firms, while customers taking some actions, might include complaining behavior, and switching provider. Abundant literature supports the commonsense expectation that satisfied customers are more likely to stay with their existing providers than dissatisfied ones (Oliver, 1997; Szymanski and Henard, 2001; Casado-Díaz, 2009).

Most researchers believe that the vast majority of the dissatisfied customers fail to complain to the provider (Stephens and Gwinner 1998; Chebat et al., 2005). In this area, some of the researchers focus on the comparative analysis studies between complainers and non-complainers (TARP; 1979; Halstead and Page, 1992; Voorhees et al., 2006; Kau and Loh, 2006; Bodey and Grace, 2006, 2007; Sharma et al., 2010) and explore the motivation of dissatisfaction customers who did not complain (Stephens and Gwinner, 1998; Snellman and Vihtkari, 2003; Chebat et al., 2005; Voorhees et al., 2006; Nimako and Mensah, 2012; Salo and Makkonen ,2014).

Although complaint behavior is "the tip-of-the-iceberg", it can represent most of the non-complainers' behavior and give service provider an opportunity to recovery and increase customer satisfaction, loyalty, long-term sales and profits (Fornell and Wernefelt, 1987; Kelley et al., 1993; Reichheld, 1993; Reichheld and Sasser, 1990). Therefore, research suggests that service provider should encourage complaints (Davidow, 2000). In general, complaint behaviors include complaint to provider, complaint to third parties, and NWOM (complain to relatives and friends).

In addition, researchers suggest that consumer dissatisfaction response options are not mutually exclusive and any dissatisfied customers may engage in multiple responses (Casado-Díaz and Nicolau-Gonzálbez, 2009).

In sum, researchers believe that customer satisfaction after recovery could influences customer's behavioral intention, such as repurchase intention, the spread of positive WOM (Blodgett et al., 1997; De Matos et al., 2009; Fornell and Wernerfelt, 1988; Harris et al., 2006; Kelley et al., 1993; Lii et al., 2012). Satisfaction arising from recovery can also affect customer behavior who makes afterwards complaints (Kelley and Davis, 1994; Tax et al., 1998; Casado-Díaz, 2009).

CHAPTER 5

CONCEPTUAL MODEL AND HYPOTHESIS

In line with the study objectives, we are going to highlight the key point in the literature that are relevant to hypothesis formulation. Five sets of hypotheses are presented below, and the conceptual model is shown below.

5.1 Service failure influences customer attribution

According to the expectation-disconfirmation paradigm, service failure is the result of negative disconfirmation where expectation exceeds reality (See 2.1.1). But arguments have been made that failures are almost inevitable in the service industry since the nature of such business involves too many variables. Therefore, researchers tend to categorize failures into types for simplification purpose. Among various of attempts, Bitner et al.'s (1990) CIT classification is considered most specific which has three major groups (service delivery system failure, not achieved customer needs and requests, unprompted and unsolicited employee action) and twelve subunits within. Other researchers look into customer satisfaction from a different angle—the severity of failure, and find out severity directly influences not only customer satisfaction, but customer expectation, recovery effects, even behavioral intention as well.

Adequate literature in service failure shows that customers would seek causes for happening, customer attribution in other words (Folkes, 1984; Folkes et al.,1987; Oliver et al., 1988; Anderson et al., 2009). In the light of Weiner's (1985a, 1986) proposal about the attribution theory, consideration on three dimensions affects customer attribution: locus of causality, controllability and stability.

Locus of control means the identification of the responsible party (Anderson et al., 2009). To protect their ego, customers tend to deny any responsibility put upon themselves (Hui and Toffoli, 2002) and often attribute bad results to situational (or external causes), while attribute good results to their own abilities (or internal causes) (Ye, 2005; Vázquez-Casielles et al., 2007).

Controllability refers to whether the organization had the power to exert control over the events of the situation (Borkowski et al., 2003). Judgements on such abilities over a certain organization are mostly based on customers' previous experience. The greater the perception of service quality from the past is, the more likely consumers will attribute to the service organization who has high levels of competence and effort to avoid service failures (Narayandas, 1998; Vázquez-Casielles et al., 2007).

The stability dimension captures if causes change over time (Oghojafor, 2012), or if the incident is likely to be repeated (Anderson et al, 2009). Weiner (2000) considers that consumers are likely to attribute a current failure to unstable, rather than stable, causes when past experiences of service quality is positive.

Based on service failure and customer attribution literature, causal attribution is the "spontaneous" behavior by customers after they have experienced negative events. Thus, we propose the first hypotheses as follows:

H1: Service failure that customer experienced in hotel influences customer attribution.

H1a: Type of service failure that customer experienced in hotel influences customer attribution (to hotel, customer and environment).

H1b: Severity of service failure that customer experienced in hotel influences customer attribution (to hotel, customer, and environment).

H1c: Stability and controllability of service failure influence customer attribution (to hotel, customer and environment).

5.2 Customer attribution influences customer recovery expectation

Customer recovery expectation is the expectation about the organization's recovery type and the efforts made prior to obtained recovery process but after failure occurs. Customer recovery expectation is influencesd by many factors including spontaneous. Hence, customer attribution (locus, controllability, stability) is one of the determinants in identifying customer recovery expectation.

Firstly, it is argued that consumer expectations of recovery may vary by the causal attributions they infer after a failure occurs. Literally, parties being regarded as responsible shall therefore solve the problem (Folkes, 1988). Once customer attribution points to the hotel, customers would rise the expectation on its solution; if the attribution lies on customer or situational environments, the expectation on the hotel lowers down naturally.

Secondly, Folkes (1984) finds out that controllability has a positive influence on customer recovery expectation. In other words, if the failure is perceived preventable that hotels are able to take certain actions to control events, expectation of recovery would be high, otherwise it would be low. Similar results are drawn from Hess et al. (2003).

Thirdly, Hess et al. (2003) suggest stability influences customer recovery expectation positively. They believe that if the service failure is perceived stable, recognizable for organizations, then policies of reaction should be made. Under such circumstances, the expectation rises, otherwise it goes down.

Recovery efforts can be divided into different categories based on various of methods. Roschk and Gelbrich (2014) come up with the resource-based compensation type classification which sorts compensations into monetary, new/exchange goods, new/re-performed service, psychological (apology) compensations. Chou et al. (2009) add service/product guarantee to strategic recovery options. Hereby we propose the second hypothesis:

H2: Customer attribution (locus, stability, controllability) influences customer recovery expectation (recovery magnitude of expectation, recovery type of expectation).

H2a: Locus of attribution influences customer expectation (recovery magnitude of expectation, recovery type of expectation).

H2b: Stability of service failure influences customer expectation (recovery magnitude of expectation, recovery type of expectation).

H2c: Controllability of service failure influences customer expectation (recovery magnitude of expectation, recovery type of expectation).

5.3   Service failure influences customer recovery expectation

In the field of antecedent of recovery expectation (See 3.3.1), many theorists believe customers' experience of service failure would then affect their expectation on recovery received (Boulding et al., 1993; Kelley et al., 1994). Justice theory suggests the severer the failure is, the higher the perceived loss will be, and the higher expectation will be (McColl-Kennedy et al., 2003; Smith et al., 1999; Li et al., 2012). The severity hence is an important indicator in customer recovery expectation.

Secondly, according to the matching hypothesis and justice theory, customers prefer "matched" compensations. For example, if the loss is about money, they would like monetary or financial compensations; if the loss is emotional, they would like apologies, explanations and respect. Based on matching hypothesis, Roschk and Gelbrich (2014) argue that the effect can be the strongest when exchanged resources match in kind, advancing that compensation type and failure type interact on the recovery effect of compensation. Therefore, we propose our third hypothesis:

H3: Service failure (type, severity) that customer experienced in hotel influences customer recovery expectation (recovery magnitude of expectation, recovery type of expectation).

H3a: Type of service failure that customer experienced in hotel influences customer recovery expectation (recovery magnitude of expectation, recovery type of expectation).

H3b: Severity of service failure that customer experienced in hotel influences customer recovery expectation (recovery magnitude of expectation, recovery type of expectation).

5.4   Disconfirmation between customer recovery expectations and obtained recovery influences customer satisfaction after recovery

Based on expectation-disconfirmation paradigm, McCollough (2000) suggested the three consequences of recovery efforts: superior recovery, adequate recovery, and inferior recovery, compared with customer recovery expectation. When there is a superior recovery, positive expectation-disconfirmation would please customers, and even "service recovery paradox" may appear (Hart et al., 1990; Krishna et al., 2011; Vázquez-Casielles et al., 2010). In this situation, the greater the gap is, the more satisfied customers would be. If organizations provide adequate recovery, which usually matches expectation type, customers would be satisfied. Yet in occasions that inferior recovery is served, a "double" deviation would cause negative expectation-disconfirmation and then dissatisfy customers. In this case, the greater the gap is, the more dissatisfied customers would be. Moreover, "matching hypotheses" suggests an unmatched compensation type would affect customer recovery satisfaction and overall satisfaction. In short, a disconfirmation gap can be caused by either extent or type. We propose the fourth hypothesis:

H4: The disconfirmation (discrepency between customer recovery expectation and obtained recovery) has effects on customer satisfaction after recovery (include recovery satisfaction and overall satisfaction).

H4a: The disconfirmation (disceipency between customer recovery expectation and obtained recovery) influences customer recovery satisfaction.

H4b: The disconfirmation (discrepency between customer recovery expectation and obtained recovery) influences customer overall satisfaction.

5.5   Customer satisfaction after recovery influences future behavioral intention

Empirical studies show that customer satisfaction affects behavioral intention. After recovery, customer's behavioral intention includes: (1) no action (non-behavioral, non-complaining, doing nothing)—it means that customers do not complain to firms; (2) complaint behavior—customers voice the dissatisfaction experience to the firms, third parties, and relatives and friends (negative word of mouth); (3) exit—customers switch provider or exit consumption; (4) multiple responses simultaneously.

Satisfied customers would be more likely to perform favorable actions in organization's perspective like re-purchase and positive WOM (Fornell, 1992; Hu et al., 2009; Matzler et al., 2006; Kandampully and Suhartanto, 2000; Dimitriades, 2006; Chi and Qu, 2008; Faullant et al., 2008). And dissatisfied customers would be more likely to perform unfavorable actions in organization's perspective, like exit, complaint, or NWOM (Bearden et al., 1983; Richins 1983; Singh, 1988; Huang et al., 1996). In an era of internet, any comments can be spread terribly quick and wide. Therefore, we propose the fifth hypothesis (See Figure 5-1):

H5: Customer satisfaction after recovery influences customer behavioral intention.

H5a: Customer satisfaction after recovery (include recovery satisfaction and overall satisfaction) positively influences the likelihood of repurchasing the services of this hotel in the future.

H5b: Customer satisfaction after recovery (include recovery satisfaction and overall satisfaction) positively influences the likelihood of recommending this hotel to other people.

H5c: Customer satisfaction after recovery (include recovery satisfaction and overall satisfaction) negatively influences the likelihood of discouraging other people to use the hotel service.

H5d: Customer satisfaction after recovery (include recovery satisfaction and overall satisfaction) negatively influences the likelihood of complaining to the hotel and manager.

H5e: Customer satisfaction after recovery (include recovery satisfaction and overall satisfaction) negatively influences the likelihood of complaining to third parties.

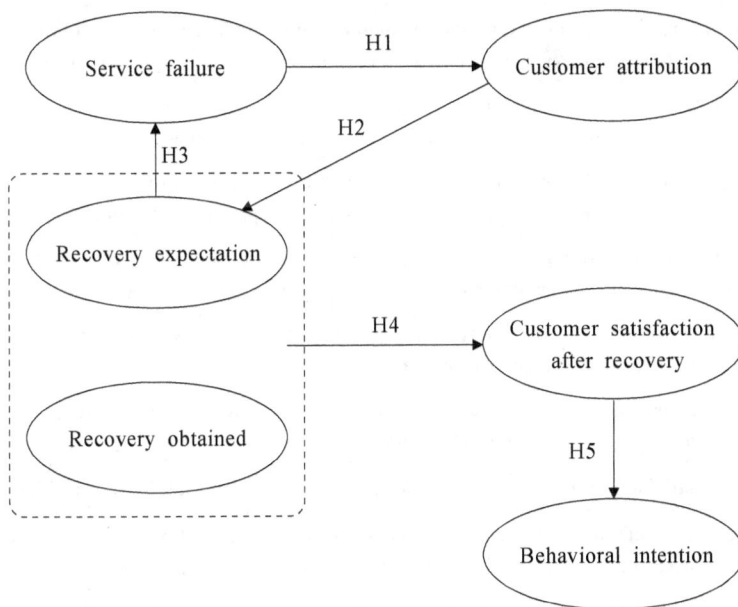

Figure 5-1   Theoretical framework of service failure, recovery, satisfaction and behavioral intention

Five sets of hypotheses are presented in Table 5-1.

Table 5-1   Hypotheses

H1: Service failure that customer experienced in hotel influences customer attribution.
H1a: Type of service failure that customer experienced in hotel influences customer attribution (to hotel, customer and environment).
H1b: Severity of service failure that customer experienced in hotel influences customer attribution (to hotel, customer, and environment).
H1c: Stability and controllability of service failure influence customer attribution (to hotel, customer and environment).
H2: Customer attribution (locus, stability, controllability) influences customer recovery expectation (recovery magnitude of expectation, recovery type of expectation).

Continued

H2a: Locus of attribution influences customer expectation (recovery magnitude of expectation, recovery type of expectation).
H2b: Stability of service failure influences customer expectation (recovery magnitude of expectation, recovery type of expectation).
H2c: Controllability of service failure influences customer expectation (recovery magnitude of expectation, recovery type of expectation).
H3: Service failure (type, severity) that customer experienced in hotel influences customer recovery expectation (recovery magnitude of expectation, recovery type of expectation).
H3a: Type of service failure that customer experienced in hotel influences customer recovery expectation (recovery magnitude of expectation, recovery type of expectation).
H3b: Severity of service failure that customer experienced in hotel influences customer recovery expectation (recovery magnitude of expectation, recovery type of expectation).
H4: The disconfirmation (discrepency between customer recovery expectation and obtained recovery) has effects on customer satisfaction after recovery (include recovery satisfaction and overall satisfaction).
H4a: The disconfirmation (discrepency between customer recovery expectation and obtained recovery) influences customer recovery satisfaction.
H4b: The disconfirmation (discrepency between customer recovery expectation and obtained recovery) influences customer overall satisfaction.
H5: Customer satisfaction after recovery influences customer behavioral intention.
H5a: Customer satisfaction after recovery (include recovery satisfaction and overall satisfaction) positively influences the likelihood of repurchasing the services of this hotel in the future.
H5b: Customer satisfaction after recovery (include recovery satisfaction and overall satisfaction) positively influences the likelihood of recommending this hotel to other people.
H5c: Customer satisfaction after recovery (include recovery satisfaction and overall satisfaction) negatively influences the likelihood of discouraging other people to use the hotel service.
H5d: Customer satisfaction after recovery (include recovery satisfaction and overall satisfaction) negatively influences the likelihood of complaining to the hotel and manager.
H5e: Customer satisfaction after recovery (include recovery satisfaction and overall satisfaction) negatively influences the likelihood of complaining to the third parties.

CHAPTER 6

RESEARCH METHODOLOGY

This Chapter introduces the process of data collection, design of the survey instrument, and measurement of constructs. The statistical methods used will also be elaborated here. The following sections are divided into four parts: (1) data collection and sampling; (2) survey instruments; (3) definition of the variables and their measurement; (4) analysis of reliability and validity; (5) statistical methods.

6.1   Data collection and sampling

The data used in this study were collected through the online distribution channel "Wenjuanxing" (https://www.wjx.cn), which is commonly acknowledged in the Chinese marketing academics. The research subject selected was Chinese hotel customers. The sampling frame consists of real hotel customers who have encountered hotel services failure and complained to service provider or manager in the past six months. The questionnaire is distributed geographically in over 25 cities across China, as is designed to be a representative sample of the Chinese hotel industry customers.

The survey was conducted in a three-month period from April 2018 to June 2018. The questionnaires were distributed to randomly selected hotel customers and collected by a professional online platform "Wenjuanxing". A total of 318 completed questionnaires were collected in this study.

In this process, to ensure the collected data is authentic and effective, the sample service provides strict quality control mechanism. According to the questionnaire, we set up the screening page to filter out the applicants who do not meet the requirements. The sample filter conditions are: (1) did you have an experience of staying in a hotel in the past six month? (2) did you experience some service failures during your stay? (3) did you complain to service provider or manager after experiencing the service failure? Thus, the respondents are the customers who have experienced service failure and complained to service provider (or manager) in a hotel in the past six month. In addition, the same IP address, the same computer, and the same user name can only be recorded once; those who are recognized as invalid answer sheets or excluded by the screening page cannot be filled in again; and set the time taken to complete too short, trap rules (e.g. in Q11 and Q15, in each of these two questions, the content of one option is reverse designed) to filter out the casually filled answer sheets. Trap rules means that a reverse answer is set in the answer item of the question. If the respondents arbitrarily answer the question, there may be inconsistencies or contradictions in the answer to the same question.

6.2 Survey instrument

The survey instrument was designed based on the literature review. The instrument was first developed in English language and then translated into Chinese using a combination of parallel blind translation and modified direct translation as described by Guthery and Lowe (1995). The instrument was first translated by two bilinguals simultaneously and the two target versions of the instrument were compared and consensus was reached. The translated instrument was then reviewed by five experts and some revisions have been made.

After that, we did a pre-test and collected 55 questionnaires. We adjusted the text expression again to ensure that participants would not have any ambiguity in their understandings. The instrument contains eight parts as displayed in Table 6-1.

Table 6-1 Structure of the survey instrument

Section	Questions included
I	Sample and filter condition
II	Types of service failure
III	Customer attribution
IV	Recovery expectation and good

continued

Section	Questions included
V	Customer satisfaction after recovery
VI	Customers' behavior/behavior intention after service recovery
VII	Others: the purpose of your trip, staying time, the hotel star-rating, reason of choose the hotel
VIII	Demographic characteristics

6.3 Variable definition and measurement

The variables used in this research included service failure, customer attribution, recovery expectation and obtained recovery, customer satisfaction after recovery, and behavioral intention. The measurement of each construct is shown below.

6.3.1 Service failure measurement

The measurement of service failure is divided into two parts, namely (1) the type of service failure, and (2) the severity of the service failure. Type of service failure is operationalized using the scales developed by Bitner et al. (1990). It includes three major groups, and a total of 12 categories. Group 1: employee response to service delivery system failure. It consists of three categories, which are (1) unavailable service; (2) unreasonably slow service; and (3) other core service failures. Group 2: employee response to customer needs and requests. There are four categories, including (1) customer's special needs; (2) customer preferences; (3) admitted customer error; and (4) potentially disruptive others. Group 3: unprompted and unsolicited employee action. The group comprises five categories, they are (1) attention paid to customers; (2) truly out-of-the-ordinary employee behavior; (3) employee behavior in the context of cultural norms; (4) gestalt evaluation (societal/cultural insult); and (3) exemplary performance under adverse circumstances.

Severity of the service failure was measured by the scale developed by Hess et al. (2003) and Cambra-Fierro et al. (2011). The respondents were asked to answer the following questions on a 1—7 Likert Scale: "Based on your experience with hotel, how would you describe the LATEST service problem? Please indicate the severity of the service problem."

6.3.2 Customer attribution measurement

The measurement for customer attribution were developed based on a literature review in attribution theories (e. g. Weiner, 1992; Oghojafor, 2012; Rotter, 1966; Folkes, 1984; Weiner, 1992; Kim et al., 2014). Customer attribution of service failure is defined as the locus and magnitude of blame a customer believes should be placed for the failure, in other words, who should be blamed for the problem and to what extent? (Maxham and Netemeyer, 2002; Dong et al., 2008). Some researchers perceive attribution of blame as the assignment of causality for failure (Choi and Mattila, 2008; Folkes, 1984). the locus of causality, controllability and stability are its three dimensions according to Folkes (1984).

The locus of causality is to decide if the cause of problem is internal or external—that is to say, whether it is in the actor or situation, and whether the cause of problem is perceived to reside within or outside of the consumer (Drach-Zahavy and Somech, 2006; Robertson, Mcquilken and Kandampully, 2012). Accordingly, the locus of causality is measured by two questions: "Regarding the service problems that you encountered, who should be responsible in your mind?" (Q6) and "The perceived cause of an event that you experience is?" (Q7) (Dong et al., 2008). The respondents were asked to evaluate the responsible of each item (hotel, customer, and situation) on a 1—7 Likert Scale.

Controllability and stability are also measured by the scale developed by Drach-Zahavy and Somech. and Robertson et al. (2012). Stability is the perceived time period lasting till the problem is solved. It assesses whether the cause of an event is permanent (stable) or temporary that could vary in time and context (unstable). Controllability on the other side is the degree to which the problem can be avoided. Controllability assesses beliefs about whether the actor can influences causes that determine the outcome of an event (controllable) or whether the causes are beyond the actor's influences (uncontrollable). (Laczniak et al., 2001; Hess et al., 2003; Drach-Zahavy and Somech, 2006; Robertson et al., 2012; Vázquez-Casielles et al., 2012).

Thus, stability (stable cause of the service failure) is measured by two questions. They are "Do you think the service failure that you experienced in this hotel happens frequently?" (Q8) and "Do you think the reason for the service failure that you experienced in this hotel is likely to be a permanent problem?" (Q9) (Hess et al., 2003; Drach-Zahavy et al., 2006; Vázquez-Casielles et al., 2012). Controllability of service failure is measured by the question "Do you think the service failure that you experienced in this hotel could be avoided?" (Q10) (Hess et al., 2003; Weiner, 2000; Drach-Zahavy et al., 2006).

6.3.3 Measurement of recovery expectation and obtained compensation

The action taken in response to a service failure is defined as service recovery by Grönroos (1988). It includes all the activities and efforts employed to rectify, amend, and restore the loss(es) incurred after the failure. Grönroos specified two dimensions of service recovery: outcome and process. The outcome, or technical, dimension is what has been done (tangible compensation), whereas the process, or functional, dimension concerns how it is done (employee interaction with the customer). Both could have an influence on customers' perception of the recovery (Dong, Evans and Zou, 2008).

In this part, the level of customer recovery expectation, the list of recovery expectation, obtained recovery, and the disconfirmation between customer recovery expectation and what they obtained from hotel are measured. All the measurements were developed base on the review of literature in service failure and recovery.

The level of customer' service recovery expectations is measured by the scale developed by Hess et al., (2003) and Cambra-Fierro et al. (2011). Respondents' expectation from the hotel was measured by the question "Given the problem you encountered in the hotel, how do you expect the hotel to respond?" (Q11).

Specific recovery expectations and obtained compensation are both listed according to the literature (Roschk and Gelbrich, 2014; Gonzalez, Hoffman, Ingram and LaForge, 2010; Chou et al., 2009). They are measured by the two questions: "Regarding the service problems that you encountered, how would you like to be compensated? Please choose the level of compensation that you expected in response to the service failure that you experienced" (Q12); and "Please list the type of compensation that you obtained from the hotel after you experienced the service failure, please choose the item(s) precisely from the following list that matched you" (Q13) (See Table 6-2).

After that, we measure the disconfirmation between expectation and obtained recovery (Hess et al., 2003) by the question "What is your opinion of the hotel's response to your complaint about the service problem or compensation provided?" (Q14).

Table 6-2 Variables and measurement

Construct	Survey questions	Measurement
Sample filter condition	1. Did you have the experience of staying in a hotel in the past six month? 2. Did you experience some service failures (error) when you stayed in the hotel? 3. Did you complain to service provider or manager after experiencing the service failure?	
Types of the service failure	4. Please list the type of service problem that you have experienced in the hotel (multiple choice). (1) Unavailable service (2) Unreasonably slow service (3) Other core service failure (4) Customer's "special need" (5) Customer preference (6) Admitted customer error (7) Potentially disruptive others (8) Attention paid to customer (9) Truly out-of-the-ordinary employee behavior (10) Employee behavior in the context of cultural norms (11) Gestalt evaluation (societal/ cultural insult) (12) Exemplary performance under adverse circumstances (13) Other service failure, please describe it	7-point Likert Scale (7 = strongly agree, 1 = strongly disagree)
Severity of the service failure	5. Based on your experience with hotel, how would you describe the LATEST service problem? Please indicate the severity of the service problem. (1) Mild—Severe (2) Major—Minor (30) Instatistically significant—Statistically significant	
Customer attribution— locus	6. Regarding the service problems that you encountered, who should be responsible in your mind? (1) The problem that I encountered was all the hotel's fault (2) The service problem that I encountered was my fault (3) The service problem that I encountered was due to the external environment; it is not my fault 7. The perceived cause of an event that you experience is: consumer(yourself)-external environmental factors.	
Customer attribution— stability, Controllability	8. Do you think the service failure that you experienced in this hotel happens frequently? 9. Do you think the reason for the service failure that you experienced in this hotel is likely to be a long-lasting problem? 10. Do you think the service failure that you experienced in this hotel could be avoided?	

Continued

Construct	Survey questions	Measurement
Recovery expectation	11. Given the problem you encountered in the hotel, how do you expect the hotel to respond? (1) I expect the hotel to do everything they can to solve the problem I encountered (2) I don't expect the hotel to exert much effort to solve the problem (R) (3) I expect the hotel to try to make up for the service failure (4) I expect the hotel to compensate me to some extent	
List of the compensation you expected	12. Regarding the service problems that you encountered, how would you like to be compensated? Please choose the level of compensation that you expected in response to the service failure that you experienced. (1) Deferred monetary compensation tied to future purchase, for example, voucher, hotel or hotel chain credit received (2) Immediate monetary compensation tied to the current purchase, for example, discount, refund (100% price reduction), free upgrades (3) New/exchanged goods, such as changing a new room for you (4) Free new/replicate service, e.g. house-keeping service (5) Psychological compensation (apology) (6) Service (or product) guarantee (7) Other compensation	7-point Likert Scale (7 = strongly agree, 1 = strongly disagree) 7-point Likert Scale (7 = strongly expect, 1 = strongly unexpected)
List of the compensation you obtained	13. Please list the type of compensation that you obtained from the hotel after you experienced the service failure, it by choosing in the following list one or more items that are correct (multiple choice). (1) Delayed-monetary (including voucher, hotel or hotel chain credit), that is tied to future purchase (2) Immediate-monetary (including discount, money back, upgrade), that is tied to the current purchase (3) New/exchanged goods, such as changed a new room for you (4) New / re-performed service, such as clean your room again (5) Psychological (apology) (6) Guarantee (7) Others compensation (8) No compensation/unresponsiveness (the hotel does not respond to your complaint)	

Continued

Construct	Survey questions	Measurement
Disconfirmation between expectation and obtained	14. What is your opinion of the hotel's response to your complaint about the service problem or compensation provided? (1) Better than my expectation—worse than my expectation (R) (2) Beyond my expectation—lower than my expectation	
Satisfaction with the recovery service	15. Please indicate your satisfaction with the recovery service (compensation) provided by the hotel. (1) I was happy with how the hotel handled my complaint (2) I was pleased with the manner in which the complaint was dealt with (3) Overall I was not satisfied with the way the complaint was handled	
Overall satisfaction	16. Please indicate the level of your overall satisfaction (pre-failure and post-recovery). (1) I am satisfied with my overall experience with the hotel (2) As a whole, I am happy with the hotel (3) Overall, I am pleased with the service experience with this hotel	7-point Likert Scale (7 = strongly agree, 1 = strongly disagree)
Behaviour intention	17. After experiencing service failure and service recovery provided by this hotel, please read the following descriptions, and choose from one of the seven numbers to express your extent of the intention to the following behaviors/actions. (1) Indicate your likelihood of staying in this hotel again in the future (2) Indicate your likelihood of recommending this hotel to others (3) Indicate your likelihood of discouraging other people to choose this hotel (4) Indicate your likelihood of complaining to the hotel and manager (5) Indicate your likelihood of complaining to third parties, e.g. customer association, etc. (6) Other behavior intention	
Others	18. Please specify your purpose of trip. 19. How long have you been staying in the hotel? 20. Please specify the hotel star-rating that you stayed in and experienced service failure. 21. Why have you chosen this hotel (multiple choice)? 22. The reason that you chose the hotel again after you experienced service problem.	

Continued

Construct	Survey questions	Measurement
Demographic characteristics	23. Please specify your gender. 24. Please specify your age group. 25. Please specify your educational level. 26. Please specify your occupation. 27. Please specify your region of residency. 28. Please specify your average monthly income?	

6.3.4 Customer satisfaction after recovery

Customer satisfaction after recovery is measured by two questions. One is "Please indicate your satisfaction with the service recovery provided by the hotel" (Q15). It is regarding customer satisfaction with the recovery service (compensation) (Dos Santos et al., 2007, 2011). Another is "Please indicate the level of your overall satisfaction (including the procedure between pre-failure and post-recovery process)," (Q16) (Ok, Back and Shanklin, 2007).

6.3.5 Customers' behavioral intention after service recovery

Customer behavior intention after recovery is measured based on the study of Vázquez-Casielles et al. (2012), and Bonifield and Cole (2008). The respondents who experienced service failure and service recovery provided by this hotel, were asked to read the descriptions, and choose a score from one to seven to express their extent of the intention to the behaviors/actions.

These behavioral intentions encompass repurchase intention, WOM intention (positive or negative), complain intention, and so on. They are measured as follows: (1) indicate your likelihood of staying this hotel again in the future; (2) indicate your likelihood of recommending this hotel to others; (3) indicate your likelihood of discouraging other people to choose this hotel; (4) indicate your likelihood of complaining to the hotel and manager; (5) indicate your likelihood of complaining to third parties, e. g. customer association etc.; and (6) other behavioral intention (Vázquez-Casielles et al.,2012; Bonifield and Cole, 2008).

6.4 Analysis of reliability and validty

In this section, we will testify the reliability and validity of the data collected. Reliability refers to the "consistency" or "repeatability" of research measures.

Validity is the degree to which it measures what it is supposed to measure.

6.4.1   Reliability analysis

Reliability analysis assesses data in three dimensions: preciseness, stability and consistency. In other words, it evaluates the extent estimates vary due to random errors. In this study, we adopt Cronbach's Alpha as main method, which measures the consistency between variables in the scale (See Table 6-3). Normally, such method fits attitude and comment style questionnaires. Additionally, the result only suggests if the measuring process is stable and reliable, yet it has nothing to do with the rightness of the experiment conclusions.

Table 6-3   Test of reliability

Variables	Items	Cronbach's Alpha
Severity of service failure	3	0.835
Customer attribution (locus of control, controllability, stability)	7	0.658
Recovery expectation (including magnitude of recovery customer expected, type of recovery customer expected)	15	0.788
Disconfirmation between expectation and obtained	2	0.823
Recovery satisfaction	3	0.912
Overall satisfaction	3	0.901
Customer future behavioral intention	6	0.769

It is argued that a Cronbach's Alpha over 0.7 shows good sample reliability, 0.6—0.7 fair, less than 0.6 unacceptable. Table 6-3 indicates that all scale measures are greater than 0.6, suggesting good modelling. But still three problems need to be paid attention to:

Firstly, in "customer attribution", controllability and stability are binary variables. Types of variables affect reliability of sorts, but as both contribution to customer attribution according to literature review, they are still put here to analyze simultaneously.

Secondly, corrected item-total correlation needs to be tested here, yet as the final results are not displayed, such test is done usually as background preparation. The problem, again, occurs in the binary variables (controllibility and stability in customer attribution). Also, they both are important aspects of customer attribution, so they are not excluded in here.

Thirdly, if during the analysis, a negative value of Cronbanch's Alpha shows up, there might exists a reverse-variable. For example, in severity of service failure test, to consistency, one of the three values resulted from questionnaires needs to be transformed (reversed) because of the negative sentences. Similar cases take place multiple times in this study, and similar solutions are employed.

6.4.2 Validity analysis

Validity analysis considers the preciseness, validity, and rightness. That is, the variation between measured values and true values, to see if a scale is measuring the right variables effectively as expected.

In assessment of validity, the usual practice is to look at KMO. When KMO > 0.9, factor analysis can be appropriately performed in the extreme; 0.8 < KMO < 0.9, factor analysis can be very suitable; 0.7 < KMO < 0.8, suitable; 0.6 < KMO < 0.7, acceptable; 0.5 < KMO < 0.6, nearly unacceptable; KMO < 0.5, unacceptable for factor analysis.

Table 6-4 suggests a good validity of the scale (KMO = 0.712). Bartlett's test concludes p < 0.01 (significance level) that most cases can be explained by the sample. As shown in Table 6-5, scales in service failure and customer attribution are also valid (KMO = 0.803, p < 0.01). As for recovery expectation and disconfirmation between expectation and obtained recovery, statistics shows statistically significant effectiveness (KMO = 0.918, p < 0.01) (See Table 6-6).

Table 6-4 KMO and Bartlett's test of service failure and customer attribution

KMO and Bartlett's test		
Kaiser-Meyer-Olkin measure of sampling adequacy		0.712
Bartlett's test of sphericity	Approx. Chi-Square	983.285
	df	45
	Sig.	0

Table 6-5   KMO and Bartlett's test of recovery expectation and
disconfirmation between expectation and the obtained

KMO and Bartlett's test		
Kaiser-Meyer-Olkin measure of sampling adequacy		0.803
Bartlett's test of sphericity	Approx. Chi-Square	1469.985
	df	153
	Sig.	0

Table 6-6   KMO and Bartlett's test of satisfaction after recovery
and behavioral intention

KMO and Bartlett's test		
Kaiser-Meyer-Olkin measure of sampling adequacy		0.918
Bartlett's test of sphericity	Approx. Chi-Square	2593.727
	df	66
	Sig.	0

6.5   Statistical analysis

In this study, we mainly adopt two analytic methods: descriptive statistics which simply aims to testify the validity of the data, and multiple linear regression analysis which deal with more detailed information.

6.5.1   Descriptive statistics

Descriptive statistics are used to present quantitative descriptions in a manageable form. In a research study, we may have lots of measure that we may measure a large number of people on any measure. Descriptive statistics help us to simplify large amounts of data in a sensible way. Each descriptive statistic transforms data into a simpler summary.

Descriptive statistics provides simple summaries about the sample and about the observations that have been made. Such summaries may be either quantitative, like summary statistics, or visual such as simple-to-understand graphs. These summaries may either form the basis of the initial description of the data as part of a more extensive statistical analysis, or they may be sufficient in and of themselves for a particular investigation.

In brief, descriptive statistics is used to describe the basic features of the data in a study. It provides simple summary about the sample and measures. Together with simple graphics analysis, it virtually forms the basis of every quantitative analysis of data. Yet there is always a risk involved when it comes to simplification—distorting the original data or losing important details. Even though given these limitations, descriptive statistics still provides a possibility of making comparisons across people or other units.

6.5.1.1   Univariate analysis

Univariate analysis involves the examination across cases of one variable at a time. There are three major characteristics of a single variable that we tend to look at: the distribution, the central tendency and the dispersion. In most situations, we would describe all three of these characteristics for each of the variables in our study.

That is, univariate analysis involves describing the distribution of a single variable, including its central tendency and dispersion (including the range and quartiles of the data-set, and measures of spread such as the variance and standard deviation variance). The distribution is a summary of the frequency of individual values or ranges of values for a variable. The simplest distribution would list every value of a variable and the number of persons who had each value. Some measures that are commonly used to describe a data-set are measures of central tendency and measures of variability or dispersion. Measures of central tendency include the mean, median and mode, while measures of variability include the standard deviation (or variance), the minimum and maximum values of the variables, kurtosis and skewness.

Thus, the shape of the distribution may also be described via indices such as skewness and kurtosis. Characteristics of a variable's distribution may also be depicted in a graphical or tabular format, including histograms and stem-and-leaf display.

6.5.1.2   Bivariate and multivariate analysis

When a sample consists of more than one variable, descriptive statistics may be used to describe the relationship between pairs of variables. In this case, descriptive statistics includes: cross-tabulations and contingency tables, graphical representation via scatterplots, quantitative measures of dependence, descriptions of conditional distributions.

The main reason for differentiating univariate and bivariate analysis is that bivariate analysis is not only simple descriptive analysis, but it also describes the relationship between two different variables (Babbie, 2009). Quantitative measures of dependence include correlation [such as Pearson's r when both variables are continuous, or Spearman's rho (ρ) if one or both are not) and covariance (which reflects the scale variables are measured on]. The slope, in regression analysis, also reflects the relationship between variables. The unstandardized slope indicates the unit change in the criterion variable for a one unit change in the predictor. The standardized slope indicates this change in standardized (z-score) units. Highly skewed data are often transformed by taking logarithms. Use of logarithms makes graphs more symmetrical and look more similar to the normal distribution, making them easier to interpret intuitively (Nick, 2007).

In statistics, the Pearson correlation coefficient, is a measure of the linear correlation between two variables X and Y. It has a value between +1 and −1, where 1 is total positive linear correlation, 0 is no linear correlation, and −1 is total negative linear correlation. Spearman's coefficient (ρ) is appropriate for both continuous and discrete ordinal variables (Lehman, 2005). It is a nonparametric measure of rank correlation (statistical dependence between the rankings of two variables). It assesses how well the relationship between two variables can be described using a monotonic function. The Spearman correlation between two variables is equal to the Pearson correlation between the rank values of those two variables; while Pearson's correlation assesses linear relationships, Spearman's correlation assesses monotonic relationships (whether linear or not). If there are no repeated data values, a perfect Spearman correlation of +1 or −1 occurs when each of the variables is a perfect monotone function of the other.

With descriptive statistics, we are able to make some simple conclusions about the basic characteristics of the main variables. It includes frequency analysis, data analysis on trends and trends in two discrete perspectives, and demographic analysis. Frequency analysis allows the locating of data and cross-frequency comparison between variables. The calculation of mean helps generating a general tendency of data. The difference across the sample therefore is meant to be reflected on the standard deviation. As an alternative means, drawing a bar chart may provide insights from another angle that is much clearer and more simplified than words. Meanwhile, a chart is favorable in observations on a macro level.

Secondly, we use correlation analysis to detect correlations between random variables. That is, when variable X has a value, the possibility of the location of variable Y changes accordingly every time, then the two variables are somehow correlated; or, if the possibility stays the same, then they are not correlated in any ways.

In descriptive statistics, to explore the demographic characteristics and testify the important variables in hypotheses, this study takes measures like gender, age, education level and income status for analysis. As demographic variables are usually coherent, we decide to go for the Pearson correlation coefficient, whose valuation lies in between -1 and 1, and the closer it gets to 0, the lower correlation the variables have. When the coefficient is positive, it means the variables are positively correlated; when it is negative, then variables are negatively correlated. Often, when the absolute value of coefficient is 0—0.09, the correlation is none; when 0.1—0.3, the correlation is weak; 0.3—0.5 means median correlation; 0.5—1.0 is strong correlation. At the same time, in the t-test, $p < 0.05$ indicates obvious correlation and $p > 0.05$ indicates otherwise.

6.5.2 Multiple regression analysis

In a multiple regression analysis, one variable is held as dependent, and other one or multiple variables are perceived as independent. The model aims to establish linear or non-linear equations to analyze the sample. Hence, there are usually more than one items influencing the dependent variable and such problems can be solved by multiple regressions.

In particular, multiple regression analysis in most cases handles: (1) to identify the existence of certain relationships; (2) to predict or control the valuation of a variable according to one or multiple variables; and (3) to do factor analysis, for example, the decision of the most important, less important factors among various independent variables.

The purpose of doing multiple regression is to interpret and make predictions. In this research, a simplified and exclusively explanative model is preferred. Therefore, we tend to value R square, collinearity and regression diagnostics, as to define if explanation being reasonable, and consistent with hypotheses.

The R square has the highest attention of ours, as it tells the fitness of the equation. A massive R square value could indicate the possibility of collinearity's being. If in a correlation test, the correlation coefficient is higher than 0.8, then there might be a multicollinearity; yet a low coefficient does not necessarily mean the denial of its presence.

Multiple regression analysis prevails among many alternative measures as it takes various independent variables into account and makes an optimal estimation of one dependent variable. In this research, such method could work out the influences of targeted independent variable has over the targeted dependent variable, with the demographic biases under control. Prior to regression, we took out the outsiders; within the process, we did collinearity diagnosis to ensure there were no multicollinearity problems caused by highly correlated independent variables. In addition, the main criterion for collinearity is Variance Inflation Factor (VIF). By empirical evidence, when $0 < VIF < 10$, there is no collinearity; when $10 < VIF < 100$, there is a rather obvious collinearity; when $VIF > 100$, there is a multicollinearity problem of very severity.

In summary, the results of this section mainly focus on unstandardized regression coefficient and its significance. The higher the absolute value of that coefficient is, the more influential the independent variable would be over the corresponding dependent variable. Besides, when $p < 0.05$, the influences talked about is obvious.

CHAPTER 7

RESULTS OF ANALYSIS

This section presents the findings from data analysis and the discussion of research findings. Descriptive analysis is conducted to identify the salient items in this study. Multiple regression analysis is used to test the hypothetical and model.

7.1 Descriptive analysis of sample

Descriptive analysis is conducted to identify the salient items in service failure, customer attribution, customer recovery expectation and obtained recovery, satisfaction after recovery, and future behavioral intention. For most parts, the profile of the respondents' characteristics and sample characteristics associated with service failures and recovery that customer experienced in hotel are examined through frequency analysis.

7.1.1 Descriptive analysis of sample-demographic characteristics

A total of 318 hotel customers were randomly selected for this study. In all, the female participants (185 counts, 58.2%) are slightly outnumbered over the counterparts (133 counts, 41.8%). As for the locus of age, there are 65.1% of the sample grouped in 25—34, which weighs the highest. Then 22% goes to age 35—44, and 10.1% goes to 18—24. Only 2.8% is recognized filled by respondents over 45 years old. 28.6% (91 counts) of the respondents had ￥5,000—7,999 (€625—999) of personal monthly income, followed by ￥10,000—30,000 (€1,250—3,750), 27.4%; ￥8,000—9,999 (€1,000—1,249), 27%; and ￥3,000—4,999 (€375—624), 11%. About the extremes, 3.5% of respondent's income is less than ¥ 2999(€374) and 2.5% respondents' income is over ¥ 30,000 (€3,750).

Among the 318 customers surveyed, 89.9% of them have a bachelor's degree or above, and 90.3% of them are managers or executives. In specific, 77.4% of the respondents have a bachelor's degree, 12.3% of them have a master's degree, and 8.5% of them have a college degree, which obviously leads to a conclusion that most of the respondents are well-educated. Regarding the occupation of respondents, 38.1% of them are professionals and technical workers; 28.9% of them are managers of enterprise; 15.1% of them are businessman (service staff, salesman); 8.2% of them are civil servants. Most of them are managers or executives. Hence, statistics tell that the majority of the respondents are well-educated white collars. (See Table 7-1).

Table 7-1   Research sample profile (demographic)

Variables	Frequency	Percent (%)	Variables	Frequency	Percent (%)
Gender			Education		
Male	133	41.8	Doctorate	1	0.3
Female	185	58.2	Master's degree	39	12.3
Total	318	100.0	Bachelor's degree	246	77.4
Age			College degree	27	8.5
18—24	32	10.1	High school level	3	0.9
25—34	207	65.1	Others	2	0.6
35—44	70	22.0	Total	318	100.0
45—54	7	2.2	Occupation		
55 and above	2	0.6	Manager of enterprise	92	28.9
Total	318	100.0	Civil servants	26	8.2
Income			Businessman (service staff, salesman)	48	15.1
Less than ¥ 2,999	11	3.5	Professionals and technical	121	38.1
¥ 3,000—4,999	35	11.0	Worker	7	2.2
¥ 5,000—7,999	91	28.6	Students	15	4.7
¥ 8,000—9,999	86	27.0	Freelancer	7	2.2

Continued

Variables	Frequency	Percent (%)	Variables	Frequency	Percent (%)
¥ 10,000—30,000	87	27.4	Retiree	1	0.3
More than ¥ 30,000	8	2.5	Others	1	0.3
Total	318	100.0	Total	318	100.0

The main research subjects, according to sample statistics, are females between 25—44 years old, who have a bachelor's degree or above in education, also with an income of ¥5,000—30,000 monthly, being a business manager, businessman or some professional technician.

Regarding the trip purposes, pleasure occupies the first place, accounting for 49.6%; followed by business, which accounts for 20%; then followed by friends/relatives, 14.8%; meeting/conference, 10%; visiting, 5.2% (See Table 7-2). The main purposes are "pleasure" and "business".

Table 7-2 Customer's trip purpose and hotel choice

Variables	Frequency	Percent
Trip-purpose	N	Percent
Pleasure	258	49.6%
Business	104	20.0%
Visiting	27	5.2%
Meeting/conference	52	10.0%
Friends/relatives	77	14.8%
Others	2	0.4%
Total	520	100.0%
Hotel star-rating	N	Percent
1-star hotel	4	1.3%
2-star hotel	17	5.3%
3-star hotel	166	52.2%
4-star hotel	115	36.2%

Continued

Variables	Frequency		Percent
5-star hotel	14		4.4%
others	2		0.6%
Total	318		100.0%
Staying time	N		Percent
1 night	53		16.7%
2—3 nights	220		69.2%
4—5 nights	38		11.9%
6 nights or more	7		2.2%
Total	318		100.0%
Reasons for choice (The factors considered in the selection of hotels)[a]	N	Percent	Percent of cases
Location of the hotel	268	35.4%	84.3%
Brand	123	16.2%	38.7%
Recommended by other people or travel agency	87	11.5%	27.4%
Online Information	151	19.9%	47.5%
Recommended by friends/relatives	75	9.9%	23.6%
Included in the package	51	6.7%	16.0%
Others	2	0.3%	0.6%
Total	757	100.0%	238.1%

a. Dichotomy group tabulated at value 1.

These customers are mainly staying in 3-star and 4-star hotels. 52.2% among them have stayed in 3-star hotels, 36.2% have experienced services in 4-star hotels; only 6.6% of those have been in 1-star hotels or 2-star hotels, and only 4.4% have stayed at least once in 5-star hotels in the past six month (See Table 7-2). This reveals the preference of Chinese hotel customers—a mid-scale hotel can mostly be ideal. In addition, 69.2% of subjects stayed for 2—3 nights, 16.7% stayed for 1 night, 11.9% stayed 4—5 nights, and only 2.2% of customers stayed for 6 nights or more.

When it comes to hotel choices, the number one determinant is location, which gets 35.4% of votes; followed by online information (comments), accounting for 19.9%. Another factor is recommendation, including travel agencies, friends, family and others, accounting for 21.4%; branding on the other side also has a considerably high importance of 16.2%. It is worth noting that with the booming population of internet users, internet WOM is now getting more important and hence needs more attention. By simple calculation, the traditional and emerging internet WOM has already taken 41.3%, whose ignorance would honestly lead to disasters.

In summary, the sample collected in this study shows that the main characteristics of the customer are: customers who have stayed at the hotel within the past 6 months, have experienced service failures, and complained to the service provider or manager, mainly under the age of 45, with a preference of 3-star and 4-star hotels. They often choose hotels based on hotel location and online information, brand, as well as word of mouth. Generally, they stayed for 2—3 days. The main reasons for their travel are leisure and business activities.

Among all the factors influencing the selection of hotels, location is the most important of common concerns; there is almost no difference in gender that male (85%) is slightly higher than female (83.8%); the brands affect male (44.4%) bit more than female (34.6%); the impact of online information, is slightly higher on women (49.2%) than men (45.1%), indicating that women are more susceptible to online information; women are more susceptible to word of mouth; as for other people or travel agencies recommended factors, female (31.4%) is more affected than male (21.8%), the influences of recommendation factors of relatives and friends, and female (26.5%) is also higher than male (19.5%). Men (18%) are more affected than women (14.6%) in whether or not this hotel is included in the package (See Table 7-3).

Therefore, compared with female customers, male customers are more affected by location and brand; women are more susceptible to online information and word of mouth.

Table 7-3 Gender—the factor considered in the selection of hotels cross tabulation

			The factors considered in the selection of hotels[a]							
			Hotel location	Brand	Recommended by travel agency	Online information	Recommended by friends/ relatives	Included in the package	Others	Total
Gender	Male	Count	113	59	29	60	26	24	2	133
		Within gender	85.0%	44.4%	21.8%	45.1%	19.5%	18.0%	1.5%	
	Female	Count	155	64	58	91	49	27	0	185
		Within gender	83.8%	34.6%	31.4%	49.2%	26.5%	14.6%	0	
Total		Count	268	123	87	151	75	51	2	318

Percentages and totals are based on respondents.

a. Dichotomy group tabulated at value 1.

7.1.2 Service failure

Table 7-4 shows the type of service failure that customers encounter in Chinese hotels. Among those 318 respondents surveyed, 26.2% (197 counts) of them experienced unreasonable lagged service, 16.3% (123 counts) experienced lack of attention, 12.5% (94 counts) experienced other core services failure, 9.0% (68 counts) experienced unavailable service (invalid service), and 8.2% (62 counts) experienced potential disruptive factors. That is, among the service failures that customers encounter in hotels, the proportion of these five types accounts for 72.2% in total.

Other types of service failures accounted for 27.8%, among which the inappropriate employee behavior related to cultural norms comprised 4.8% (36 counts), followed by customer preferences cannot be met (4.6%,35 counts), customers' special requests cannot be satisfied (4.2%, 32 counts), inappropriate and disruptive employee behavior (4.1%, 31 counts), gestalt evaluation (societal/ cultural insult) (3.9%, 29 counts), exemplary performance under adverse/extra-ordinary circumstances (3.1%, 23 counts), inventory loss due to customers' fault (2.8%, 21 counts), and others service failure (0.3%, 2 counts). The standard deviations of these types of failure are all below 1, indicating a low internal difference among variables—that is, the data is close to the mean (See Table 7-4).

The results of the frequency analysis show that the bitter classification method (Bittner, 1990) covers almost all the service failures that customers encounter in the Chinese hotel industry.

Table 7-4 Types of service failure

Types of service failure[a]	Frequencies	Percent of cases	Percent	Std. Deviation
Unavailable service (invalid service)	68	21.4%	9.0%	0.411
Unreasonable lagged service	197	61.9%	26.2%	0.486
Other core services failure	94	29.6%	12.5%	0.457
Customers' special requests cannot be satisfied	32	10.1%	4.2%	0.301
Customer preferences cannot be met	35	11.0%	4.6%	0.313
Inventory loss due to customers' fault	21	6.6%	2.8%	0.249
potential disruptive factors	62	19.5%	8.2%	0.397
Lack of attention	123	38.7%	16.3%	0.488
Inappropriate and disruptive employee behavior	31	9.7%	4.1%	0.297
Inappropriate employee behavior related to cultural norms	36	11.3%	4.8%	0.317
Gestalt evaluation (societal/cultural insult)	29	9.1%	3.9%	0.288
Exemplary performance under adverse / extra-ordinary circumstances	23	7.2%	3.1%	0.259
Others service failure	2	0.6%	0.3%	0.079
Total	753	236.8%	100.0%	

N of case = 318.

a. Dichotomy group tabulated at value 1.

In addition, among those 318 respondents surveyed, 71.7% (228 counts) of them experienced more than one type of service failure in the hotel in this study, and only 28.3% of them encounter one type of service failure, as shown in Table 7-5. That further explains that most complainers are customers who encounter more than one type of failure.

Table 7-5 Frequency of single versus multiple service failure

Type of service failure	Frequency	Percentage (%)
Single service failure	90	28.3
Multiple service failure	228	71.7
Total	318	100.0

Table 7-6 shows the severity of service failure, which is measured by three items: the first one is from Mild to Severe with mean values of 4.45; the second one is from Minor to Major with mean values of 4.46; the third one is from Instatistically significant to Statistically significant with mean values of 4.85. The three items all have an average mean over four. Thus the complainers perceive the severity of failure is more than Mild. A further investigation revealed that, the standard deviations of the three items are all over 1.3, indicating that differences may exist among different demographic groups for those four items.

Table 7-6 Mean and Std. Deviation of the severity of service failure

The severity of service failure	N	Mean	Std. Deviation
Mild—Severe	318	4.45	1.332
Minor—Major	318	4.46	1.463
Instatistically significant—Statistically significant	318	4.85	1.323

7.1.3 Customer attribution

As is displayed in Table 7-7, it is common for surveyed subjects to attribute failures to the hotel and external environments, instead of themselves. The means are 5.64 and 5.43 respectively, and the standard deviation is bit higher than 1, being 1.158 and 1.181. Meanwhile, customers who blame themselves for the cause of failure accounts for 1.93 (mean value), with a standard deviation of 0.985, showing that internal figures do not quite vary.

Table 7-7 Mean and Std. Deviation of customer attribution

Customer attribution	N	Mean	Std. Deviation
The service problem that I encountered was totally the hotel's fault	318	5.64	1.158

Continued

Customer attribution	N	Mean	Std. Deviation
The service problem that I encountered was my fault	318	1.93	0.985
The service problem that I encountered was due to the external environment, it is not my fault	318	5.43	1.181

Overall, the average mean for causal attribution is 5.7, indicating that subjects tend to blame external environments. In detail, the figure for males is 5.77, for females is 5.65, and t-test results in 0.235, all together showing very little difference in gender. According to Table 7-8, customer attribution is positively correlated with age and income, which possibly means more experienced customers with higher income would more likely attribute failure to externalities.

Table 7-8   Correlation coefficient of attribution, age group, education and income

	Attribution to customer or external factors	Age group	Education	Income
Attribution to customer or external factors	1	0.136*	−0.034	0.131*
		0.016	0.548	0.019
	318	318	318	318
Age group	0.136*	1	0.157**	0.197**
	0.016		0.005	0
	318	318	318	318
Education	−0.034	0.157**	1	−0.251**
	0.548	0.005		0
	318	318	318	318
Income	0.131*	0.197**	−0.251**	1
	0.019	0	0	
	318	318	318	318

* At the 0.05 level (two-tailed), the correlation is statistically significant.
** At the 0.01 level (two-tailed), the correlation is statistically significant.

Table 7-9 shows that, from the dimension of stability of failure, 48% of surveyed customers perceive failures they have encountered as frequent situations; whereas 52% think otherwise, who slightly outnumber their counterparts, identifying failures as occasional accidents. 35.2% of customers believe that in a considerably long run, the problems seem to be stable (unchangeable), but 64.8% take time or environments into account, saying the situation might change accordingly.

As discussed in literature review, the customer perception of stability would have an impact on their expectation on the hotel service. When the perception of failure occurring becomes consistent, in a long-term and hence stable, customers either choose to switch servicer for good, or they might still make the same choice but with certain level of tolerance. If the customer perceives failure to be rare, or dependable on timing and environments, and the service fails unfortunately, the customer expectation would be broken and therefore affects satisfaction. The study measures stability from two aspects—whether the failure happens frequently, and if the possibility of its occurring changes over time. Which means, the results indicate most customers believe service failures are unstable, that is, occasionally taken place.

Table 7-9   Stability of service failure

	Stability of service failure	Frequency	Percent
Frequently	Yes, it is occurred frequently in the hotel	152	47.8%
	No, it is happened rarely in the hotel	166	52.2%
	Total	318	100.0%
Stable	Yes, it is a permanent problem (stable)	112	35.2%
	No, it varies over time and context (unstable)	206	64.8%
	Total	318	100.0%

As can be observed from Table 7-10, only 5.3% of customers are convinced that the failures they have experienced are unavoidable, which leaves 94.7% of total sample considering otherwise. Hotels can always take certain precautions and thus the service failures tend to be containable and avoidable.

Table 7-10   Controllability of service failure

Preventable	Frequency	Percent
Yes, it could be avoided by taking precaution actions	301	94.7%
No, it cannot be avoided	17	5.3%
Total	318	100.0%

As a matter of fact, by the evidence collected, most customers who claimed service failure experience have encountered at least more than two types of service failure, with the severity level higher than Mild (total mean = 4.59). In specific, 26.2% values the service timing, which is the highest among all measures; followed by core service failure (21.5%); and attention obtained from the service provider ranks the third (16.3%). Customers who experienced service failure are likely to seek causes and they usually attribute failure to the hotel or environment (external), instead of themselves (internal) which fits the attribution theory.

There are three dimensions in terms of attribution according to the relevant literature—locus, stability and controllability. Hotels and external environments are to blame instead of customers themselves; frequency analysis in stability shows that more customers are convinced the service failure should be occasional; as for controllability, 95% of surveyed customers believe failures can be avoidable by hotels taking certain actions.

7.1.4   Recovery expectation

Table 7-11 showed that respondents generally had a stronger desire for the hotel to try to solve the problems encountered and make up for them, but a slightly lower expectation of compensation.

Table 7-11   The levels of customer recovery expectation

	Recovery expectation	Mean	Std. Deviation
Item 1	I expect the hotel to do everything they can to solve the problem I encountered	5.09	1.261
Item 2	I don't expect the hotel to exert much effort to solve the problem (R)	4.78	1.510
Item 3	I expect the hotel to try to make up for the service failure	5.06	1.335
Item 4	I expect the hotel to compensate me to some extent	4.64	1.415

Note: Item 2 is a negative sentence, therefore we did transformation on the data to ensure consistency.

In terms of compensation expectations, "Deferred monetary compensation tied to future purchase" is Mild (mean = 4.37); "Immediate monetary compensation tied to the current purchase" is rather desirable (mean = 5.30), especially a refund (mean = 5.49) (Table 7-12). Obviously, customers prefer to have the monetary compensation immediately if there is one, yet hotels prefer deferred compensation as it implies future purchase. However, the second option is far less desirable because customers are unsure about if they might again purchase the service. This gap would lower the actual effects of recovery.

Table 7-12   The types of recovery expected by customer

List of the compensation you expected	Mean	Std. Deviation
A. Deferred monetary compensation tied to future purchase	4.37	1.643
(1) Voucher	4.30	1.490
(2) Hotel or hotel chain credit received	4.25	1.570
B. Immediate monetary compensation tied to the current purchase	5.30	1.408
(1) Discount	5.44	1.258
(2) Refund	5.49	1.453
(3) Free upgrades	5.29	1.329
C. New/exchanged goods, such as changed a new room for you	5.39	1.343
D. Free new/replicate service, e.g. house-keeping service	4.92	1.415
E. Psychological compensation (apology)	5.44	1.376
F. Service (or product) guarantee	5.20	1.339
G. Other compensation	2.26	1.825

In addition, "New/exchanged goods" is favorable (mean = 5.39), so is "psychological compensation (apology)" (mean = 5.44). Also, customers have high expectations on "Service or product guarantee" (mean = 5.20) and "Free new/replicate service" (mean = 4.92). The option of "Free new/replicate service" scores bit lower because of the nature of service type where the supply and consumption happen at the same time. It means not only hotels need to pay extra costs on reproduction, but also customers would spend extra time waiting for like room cleaning service or a meal.

In a word, by looking into the means of all measures, the most preferable compensation is immediate payback (mean = 5.30), followed by replacement (mean = 5.39), then the apology (mean = 5.44) (See Table 7-12).

7.1.5 Recovery that customer obtained from the hotel

Table 7-13 shows that customers receive usually more than one type of compensation, and in the obtained compensations, the three highest options are "Psychological compensation (apology)(21.4%)", "Immediate monetary compensation (20.3%)" and "Free product/services upgrade (19.6%)", the order being basically consistent with the customer expectation.

Table 7-13 Frequencies of compensation obtained by customer

		Responses		Percent of cases
		N	Percent	
Compensation obtained by customer[a]	A. Deferred monetary compensation	113	12.7%	35.5%
	B. Immediate monetary compensation	180	20.3%	56.6%
	C. Free product/services upgrade	174	19.6%	54.7%
	D. Free new/replicate service	122	13.8%	38.4%
	E. Psychological compensation (apology)	190	21.4%	59.7%
	F. Product/service guarantee	104	11.7%	32.7%
	G. Others compensation	2	0.2%	0.6%
	H. No compensation/no respondent	2	0.2%	0.6%
Total		887	100.0%	278.9%

a. Dichotomy group tabulated at value 1.

Meanwhile, customers are getting immediate rather than deferred monetary compensation just as they have expected. Evidence can be found in Table 7-14 that 35.5% of surveyed customers have had deferred monetary compensation whereas 56.6% have had immediate monetary compensation.

Table 7-14 Case summary of customer obtained recovery

	Cases					
	Valid		Missing		Total	
	N	Percent	N	Percent	N	Percent
Obtained immediate monetary compensation[a]	180	56.6%	138	43.4%	318	100.0%

Continued

	Cases					
	Valid		Missing		Total	
	N	Percent	N	Percent	N	Percent
Obtained deferred monetary compensation[a]	113	35.5%	205	64.5%	318	100.0%

a. Dichotomy group tabulated at value 1.

If we go down to very specifics, 78.8% of customers who had deferred monetary compensation were given voucher, and 71.7% had hotel credit. The two types cover most of the cases, and only left 0.9% for other deferred monetary compensations (See Table 7-15).

Table 7-15 Frequencies of obtained deferred monetary compensation

		Responses		Percent of cases
		N	Percent	
Obtained deferred monetary compensation [a]	Voucher	89	52.0%	78.8%
	Hotel credit	81	47.4%	71.7%
	Others	1	0.6%	0.9%
Total		171	100.0%	151.3%

a. Dichotomy group tabulated at value 1.

Table 7-16 indicates that 77.2% of surveyed customers who had immediate monetary compensation were compensated with discounts, and 58.9% were refunded, 55.0% had "Free product/service upgrade". The three options include most of the cases.

Table 7-16 Frequencies of obtained Immediate monetary compensation

		Responses		Percent of cases
		N	Percent	
Obtained immediate monetary compensation [a]	Discount	139	40.1%	77.2%
	Refund	106	30.5%	58.9%
	Free product/service upgrade	99	28.5%	55.0%
	Others	3	0.9%	1.7%
Total		347	100.0%	192.8%

a. Dichotomy group tabulated at value 1.

Nevertheless, does the obtained recovery or compensation match expectation? According to the "expectation-disconfirmation paradigm", the customer satisfaction rises when there is a match. First of all, we did some data processing for the match analysis. We extract every highest sub-option in the customer expectation variables and transform it into 1, as being most desirable; and the rest all become 0. Despite the orders are similar, they are actually very different (See Table 7-17, Table 7-18). The expectation-disconfirmation from high to low is listed as follows (See Table 7-18): "Immediate monetary compensation tied to the current purchase" (12.9%); "New / exchanged goods, such as changed a new room for you" (11.4%); "Psychological compensation (apology)" (11.2%); and "Deferred monetary compensation tied to future purchase" (10.7%).

Table 7-17 Case summary of matching

	Cases					
	Valid		Missing		Total	
	N	Percent	N	Percent	N	Percent
Matching[a]	284	89.3%	34	10.7%	318	100.0%

a. Dichotomy group tabulated at value −1.

Table 7-18   Matching frequencies

		Responses		Percent of cases	Match inconsistent rankings
		N	Percent		
Matching[a]	A. Deferred monetary compensation tied to future purchase	99	10.7%	34.9%	4
	(1) Voucher	71	7.7%	25.0%	
	(2) Hotel or hotel chain credit received	65	7.0%	22.9%	
	B. Immediate monetary compensation tied to the current purchase	120	12.9%	42.3%	1
	(1) Discount	88	9.5%	31.0%	
	(2) Refund	59	6.4%	20.8%	
	(3) Free upgrades	65	7.0%	22.9%	
	C. New/exchanged goods, such as changed a new room for you	106	11.4%	37.3%	2
	D. Free new/replicate service, e.g. house-keeping service	82	8.8%	28.9%	
	E. Psychological compensation (apology)	104	11.2%	36.6%	3
	F. Service (or product) guarantee	66	7.1%	23.2%	
	G. Other compensation	2	0.2%	0.7%	
Total		927	100.0%	326.4%	

a. Dichotomy group tabulated at value −1.

The dissatisfaction from Table 7-19 can be explained from two aspects: either hotels provide something customers do not desire (provide undesired), or the compensation fits the expectation, but in an inadequate way (do not provide desired). Table 7-20 elaborates such situations in more details; the main "undesired compensations" are "New/exchanged goods, such as changed a new room" and "Psychological compensation (apology)". And facts can be told by Table 7-21; the most "desirable but did not have" compensations are "Refund" (18.3%), "Free upgrades" (11.9%) and "Discount", (8.9%), which all belong to the category of "Immediate monetary compensation tied to the current purchase"; followed by

"Service (or product) guarantee" (11.2%).

Table 7-19 summary of "provide undesired" and "do not provide desired"

	Cases					
	Valid		Missing		Total	
	N	Percent	N	Percent	N	Percent
Provide undesired[a]	284	89.3%	34	10.7%	318	100.0%
Do not provide desired[b]	231	72.6%	87	27.4%	318	100.0%

a. Dichotomy group tabulated at value −1.
b. Dichotomy group tabulated at value 1.

Table 7-20 "Provide undesired" frequencies

		Responses		Percent of cases
		N	Percent	
Provide undesired[a]	A. Deferred monetary compensation tied to future purchase	99	10.7%	34.9%
	(1) Voucher	71	7.7%	25.0%
	(2) Hotel or hotel chain credit received	65	7.0%	22.9%
	B. Immediate monetary compensation tied to the current purchase	120	12.9%	42.3%
	(1) Discount	88	9.5%	31.0%
	(2) Refund	59	6.4%	20.8%
	(3) Free upgrades	65	7.0%	22.9%
	C. New/exchanged goods, such as changed a new room for you	106	11.4%	37.3%
	D. Free new/replicate service, e.g. house-keeping service	82	8.8%	28.9%
	E. Psychological compensation (apology)	104	11.2%	36.6%
	F. Service (or product) guarantee	66	7.1%	23.2%
	G. Other compensation	2	0.2%	0.7%
Total		927	100.0%	326.4%

a. Dichotomy group tabulated at value −1.

Table 7-21 "Do not provide desired" frequencies

		Responses		Percent of Cases
		N	Percent	
Do not provide desired[a]	A. Deferred monetary compensation tied to future purchase	28	6.4%	12.1%
	(1) Voucher	19	4.4%	8.2%
	(2) Hotel or hotel chain credit received	19	4.4%	8.2%
	B. Immediate monetary compensation tied to the current purchase	37	8.5%	16.0%
	(1) Discount	39	8.9%	16.9%
	(2) Refund	80	18.3%	34.6%
	(3) Free upgrades	52	11.9%	22.5%
	C. New/exchanged goods, such as changed a new room for you	34	7.8%	14.7%
	D. Free new/replicate service, e.g. house-keeping service	28	6.4%	12.1%
	E. Psychological compensation (apology)	35	8.0%	15.2%
	F. Service (or product) guarantee	49	11.2%	21.2%
	G. Other compensation	16	3.7%	6.9%
Total		436	100.0%	188.7%

a. Dichotomy group tabulated at value 1.

As shown in tables, customers want immediate monetary compensations, yet hotels prefer to provide comparatively low-costing alternatives like less-valuable product/service recovery and psychological compensations. The gap between the customer expectation and the hotel behavior is caused by the difference in interests of the two parties, and will then affect the overall satisfaction level on recovery. Based on expectation-disconfirmation paradigm, if customers are getting exceeding compensations after service failure, the satisfaction level rises; or in contrast, it works on the opposite.

In Table 7-22, we used a 1-7 Likert Scale as 1 being "Better than my expectation" and "Beyond my expectation", and 7 being "worse than my expectation" and "Lower than my expectation". The means are 3.52 and 3.81 respectively, indicating that customers are compensated slightly better than expected. Figure 7-1 shows Chinese customers tend to give median scores.

Table 7-22 Mean and Std. Deviation of disconfirmation between recovery expectation and obtained recovery

		Better or worse than expectation	Beyond or lower than expectation
N	Valid	318	318
	Missing	0	0
Mean		3.520	3.810
Std. Deviation		1.347	1.315

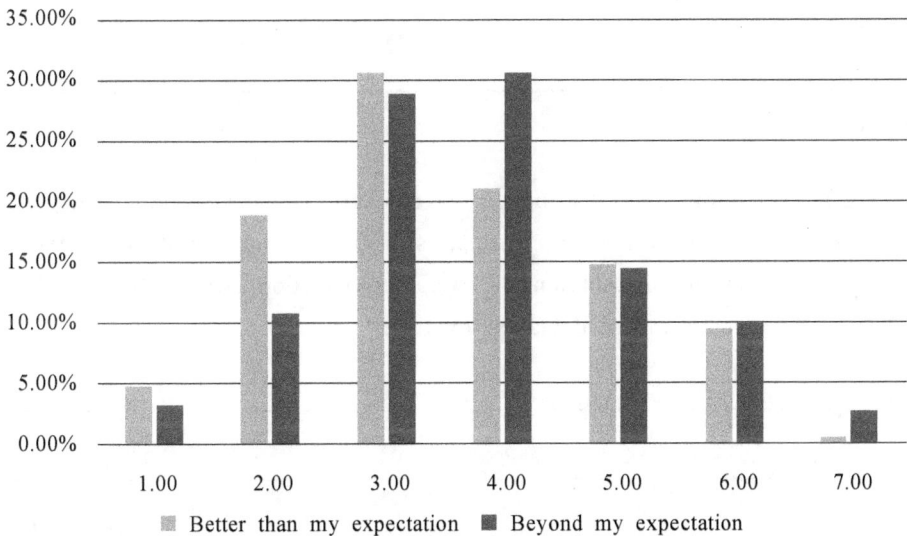

Figure 7-1 The distribution of disconfirmation between recovery expectation and obtained recovery

7.1.6 Satisfaction after recovery

By the discussion of literature, the satisfaction level after recovery includes the satisfaction about recovery process that hotel provides, on the result of recovery, and the overall satisfaction level on the whole flow.

The three measures on recovery satisfaction have a considerably high consistency (mean = 4.62, 4.92, 4.67 in Table 7-23), implying that customers are decently satisfied with the recovery itself, not highly though. The overall satisfaction level is fairly satisfying (mean = 4.50, 4.58, 4.54), but again not much.

Table 7-23   Mean and Std. Deviation of satisfaction to the service recovery

Recovery satisfaction	Mean	Std. Deviation
I am happy with the way that the hotel handled my complaint	4.62	1.267
I am satisfied with the attitude and manner in which the complaint was dealt with	4.92	1.463
Overall I am not satisfied with the way the complaint was handled by the hotel (R)	4.67	1.504
Overall satisfaction	Mean	Std. Deviation
I am satisfied with my overall experience with the hotel	4.50	1.384
Overall, I am satisfied with the hotel	4.58	1.496
To sum up, I am pleased with the service experienced in this hotel	4.54	1.442

N = 318.

Figure 7-2 shows the distribution of recovery satisfaction after categorizing the variables. The mean is 4.29, median is 4.33 and standard deviation is 0.51. Figure 7-3 shows the distribution of overall satisfaction, with a mean of 4.54, median of 4.83 and standard deviation of 1.31.

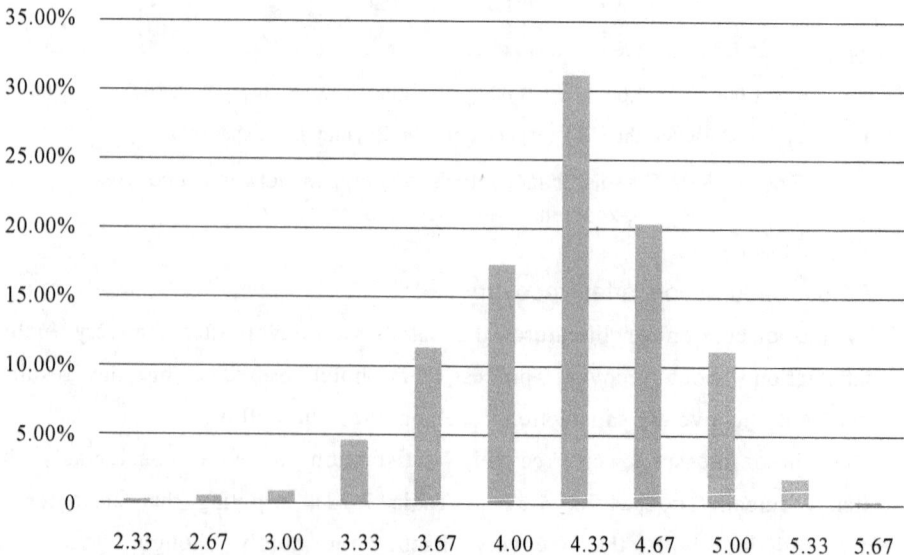

Figure 7-2   The distribution of recovery satisfaction

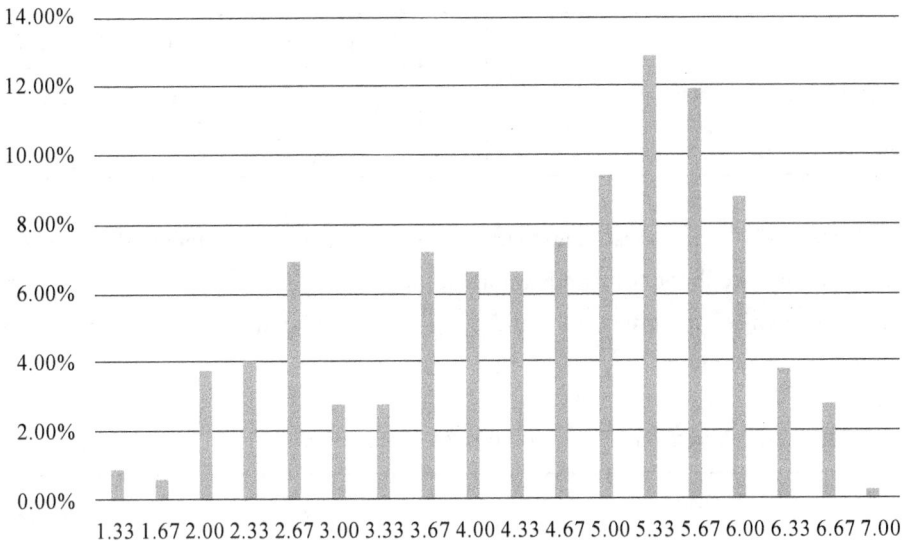

Figure 7-3 The distribution of overall satisfaction

7.1.7 Behavioural intention

As indicated by Table 7-24, the customer intentions are quite insightful. Surveyed customers are probably once again choosing the hotel in the future (mean = 4.49); the recommendation intention is neutral (mean = 3.98); the will of discouraging is unlike (mean = 3.48); complaint to hotel managers is neutral; the desire to complaining to third parties is low (mean = 3.08).

Table 7-24 Mean and Std. Deviation of behavioral intention

	N	Minimum	Maximum	Mean	Std. Deviation
Likelihood of staying this hotel again in the future	318	1	7	4.49	1.455
Likelihood of recommending this hotel to others	318	1	7	3.98	1.729
Likelihood of discouraging other people to choose this hotel	318	1	7	3.48	1.546
Likelihood of complaining to the hotel and manager	318	1	7	4.01	1.462
Likelihood of complaining to third parties	318	1	7	3.08	1.487

Continued

	N	Minimum	Maximum	Mean	Std. Deviation
Other behavior intention	318	1	7	1.88	1.516
Valid N (listwise)	318				

Table 7-25 and t-test together prove the fact that gender does have an effect on the likelihood of complaining to the hotel and manager ($\beta = 0.007$, *p < 0.05); meanwhile the effect of gender on the likelihood of complaining to third parties is also obvious ($\beta = 0.072$, *p < 0.1).

Table 7-25 Mean and Std. Deviation of customer behavioral intention (gender)

	Gender	N	Mean	Std. Deviation
Likelihood of staying this hotel again in the future	Male	133	4.56	1.373
	Female	185	4.44	1.514
Likelihood of recommending this hotel to others	Male	133	3.92	1.656
	Female	185	4.03	1.783
Likelihood of discouraging other people to choose this hotel	Male	133	3.64	1.554
	Female	185	3.37	1.535
Likelihood of complaining to the hotel and manager	Male	133	4.27	1.488
	Female	185	3.83	1.419
Likelihood of complaining to third parties	Male	133	3.26	1.584
	Female	185	2.95	1.404

Table 7-26 shows that age has a rather evident positive influences on the likelihood of recommending this hotel to others, meaning the elder customers are, the more willing to recommend. As for education level, the influence tends to be negative—the more educated the subjects are, the less likely they would go for recommendation or discouragement.

Table 7-26 Correlation coefficient among customer behavioral
intention and age group, education, and income

		Staying this hotel again	Recommending this hotel to others	Discouraging other people to choose this hotel	Complaining to the hotel and manager	Complaining to third parties
Age group	Pearson correlation	0.107	0.125*	−0.025	0.014	-0.002
	Sig. (2-tailed)	0.056	0.026	0.656	0.804	0.974
	N	318	318	318	318	318
Education	Pearson correlation	−0.046	0.036	−0.142*	−0.027	0.084
	Sig. (2-tailed)	0.41	0.527	0.011	0.634	0.136
	N	318	318	318	318	318
Income	Pearson correlation	0.039	−0.007	0.08	0.039	−0.04
	Sig. (2-tailed)	0.491	0.895	0.157	0.483	0.476
	N	318	318	318	318	318

7.2 Test of hypothesis

In this section, we test five hypotheses regarding service failure, customer attribution, recovery expectation and obtained recovery, satisfaction after recovery and customer future behavioral intention using hierarchical regression. In the first layer, we put demographic variables into the regression model and then add other research independent variables in the second layer. This approach effectively eliminates the potential biases by containing certain variables (gender, age, education, occupation, income). The results are presented as follows.

7.2.1 Service failure influences customer attribution

Regarding the types of service failure, Bitner et al. (1990) categorize it into three major classes: the first group is service delivery system failure, including (1) unavailable service, (2) unreasonably slow service, and (3) other core service failures; the second group is the failure due to not achieved customer needs and requests, including (1) customer's special need, (2) customer preferences, (3) admitted customer error, and (4) potentially disruptive others; the third group is due to unprompted and unsolicited employee action, including (1) attention paid to customer, (2)truly out-of-the-ordinary employee behavior, (3) employee behavior in the context of cultural norms, (4) gestalt evaluation (societal/cultural insult), and (5) exemplary performance under adverse circumstances (See 2.1.2). As for customer's attribution, Weiner (1985a, 1986) proposed three dimensions as the basis of consumer causal attribution inferences. That is, customer attribution inferences are made according to locus of causality, stability and controllability (Weiner 1985a, 1986; Vázquez-Casielles et al., 2007) (See 2.2.4). Thus, Hypothesis 1 is regarding the relationship between service failure and customer attribution. H1a is about the influence that the type of failure has over customer attribution to hotel, customer or environment; H1b is about the influence that the severity of failure has over customer attribution to hotel, customer or environment; H1c is about the influence that the stability and controllability of service failure have over customer attribution to hotel, customer, and environment.

7.2.1.1 The relationship between the types and severity of failure and customer attribution

Empirical studies suggest that the service failure affects the causal attribution of customers in types of failure and the severity of failure (See 2.1, 2.2). Thus, we aim to understand the relationship between the twelve types of failure (Bitner et al., 1990) and the customer attribution (to hotel, customer, and environment); and the relationship between the severity of failure (e.g. Hirschman, 1970; Smith et al., 1999; Smith and Bolton, 2002; Hess et al., 2003) and the customer attribution (to hotel, customer, and environment).

At this point, we add up all the four variables related to customer attribution (attribution to hotel, to customer, to environment, and customer-environment). As the measure for attribution is 1—7 Likert Scale, with 1 being internal factors (customer) and 7 being external factors (hotel or environment). Thus, the higher the score of attribution is, the more likely customers are to blame hotels or external environment for failure. Then, we apply a multiple hierarchical regression model to specifically analyze the different twelve types of failure, of their impacts on customer attribution. The results show that six of the twelve types of service failures statistically significant affect customer attribution (from Table 7-27 to Table 7-32). They are: (1) unavailable service failure; (2) other core or main services failure; (3) the failure due to customers' special needs cannot be satisfied; (4) the failure due to customer preferences cannot be met; (5) the failure due to admitted customer error; and (6) the failure due to lack of the attention paid to customer. And the other six types of service failures have no statistically significant impact on customer attribution, such as unreasonably slow service, gestalt evaluation (societal/cultural insult). This may be because in the Chinese hotel industry, the content of customer concern is different; it may also be because some types contain too complex content, and it is difficult for customers to determine who is causing them, so it is difficult to attribute them to hotel and environment or themselves. Thus, the classification of service failure can be further studied and refined in the future. But in any case, the type of service failure does affect customer attribution. The specific analysis process and results are as follows.

The results displayed from Table 7-27 to Table 7-34, are in all of the regressions, VIF < 1.5, indicating a non-existence of sever collinearity. In regression equation 1 of all tables, the involvement of 5 demographic factors has explained only 5% of the variation in customer attribution. By the minor account of variation, we can tell with quite confidence that demographic factors are not influential. Yet in regression equation 2, the results are different.

The first argument focuses on the effects that unavailable service failure has on customer attribution (to hotel, customer, and external environment). Unavailable service (invalid service), that is, the hotel is unable to provide services to customers. It is one of the service delivery system failure (Bitner et al., 1990). For example, the hotel room is unavailable to customer due to untraceable reservation information or overbooked situation; the window table customer reserved for the hotel restaurant is occupied by other customers. In this point, unavailable service failure is perceived as independent variable and customer attribution is perceived as dependent variable, and controlling variables for hierarchical regression are gender, age, education, occupation, income. Table 7-27 shows that in regression equation 1, five demographic factors have explained 5% of the variation in customer attribution. In regression 2, five demographic factors and unavailable service failure have explained 9% of the variation. That is, unavailable service failure alone explains 4% of the variation in customer attribution. According to previous literature, the antecedents of customer attribution include information, belief, and motivation (Bierhoff, 1989; Wang, 2008). That is, there are many factors that affect customer attribution. And the failure to provide service is only one of the 12 service failure, so it is not surprising that only 4% can be explained.

Table 7-27   The influence of unavailable service failure on customer attribution

Variable name	Regression equation 1					Regression equation 2				
	B	SE	β	t	VIF	B	SE	β	t	VIF
Gender	−0.05	0.09	−0.03	−0.50	1.05	−0.08	0.09	−0.05	−0.88	1.06
Age	0.20	0.07	0.16	2.82**	1.09	0.20	0.07	0.16	2.83**	1.09
Education	−0.07	0.10	−0.04	−0.67	1.10	−0.08	0.10	−0.05	−0.83	1.11
Occupation	0.003	0.04	0.01	0.08	1.23	−0.01	0.04	−0.02	−0.36	1.25
Income	0.08	0.05	0.11	1.68	1.34	0.08	0.04	0.11	1.71	1.34
Unavailable service or invalid service						−0.40	0.11	−0.20	−3.69***	1.03
R^2	0.05					0.09				
F	3.24**					5.08***				

a. Dependent variable: customer attribution.
Note: *$p < 0.05$; **$p < 0.01$; ***$p < 0.001$.

The result also indicates that the influence that unavailable service failure has over customer attribution is proved to be negative and statistically significant ($β = -0.20$, $t = -3.69$, $p < 0.001$). It means that when the situation where hotels are unable to provide corresponding service occurs, customers might attribute causes to themselves instead of environments or hotels. Such circumstance contradicts the proposition of attribution theory that customers prefer to attribute failures to external factors rather than themselves (e.g. Weiner, 1979; Borkowski et al., 2003; Hui and Toffoli, 2002; Ye, 2005; Vázquez-Casielles et al., 2007). Probably, in Chinese customers' mind, as quality service / product is far too popular that receiving service failure can be a fault of themselves for not booking a good enough service in advance. Or it could be the idea of restraining oneself originated from the traditional Chinese Confucianism that makes customers think in a more rational way ("deny self and return to propriety" and "self-introspection consciousness" of The Analects of Confucius) while encountering service failure. The future research may look into this phenomenon.

The second argument is regarding the effects that other core service failures have on customer attribution (to hotel, customer, and external environment). Other core or main services failure refers to some important systemic service failure that involve the core value of the product or service. For example, the room that customer stayed is not clean; the food is expired or not safe; money is stolen during customer stay in hotel. In this point, other core services failure is perceived as independent variable and customer attribution is perceived as dependent variable, and controlling variables for hierarchical regression are gender, age, education, occupation, income. As displayed in Table 7-28, in regression 1, the involvement of five demographic factors have explained 5% of the variation in customer attribution, and in regression 2, five demographic factors and other core service failures have explained 7% of the variation. That is, other core service failures alone explain 2%. In addition, the influence that other core service failures have over customer attribution is proved to be positive and statistically significant ($\beta = 0.15$, $t = 2.75$, $p < 0.01$). It means that customers tend to attribute causes to hotels or to environments when the encountered failure happens to be in the category of "other core or main service failure". Hence, hotels should avoid such kind of failures as hard as possible. For example, issues about the cleanness, customer's personal and property safety are of vital priorities.

Table 7-28 The influence of other core service failures on customer attribution

Variable name	Regression equation 1					Regression equation 2				
	B	SE	β	t	VIF	B	SE	β	t	VIF
Gender	−0.05	0.09	−0.03	−0.50	1.05	−0.04	0.09	−0.03	−0.44	1.05
Age	0.20	0.07	0.16	2.82**	1.09	0.22	0.07	0.17	3.03**	1.10
Education	−0.07	0.10	−0.04	−0.67	1.10	−0.05	0.10	−0.03	−.052	1.11
Occupation	0.003	0.04	0.01	0.08	1.23	0.01	0.04	0.01	0.19	1.23
Income	0.08	0.05	0.11	1.68	1.34	0.08	0.05	0.11	1.69	1.34
Other core service failures						0.27	0.10	0.15	2.75**	1.01
R²	0.05					0.07				
F	3.24**					4.01***				

a. Dependent variable: customer attribution.
Note: *p < 0.05; **p < 0.01; ***p < 0.001.

The third argument is regarding the effects that the failure due to customers' special needs cannot be satisfied has on customer attribution (to hotel, customer, and external environment). The failure due to customers' special needs or requests cannot be met refers to the situation that customers request something other than regular services, and the hotel cannot meet these requirements. For example, the hotel cannot provide "extra-bed service" for kids; offering "nursery services" while occasionally leaving babies alone in the hotel room. At this point, the failure due to customers' special needs or requests cannot be satisfied is perceived as independent variable and customer attribution is perceived as dependent variable, and controlling variables for hierarchical regression are gender, age, education, occupation, and income. As displayed in Table 7-29, in regression 1, the involvement of five demographic factors has explained 5% of the variation in customer attribution, and in regression 2, five demographic factors and the failure due to customers' special need cannot be satisfied have explained 7% of the variation. That is, the failure due to customers' special need cannot be satisfied alone explains 2%. In addition, the influence that the failure due to customers' special need cannot be satisfied has over customer attribution is proved to be negative and statistically significant ($\beta = -0.16$, $t = -2.82$, $p < 0.01$). It means that when the hotel is unable to meet customers' special need or requests, customers are likely to attribute causes to themselves instead of environments or hotels. This shows that customers in Chinese hospitality are more objective and rational, and they will not blame the hotel for the situation that their additional requirements cannot be fulfilled.

Table 7-29 The influence of the failure that customers' special need cannot be satisfied on customer attribution

Variable name	Regression equation 1					Regression equation 2				
	B	SE	β	t	VIF	B	SE	β	t	VIF
Gender	−0.05	0.09	−0.03	−0.50	1.05	−0.05	0.09	−0.03	−0.54	1.05
Age	0.20	0.07	0.16	2.82**	1.09	0.20	0.07	0.16	2.77**	1.09
Education	−0.07	0.10	−0.04	−0.67	1.10	−0.07	0.10	−0.04	−0.66	1.10
Occupation	0.003	0.04	0.01	0.08	1.23	−0.004	0.04	−0.01	−0.10	1.24
Income	0.08	0.05	0.11	1.68	1.34	0.06	0.05	0.08	1.29	1.36
customers' special requests cannot be satisfied						−0.42	0.15	−0.16	−2.82**	1.02
R^2	0.05					0.07				
F	3.24**					4.08***				

a. Dependent variable: customer attribution.
Note: *$p < 0.05$; **$p < 0.01$; ***$p < 0.001$.

The fourth argument is regarding the effects that the failure due to customer preferences cannot be met on customer attribution (to hotel, customer, and external environment). The failure due to customer preferences cannot be met refers to the hotel is not able to accommodate some of the guests' special preferences. For example, pets are not allowed; accommodation types are not flexible to change from a mountain-view room to a sea-view room. In this point, the failure due to customer preferences cannot be met is perceived as independent variable and customer attribution is perceived as dependent variable, and controlling variables for hierarchical regression are gender, age, education, occupation, and income. As displayed in Table 7-30. In regression 1, the involvement of five demographic factors has explained 5% of the variation in customer attribution, and in regression 2, five demographic factors and the failure due to customer preferences cannot be met have explained 8% of the variation. That is, the failure due to customer preferences cannot be met alone explains 3%. In addition, the influence that the failure due to customer preferences cannot be met has over customer attribution is proved to be negative and statistically significant ($\beta = -0.16$, $t = -2.93$, $p < 0.01$). It means that when the hotel is unable to meet customer's preferences, customers might attribute causes to themselves instead of environments or hotels. This result indicates that the customer believes that personal preferences cannot be met, not the fault of the hotel.

Table 7-30 The influence of the failure that customer preferences cannot be met on customer attribution

Variable name	Regression equation 1					Regression equation 2				
	B	SE	β	t	VIF	B	SE	β	t	VIF
Gender	−0.05	0.09	−0.03	−0.50	1.05	−0.05	0.09	−0.03	−0.54	1.05
Age	0.20	0.07	0.16	2.82**	1.09	0.19	0.07	0.15	2.62**	1.10
Education	−0.07	0.10	−0.04	−0.67	1.10	−0.08	0.10	−0.05	−0.86	1.11
Occupation	0.003	0.04	0.01	0.08	1.23	−0.003	0.04	−0.01	−0.09	1.23
Income	0.08	0.05	0.11	1.68	1.34	0.07	0.05	0.10	1.61	1.34
Customer preferences cannot be met						−0.42	0.14	−0.16	−2.93**	1.01
R^2	0.05					0.08				

Continued

Variable name	Regression equation 1					Regression equation 2				
	B	SE	β	t	VIF	B	SE	β	t	VIF
F	3.24**					4.19***				

a. Dependent variable: customer attribution.
Note: *p < 0.05; **p < 0.01; ***p < 0.001.

The fifth argument is regarding the effects that the failure due to admitted customer error has on customer attribution (to hotel, customer, and external environment). The failure due to admitted customer error refers to inventory loss due to customers' fault. For example, customer break the table lamp in the hotel room and being requested to reimburse for it; customer lost personal items like glasses in the hotel lobby and unable to retrieve. In this point, the failure due to admitted customer error is perceived as independent variable and customer attribution is perceived as dependent variable, and controlling variables for hierarchical regression are gender, age, education, occupation, and income. As displayed in Table 7-31. In regression 1, the involvement of five demographic factors has explained 5% of the variation in customer attribution, and in regression 2, five demographic factors and the failure due to admitted customer error have explained 7% of the variation. That is, the failure due to admitted customer error explains 2%. In addition, the influence that the failure due to admitted customer error has over customer attribution is proved to be negative and statistically significant ($\beta = -0.15$, $t = -2.75$, $p < 0.01$). It means that when the customer perceived the failure due to admitted customer error, they might attribute causes to themselves instead of environments or hotels.

Table 7-31   The influence of the failure due to admitted customer
error on customer attribution

Variable name	Regression equation 1					Regression equation 2				
	B	SE	β	t	VIF	B	SE	β	t	VIF
Gender	−0.05	0.09	−0.03	−0.50	1.05	−0.07	0.09	−0.004	−0.73	1.05
Age	0.20	0.07	0.16	2.82**	1.09	0.18	0.07	0.15	2.59**	1.10
Education	−0.07	0.10	−0.04	−0.67	1.10	−0.07	0.10	−0.04	−0.68	1.10
Occupation	0.003	0.04	0.01	0.08	1.23	−0.012	0.04	−0.02	−0.35	1.26

continued

Variable name	Regression equation 1					Regression equation 2				
	B	SE	β	t	VIF	B	SE	β	t	VIF
Income	0.08	0.05	0.11	1.68	1.34	0.07	0.05	0.10	1.64	1.34
Admitted customer error						−0.50	0.18	−0.15	−2.75**	1.04
R^2	0.05					0.07				
F	3.24**					4.02***				

a. Dependent variable: customer attribution.

Note: $*p < 0.05$; $**p < 0.01$; $***p < 0.001$.

According to the customer's attribution to the above three types of failure, the failure due to customers' special needs and preferences cannot be met, the failure due to admitted customer error is all customer-caused. The results show that hotel customers do not always attribute the responsibility of the fault to the hotel. When the mistake is caused by themselves, they will self-attribute. Customers tend to objectively admit that they are the cause of the failure.

The sixth argument is regarding the effects that the failure due to lack of the attention paid to customer has on customer attribution (to hotel, customer, and external environment). Lack of attention paid to customers means that the attention of the hotel or employee is not placed on the customer, ignoring the customer. For example, some hotel staff at the front desk keep focusing on their mobile phones, acting like those hotel guests are bothering them. In this case, the failure due to lack of the attention paid to customer is perceived as independent variable and customer attribution is perceived as dependent variable, and controlling variables for hierarchical regression are gender, age, education, occupation, and income. As displayed in Table 7-32. In regression 1, the involvement of five demographic factors has explained 5% of the variation in customer attribution, and in regression 2, five demographic factors and the failure due to lack of the attention paid to customer have explained 6% of the variation. That is, the failure due to lack of the attention paid to customer explains 1%. In addition, the influence that the failure due to lack of the attention paid to customer has over customer attribution is proved to be negative and statistically significant ($\beta = -0.11$, $t = -2.03$, $p < 0.05$). It means that when the customer perceived the failure due to the hotel lack of the attention paid to customer, they might attribute causes to themselves instead of environments or hotels. Similar to the result of unavailable service failure, the failure due to lack of the attention paid to customer is obviously the fault of the hotel, however, the customer attributes the fault of the hotel to himself, such circumstance contradicts the proposition of attribution theory that customers prefer to attribute failures to external factors rather than themselves (Weiner, 1979; Borkowski et al., 2003; Hui and Toffoli, 2002; Ye, 2005; Vázquez-Casielles et al., 2007). Perhaps, because the general practice in environment of the hotel is like such, the hotel staff is not paying enough attention to customers. Thus, the Chinese customers are more used to being ignored, so they do not consider it to be a hotel problem, they may just think that it is their own selective mistake. Another possible reason is the low-key habits of Chinese customers, so that they do not think there is anything wrong with being ignored.

Table 7-32   The influence of the failure due to lack of the attention
paid to customer on customer attribution

Variable name	Regression equation 1					Regression equation 2				
	B	SE	β	t	VIF	B	SE	β	t	VIF
Gender	−0.05	0.09	−0.03	−0.50	1.05	−0.05	0.09	−0.03	−0.49	1.05
Age	0.20	0.07	0.16	2.82**	1.09	0.18	0.07	0.15	2.49*	1.12
Education	−0.07	0.10	−0.04	−0.67	1.10	−0.07	0.10	−0.04	−0.70	1.10
Occupation	0.003	0.04	0.01	0.08	1.23	0.001	0.04	0.002	0.04	1.23
Income	0.08	0.05	0.11	1.68	1.34	0.08	0.05	0.11	1.74	1.34
Lack of the attention						−0.19	0.09	−0.11	−2.03*	1.03
R^2	0.05					0.06				
F	3.24**					3.41**				

a. Dependent variable: customer attribution.
Note: *$p < 0.05$; **$p < 0.01$; ***$p < 0.001$.

In a word, Table 7-27 to Table 7-32 show that "unavailable service (invalid service)", "customers' special need cannot be satisfied", "customer preferences cannot be met", the failure due to "admitted customer error", and "lack of the attention paid to customer" all negatively influence customer's attributing to the hotel or environment. "Other core service failures" positively influences customer attribution to hotel and environment. Therefore, the types of service failure that customer experienced in hotel statistically significant influence customer attribution. In addition, based on previous literature, the antecedents of customer attribution include information, beliefs, and motivation (Bierhoff, 1989; Wang, 2008). That is, there are many factors that affect customer attribution. And each failure to provide service is only one of the twelve service failure, so it is not surprising that only 1%—4% can be explained.

Finally, we analyze the impact of six service failures as a whole on customer attribution (to hotel, customer, and external environment). The previous analysis has shown that the six types of service failures statistically significant affect customer attribution. Specifically, the six types of failures include: (1) the failure due to unavailable service or invalid service; (2) the failure due to core service failure; (3) the failure due to customers' special requests cannot be satisfied; (4) the failure due to customer preferences cannot be met; (5) the failure due to admitted customers' fault; and (6) the failure due to lack of attention paid to customer. We use hierarchical regression analysis, and the six types of failure are perceived as independent variable and customer attribution is perceived as dependent variable, and controlling variables for hierarchical regression are gender, age, education, occupation, and income. As displayed in Table 7-33. In regression 1, the involvement of five demographic factors has explained 5% of the variation in customer attribution, while in regression 2, five demographic factors and the six types of failure have explained 16% of the variation. That is, the six types of failure explain 11%. Although the explanatory power of the six types is not very large, it does indicate that the type of service failure has an impact on customer attribution.

Table 7-33 The influence of service failure types on customer attribution

Variable name	Regression equation 1					Regression equation 2				
	B	SE	β	t	VIF	B	SE	β	t	VIF
Gender	−0.05	0.09	−0.03	−0.05	1.05	−0.09	0.09	−0.06	−1.05	1.06
Age	0.20	0.07	0.16	2.82*	1.09	0.16	0.07	0.13	2.32*	1.14
Education	−0.07	0.10	−0.04	−0.67	1.10	−0.08	0.10	−0.05	−0.89	1.12
Occupation	0.003	0.04	0.01	0.08	1.23	−0.03	0.03	−0.05	−0.84	1.29
Income	0.08	0.05	0.11	1.68	1.34	0.06	0.04	0.09	1.49	1.36
Unavailable service or invalid service						−0.39	0.11	−0.20	−3.69***	1.04

Continued

Variable name	Regression equation 1					Regression equation 2				
	B	SE	β	t	VIF	B	SE	β	t	VIF
Other core services failure						0.19	0.10	0.11	1.98*	1.04
Customers' special requests cannot be satisfied						−0.22	0.16	−0.08	−1.43	1.21
Customer preferences cannot be met						−0.28	0.14	−0.11	−1.93	1.10
Inventory loss due to customers' fault						−0.36	0.19	−0.11	−1.92	1.18
Lack of attention						−0.18	0.09	−0.11	−1.95*	1.05
R^2	0.05					0.16				
F	3.24**					5.33***				

a. Dependent variable: customer attribution.
Note: *$p < 0.05$; **$p < 0.01$; ***$p < 0.001$.

Based on the above analysis, in all service failure types, we find that the failure due to unavailable service has the greatest explanatory power in customer attribution (4%), followed by the failure due to customer preference cannot be met (3%), and then the failure due to other core service (2%), the failure due to customer's special needs cannot be satisfied (2%), and the failure due to admitted customer error have the same explanatory power (2%). The smallest explanatory power on the variance occurs in the failure due to lack of the attention paid to customer (1%). The overall explanatory power of all six failures types is 11%, which manifests that the service failure type is indeed a very important factor in affecting customer attribution.

Severity of failure is the customer's perceived magnitude of the problem (Smith and Bolton, 1998). There are many researchers have made attempts to analyze the effects of severity of failure (also called the magnitude of the failure/ dissatisfaction problem) in a service failure / recovery encounter context (Hirschman, 1970; Smith et al., 1999; Smith and Bolton, 2002; Hess et al., 2003). In this study, we focused on the impact of the severity of failure on customer attribution. In the hierarchical regression, the severity of service failure is perceived as independent variable and customer attribution is perceived as dependent variable, and controlling variables for hierarchical regression are gender, age, education, profession, and income. As displayed in Table 7-34, in both of the regressions, VIF < 1.5, indicating a non-existence of sever collinearity. In regression 1, the involvement of five demographic factors has explained only 5% of the variation in customer attribution. By the minor account of variation, we can tell with quite confidence that demographic factors are not influential. In regression 2, five demographic factors and the severity of service failure have explained 15% of the variation. That is, the severity of service failure alone explains 10%. Although the explanatory power of 10% is not very large, it is sufficient to indicate that the severity of service failure does affect the customer's attribution.

Table 7-34　The influence of severity of service failure on customer attribution

Variable name	Regression equation 1					Regression equation 2				
	B	SE	β	t	VIF	B	SE	β	t	VIF
Gender	−0.05	0.09	−0.03	−0.50	1.05	−0.06	0.09	−0.04	−0.67	1.05
Age	0.20	0.07	0.16	2.82**	1.09	0.24	0.07	0.19	3.51**	1.10
Education	−0.07	0.10	−0.04	−0.67	1.10	−0.06	0.09	−0.03	−0.60	1.10
Occupation	0.003	0.04	0.01	0.08	1.23	0.02	0.03	0.03	0.57	1.24
Income	0.08	0.05	0.11	1.68	1.34	0.06	0.04	0.09	1.51	1.34
Severity						0.22	0.04	0.32	6.12***	1.02
R^2	0.05					0.15				
F	3.24**					9.27***				

a. Dependent variable: customer attribution.
Note: *$p < 0.05$; **$p < 0.01$; ***$p < 0.001$.

In addition, the influence that severity of service failure has over customer attribution is proved to be positive and statistically significant ($\beta = 0.32$, $t = 6.12$, $p < 0.001$). This shows that the higher the level of service failure is, the more likely would the customer attribute the responsibility to hotels. Therefore, hotels should try to avoid serious mistakes, as far as possible to deal with it before the magnitude of the service failure is not serious. In the existing literature, there is considerable evidence to indicate that the magnitude of service failure (Harris et al., 2006; Hoffman et al., 1995) plays an important role in customer perceptions (Chuang et al., 2012). Therefore, many investigators have used the magnitude of service failure to measure a customer's evaluation of the perceived intensity of the service problem (Blodgett et al., 1997; Blodgett et al., 1995; Tax et al., 1998). However, there is very little empirical research on the impact of service failure severity on customer attribution.

7.2.1.2 The relationship between stability, controllability of service failure and customer attribution to hotel, customer or environment

Customer attribution is the "spontaneous" behavior by customers after experiencing negative events. The researchers believe that customer attribution is based on three dimension: locus of control, stability, and controllability (Rotter, 1966; Folkes, 1984; Weiner, 1992; Kim et al., 2014) (See 2.2.4). Thus, we aim to understand the relationship between stability, controllability and customer attribution to hotel, customer and environment. The results displayed from Table 7-35 to Table 7-38, in all of the regressions, VIF < 1.5, indicating a non-existence of sever collinearity.

First is regarding stability and controllability having effects on customer attribution to hotel. Stability refers to the extent to which a cause is viewed as temporary or predictable and permanent (Vázquez-Casielles et al., 2007; Anderson et al, 2009; Oghojafor, 2012). Controllability refers to whether the service provider had the power to exert control over the events of the situation (Borkowski et al., 2003), or whether the firm could avoid a failure from occurring (Weiner, 1985a, 2000; Hui et al., 2006; Vázquez-Casielles et al., 2007). We analyzed the influence of stability and controllable type on attribution to hotel respectively.

Table 7-35 shows that stability is perceived as independent variable and customer attribution to hotel is perceived as dependent variable, and controlling variables for hierarchical regression are gender, age, education, occupation, and income. In regression equation 1, the involvement of five demographic factors has explained only 5% of the variation in customer attribution to hotel. In regression 2, five demographic factors and stability have explained 6% of the variation. That is, stability alone explains 1%. The explanatory power of stability is very small, but it does have an impact on the customer's attribution to the hotel. In addition, stability has over customer attribution to hotel is proved to be negative and statistically significant ($\beta = -0.11$, $t = -2.01$, $p < 0.05$). The result shows that when customers believe that the service failures they encounter are stable, they usually do not attribute the responsibility to the hotel, conversely, if they consider the failure is unstable, they will attribute the responsibility to the hotel.

Table 7-35 The influence of stability on attribution to hotel

Variable name	Regression equation 1					Regression equation 2				
	B	SE	β	t	VIF	B	SE	β	t	VIF
Gender	−0.17	0.13	−0.07	−1.30	1.05	−0.16	0.13	−0.07	−1.21	1.05
Age	0.30	0.10	0.17	2.93**	1.09	0.30	0.10	0.17	2.94**	1.09
Education	−0.09	0.14	−0.04	−0.66	1.10	−0.08	0.14	−0.03	−0.57	1.11
Occupation	−0.04	0.05	−0.05	−0.88	1.23	−0.06	0.05	−0.07	−1.14	1.25
Income	0.03	0.06	0.03	0.42	1.34	0.03	0.06	0.03	0.39	1.34
Stability						−0.30	0.15	−0.11	−2.01*	1.03
R^2	0.05					0.06				
F	3.24**					3.40**				

a. Dependent variable: attribution to hotel.
Note: *$p < 0.05$; **$p < 0.01$; ***$p < 0.001$.

Table 7-36 shows that controllability is perceived as independent variable and customer attribution to hotel is perceived as dependent variable, and controlling variables for hierarchical regression are gender, age, education, occupation, and income. In regression equation 1, the involvement of five demographic factors has explained only 5% of the variation in customer attribution to hotel. In regression 2, five demographic factors and controllability have explained 7% of the variation. That is, controllability alone explains 2%. Although Controllability has a relatively small explanatory power on customer attribution to hotel, it does have an impact. Moreover, controllability has over customer attribution to hotel is proved to be positive and statistically significant ($β = 0.16$, $t = 2.85$, $p < 0.05$). This means that when the customer perceives that the hotel can control and prevent the failure of the service, they tend to attribute the responsibility of service failure to the hotel.

Table 7-36   The influence of controllability on attribution to hotel

Variable name	Regression equation 1					Regression equation 2				
	B	SE	β	t	VIF	B	SE	β	t	VIF
Gender	−0.17	0.13	−0.07	−1.30	1.05	−0.17	0.13	−0.07	−1.30	1.05
Age	0.30	0.10	0.17	2.93**	1.09	0.30	0.10	0.17	2.97**	1.09
Education	−0.09	0.14	−0.04	−0.66	1.10	−0.10	0.14	−0.04	−0.71	1.10
Occupation	−0.04	0.05	−0.05	−0.88	1.23	−0.04	0.05	−0.05	−0.85	1.23
Income	0.03	0.06	0.03	0.42	1.34	0.03	0.06	0.03	0.43	1.34
Controllability						0.80	0.28	0.16	2.85**	1.00
R^2	0.05					0.07				
F	3.24**					4.11**				

a. Dependent variable: attribution to hotel.
Note: *$p < 0.05$; **$p < 0.01$; ***$p < 0.001$.

In brief, regarding the relationship between stability, controllability and customer attribution to hotel, the results indicate that stability and controllability are evident indicators for customer's attributing to hotels. Specifically, the explanatory power of controllability (2%) is stronger than the explanatory power of stability (1%) in customer attribution to hotel. That means the controllability of service failure has a greater impact on customer attribution than the stability of service failure. Stability statistically and negatively influences such attribution, while controllability has a positive influence. That is, as for stability, customers would blame hotels only if the failure is perceived unstable. Pertaining to controllability, when the failure is perceived controllable, meaning hotels can act accordingly to prevent it from happening, customers would then attribute the cause to hotels; if the failure is uncontrollable, hotels are less likely to be blamed.

Second is regarding the effects that stability and controllability have on attribution to customer. In this section, we separately analyze the impact of stability and controllability on the customer's attribution to their own. The results indicate that the effect that stability has on attribution to customer is proved to be statistically insignificant ($p > 0.05$); but controllability statistically significant and negatively influences customer attribution towards themselves ($\beta = -0.21$, $t = -3.89$, $p <$ 0.001) (See Table 7-37). This means that when the customer perceives that the hotel can control and prevent the failure of the service from happening, they do not attribute the responsibility of service failure to their own. Specifically, as displayed in Table 7-37, controllability is perceived as independent variable and customer attribution to themselves is perceived as dependent variable, and controlling variables for hierarchical regression are gender, age, education, occupation, and income. In regression equation 1, the involvement of 5 demographic factors has explained only 2% of the variation in customer attribution to themselves. In regression 2, five demographic factors and controllability have explained 6% of the variation. That is, controllability alone explains 4%. Although controllability has a small explanatory power on customer attribution to themselves, it does have an impact.

Table 7-37 The influence of controllability on attribution to customer

Variable name	Regression equation 1					Regression equation 2				
	B	SE	β	t	VIF	B	SE	β	t	VIF
Gender	0.04	0.11	0.02	0.34	1.05	0.04	0.11	0.02	0.33	1.05
Age	−0.08	0.09	−0.06	−0.94	1.09	−0.08	0.09	−0.06	−0.97	1.09
Education	−0.05	0.12	−0.03	−0.42	1.10	−0.04	0.12	−0.02	−0.36	1.10
Occupation	0.03	0.04	0.04	0.67	1.23	0.03	0.04	0.04	0.64	1.23
Income	−0.07	0.06	−0.08	−1.24	1.34	−0.07	0.05	−0.08	−1.26	1.34
Controllability						−0.94	0.24	−0.21	−3.89***	1.00
R^2	0.02					0.06				
F	1.12					3.51**				

a. Dependent variable: attribution to customer.
Note: *$p < 0.05$; **$p < 0.01$; ***$p < 0.001$.

Third is regarding the effects that stability and controllability have on customer attribution to external environment. We also separately analyze the impact of stability and controllability on the customer's attribution to external environment. the results indicate that controllability statistically significant and positively influences customer attribution to environment ($\beta = 0.12$, $t = 2.24$, $p <$

0.05) (See Table 7-38), while stability appears to be statistically insignificant in influencing customer attribution to environment ($p > 0.05$). If customers believe the idea that failures can be avoided by certain precautions then, the more they would likely to blame external factors (environment). Specifically, as displayed in Table 7-38, controllability is perceived as independent variable and customer attribution to external environment is perceived as dependent variable, and controlling variables for hierarchical regression are gender, age, education, occupation, and income. In regression equation 1, the involvement of five demographic factors has explained only 4% of the variation in customer attribution to themselves. In regression 2, five demographic factors and controllability have explained 6% of the variation. That is, controllability alone explains 2%. Although controllability has a small explanatory power on customer attribution to external environment, it does have an impact.

Table 7-38   The influence of controllability on attribution to environment

Variable name	Regression equation 1					Regression equation 2				
	B	SE	β	t	VIF	B	SE	β	t	VIF
Gender	0.08	0.14	0.03	0.60	1.05	0.08	0.14	0.03	0.61	1.05
Age	0.26	0.10	0.14	2.45*	1.09	0.26	0.10	0.14	2.47*	1.09
Education	−0.09	0.15	−0.04	−0.60	1.10	−0.09	0.14	−0.04	−0.64	1.10
Occupation	0.08	0.05	0.10	1.58	1.23	0.08	0.05	0.10	1.61	1.23
Income	0.14	0.07	0.13	2.08*	1.30	0.14	0.07	0.13	2.10*	1.34
Controllability						0.65	0.29	0.12	2.24*	1.00
R^2	0.04					0.06				
F	2.64*					3.06**				

a. Dependent variable: attribution to environment.
Note: *$p < 0.05$; **$p < 0.01$; ***$p < 0.001$.

Overall, in terms of the explanatory power of controllability, it has the strongest explanatory power (4%) in customer attribution, followed by in attribution to environment (2%) and attribution to hotel (2%). On the other hand, the explanatory power of controllability (2%) is greater than stability (1%) in attribution to hotel.

In summary, types of service failure statistically significant affect customer attribution. H1a is supported. Next, when the severity increases, the more likely customers would attribute to hotels and environments, instead of themselves. H1b—severity of service failure that customer experienced in hotel influences customer attribution—is supported. Thirdly, stability and controllability statistically significant affect customer attribution. H1c is supported. Therefore, Hypothesis 1 service failure that customer experienced in hotel influences customer attribution. The results in line with Weiner's research (1980, 1985a, 1985b, 1986), hospitality customer causal attribution inferences based on three dimensions (locus of causality, stability and controllability) (Vázquez-Casielles et al., 2007). In accordance with the above test results, we conclude as follows (See Table 7-39).

Table 7-39 The test results of Hypothesis 1

Hypothesis 1	Results
H1: Service failure that customer experienced in hotel influences customer attribution	Supported
H1a: Type of service failure that customer experienced in hotel influences customer attribution (to hotel, customer and environment)	Supported
H1b: Severity of service failure that customer experienced in hotel influences customer attribution (to hotel, customer and environment)	Supported
H1c: Stability and controllability of service failure influence customer attribution (to hotel, customer and environment)	Supported

7.2.2 Customer attribution influences customer recovery expectation

As discussed before, there are three dimensions when discussing customer attribution: locus of control, stability and controllability (Weiner, 1980, 1985a, 1985b). Customer recovery expectation includes the magnitude of recovery that customer expected and the type of obtained recovery (Miller et al., 2000; Hess et al., 2003; Craighead et al., 2004).

7.2.2.1 The relationship between the locus of causality and customer recovery expectation

Locus of control implies the identification of the responsible party (Anderson et al., 2009). According to Weiner (1979), Borkowski et al. (2003) proposed that when one tries to describe the processes of explaining events and the relating behavior, external or internal attributions can be given. In this case, we focus on the relationship between locus of causality and customer expectation. It includes two aspects, that is, the impact on recovery magnitude of expectation and the impact on recovery types of expectation.

Regarding the relationship between locus attribution and the recovery magnitude of expectation, locus attribution is perceived as independent variable and recovery magnitude of expectation is perceived as dependent variable, and controlling variables for hierarchical regression are gender, age, education, profession, and income. As displayed in Table 7-40, in both of the regressions, VIF < 1.5, indicating a non-existence of sever collinearity. In regression 1, the involvement of 5 demographic factors has explained only 7% of the variation in recovery magnitude of expectation. In regression 2, five demographic factors and locus of causality have explained 10% of the variation. That is, locus of causality alone explains 3%. Although locus of causality has a small explanatory power on recovery magnitude of expectation, it does have an impact. In addition, the influence that locus attribution has over recovery magnitude of expectation is proved to be positive and statistically significant ($\beta = 0.19$, $t = 3.40$, $p < 0.001$). This means that the more a customer is inclined to attribute to the hotel or environment, the more likely they are to have a higher recovery expectation.

Table 7-40   The influence of customer locus attribution on recovery magnitude of expectation

Variable name	Regression equation 1					Regression equation 2				
	B	SE	β	t	VIF	B	SE	β	t	VIF
Gender	0.28	0.13	0.12	2.21*	1.05	0.30	0.13	0.13	2.34*	1.05
Age	−0.01	0.10	−0.01	−0.12	1.09	−0.06	0.10	−0.04	−0.66	1.12
Education	0.28	0.14	0.12	2.06*	1.10	0.30	0.13	0.13	2.22*	1.11
Occupation	−0.14	0.05	−0.18	−2.97**	1.23	−0.14	0.05	−0.18	−3.03	1.23
Income	0.05	0.06	0.05	0.73	1.34	0.03	0.06	0.03	0.42	1.35
Customer locus attribution						0.26	0.08	0.19	3.40**	1.05
R²	0.07					0.10				
F	4.36**					5.68***				

a. Dependent variable: recovery magnitude of expectation.
Note: *p < 0.05; **p < 0.01; ***p < 0.001.

Regarding the relationship between locus attribution and recovery types of customer expectation, the types of customer's recovery expectation are divided into six categories mainly according to the resource-based classifications of Roschk and Gelbrich (2014). They are (1) deferred monetary compensation tied to future purchase, include voucher and credit of hotel or hotel chain; (2) immediate monetary compensation tied to the current purchase, include discount, refund and free upgrades; (3) new / exchanged goods, such as changed a new room for customer; (4) free new/replicate service, e.g. house-keeping service; (5) psychological compensation (apology); (6) service (or product) guarantee. In this section, customer locus of causality is perceived as independent variable and six types of expectation are perceived as dependent variable respectively, and controlling variables for hierarchical regression are gender, age, education, profession, and income. As displayed from Table 7-41 to 7-45, in both of the regressions, VIF < 1.5, indicating a non-existence of sever collinearity.

Firstly, regarding the relationship between customer locus of causality and the recovery expectation of deferred monetary compensation tied to future purchase, including voucher and credit of hotel or hotel chain (Roschk and Gelbrich, 2014), as displayed in Table 7-41, in regression 1, the involvement of five demographic factors has explained only 4% of the variation in the expectation of deferred monetary compensation. In regression 2, five demographic factors and locus of causality have explained 5% of the variation. That is, locus of causality alone explains 1%. Although locus of causality has a small explanatory power on the expectation of deferred monetary compensation, it does have an impact. In addition, the results indicate that locus of attribution statistically significant and negatively influences the expectation of deferred monetary compensation ($\beta = -0.11$, $t = -2.01$, $p < 0.05$). That is, the more the customer believes that the mistake is caused by the hotel, the less the customer prefers to the delay monetary compensation. This means the customer lacks confidence in returning to the hotel when they convinced that the failure was caused by the hotel.

Table 7-41 The influence of locus of attribution on the expectation of deferred monetary compensation

Variable name	Regression equation 1					Regression equation 2				
	B	SE	β	t	VIF	B	SE	β	t	VIF
Gender	0.29	0.19	0.09	1.55	1.05	0.28	0.19	0.09	1.50	1.05

Continued

Variable name	Regression equation 1					Regression equation 2				
	B	SE	β	t	VIF	B	SE	β	t	VIF
Age	0.26	0.15	0.11	1.81	1.09	0.31	0.15	0.12	2.11	1.12
Education	−0.03	0.20	−0.01	−0.17	1.10	−0.05	0.20	−0.01	−0.25	1.11
Occupation	−0.15	0.07	−0.13	−2.08*	1.23	−0.15	0.07	−0.13	−2.08	1.23
Income	0.02	0.09	0.01	0.22	1.34	0.04	0.09	0.03	0.41	1.35
Locus of attribution						−0.23	0.11	−0.11	−2.01	1.05
R^2	0.04					0.05				
F	2.41*					2.71*				

a. Dependent variable: the expectation of deferred monetary compensation.
Note: $*p < 0.05$; $**p < 0.01$; $***p < 0.001$.

Secondly, regarding the relationship between customer locus of causality and the recovery expectation of immediate monetary compensation tied to the current purchase, including discount, refund and free upgrades (Roschk and Gelbrich, 2014), as displayed in Table 7-42, in regression 1, the involvement of five demographic factors has explained only 4% of the variation in the expectation of immediate monetary compensation. In regression 2, five demographic factors and locus of causality have explained 9% of the variation. That is, locus of causality alone explains 5%. Although locus of causality has a small explanatory power on the expectation of immediate monetary compensation, it does have an impact. In addition, locus of attribution statistically significant and positively influences customer's expectation of immediate monetary compensation ($β = 0.23$, $t = 4.20$, $p < 0.001$). That is, the more the customer considers the failure is caused by the hotel, the more the customer prefers to have the immediate monetary compensation. This also means the customer lacks confidence in returning to the hotel when they perceived the failure caused by hotel.

Table 7-42 The influence of locus of attribution on the expectation of immediate monetary compensation

Variable name	Regression equation 1					Regression equation 2				
	B	SE	β	t	VIF	B	SE	β	t	VIF
Gender	0.18	0.16	0.06	1.12	1.05	0.20	0.16	0.07	1.27	1.05
Age	0.37	0.12	0.17	2.99**	1.09	0.29	0.12	0.14	2.37*	1.12
Education	−0.26	0.17	−0.09	−1.50	1.10	−0.23	0.17	−0.08	−1.38	1.11
Occupation	0.05	0.06	0.05	0.73	1.23	0.04	0.06	0.04	0.73	1.23
Income	0.004	0.08	0.003	0.05	1.34	−0.03	0.08	−0.02	−0.35	1.35
Locus of attribution						0.40	0.10	0.23	4.20***	1.05
R^2	0.04					0.09				
F	2.24*					4.90***				

a. Dependent variable: the expectation of immediate monetary compensation.
Note: *$p < 0.05$; **$p < 0.01$; ***$p < 0.001$.

Thirdly, regarding the relationship between customer locus of causality and the recovery expectation of new/exchanged goods, such as changing a new room for customer (Roschk and Gelbrich, 2014), as displayed in Table 7-43, in regression 1, the involvement of five demographic factors has explained only 2% of the variation in the expectation of new/exchanged goods. In regression 2, five demographic factors and locus of causality have explained 4% of the variation. That is, locus of causality alone explains 2%. Although locus of causality has a small explanatory power on the expectation of new/exchanged goods, it does have an impact. In addition, locus of attribution statistically significant and positively influences customer's expectation of new/exchanged goods (β = 0.11, t = 1.96, p < 0.05).That is, when customers perceive that the mistake is caused by the hotel, they will expect the hotel to provide the product replacement, they are willing to accept the new/exchanged goods.

Table 7-43   The influence of locus of attribution on the
expectation of new/exchanged goods

Variable name	Regression equation 1					Regression equation 2				
	B	SE	β	t	VIF	B	SE	β	t	VIF
Gender	0.30	0.16	0.11	1.95	1.05	0.31	0.16	0.16	2.02*	1.05
Age	−0.04	0.12	−0.02	−0.37	1.09	−0.08	0.12	−0.04	−0.68	1.12
Education	0.07	0.17	0.02	0.40	1.10	0.08	0.17	0.03	0.48	1.11
Occupation	−0.02	0.06	−0.02	−0.38	1.23	−0.02	0.06	−0.02	−0.39	1.23
Income	0.14	0.08	0.12	1.83	1.34	0.12	0.08	0.11	1.65	1.35
Locus of attribution						0.18	0.09	0.11	1.96*	1.05
R^2	0.02					0.04				
F	1.56*					1.96***				

a. Dependent variable: the expectation of new/exchanged goods.
Note: *$p < 0.05$; **$p < 0.01$; ***$p < 0.001$.

Fourthly, regarding the relationship between customer locus of causality and the recovery expectation of psychological compensation (apology) (Roschk and Gelbrich, 2014), as displayed in Table 7-44, in regression 1, the involvement of five demographic factors has explained only 4% of the variation in the expectation of psychological compensation (apology). In regression 2, five demographic factors and locus of causality have explained 7% of the variation. That is, locus of causality alone explains 3%. Although locus of causality has a small explanatory power on the expectation of psychological compensation (apology), it does have an impact. In addition, locus of attribution statistically significant and positively influences customer's expectation of psychological compensation (apology) ($\beta = 0.19$, t = 3.41, $p < 0.001$). That is, when customers perceive that the mistake is caused by the hotel, they will expect the hotel to provide the psychological compensation (apology), they are willing to accept psychological compensation (apology) from hotel. In all compensation methods, the material cost of apologizing is the lowest, but it can satisfy the guest's self-esteem, so the hotel should pay more attention to it.

Table 7-44   The influence of locus of attribution on the expectation
of psychological compensation (apology)

Variable name	Regression equation 1					Regression equation 2				
	B	SE	β	t	VIF	B	SE	β	t	VIF
Gender	0.16	0.16	0.06	1.04	1.05	0.18	0.16	0.06	1.15	1.05
Age	0.08	0.12	0.04	0.61	1.09	0.01	0.12	0.01	0.08	1.12
Education	0.17	0.17	0.06	0.98	1.10	0.19	0.17	0.07	1.12	1.11
Occupation	−0.15	0.06	−0.16	−2.51*	1.23	−0.15	0.06	−0.16	−2.57*	1.23
Income	0.02	0.08	0.01	0.21	1.34	−0.01	0.08	−0.01	−0.11	1.35
Locus of attribution						0.32	0.10	0.19	3.41***	1.05
R^2	0.04					0.07				
F	2.23					3.86***				

a. Dependent variable: the expectation of psychological compensation (apology).
Note: *$p < 0.05$; **$p < 0.01$; ***$p < 0.001$.

Fifthly, regarding the relationship between customer locus of causality and the recovery expectation of service (or product) guarantee, a service guarantee is defined as an extension of a product warranty in the background of service settings (Wong et al., 2009). It provides what the customer can expect (the promise or coverage) and the actions the company will take when it fails to deliver what is promised before (the payout) (Hart et al., 1992; McDougall et al., 1998; Wong et al., 2009). As displayed in Table 7-45, in regression 1, the involvement of five demographic factors has explained only 2% of the variation in the expectation of Service (or product) guarantee. In regression 2, five demographic factors and locus of causality have explained 5% of the variation. That is, locus of causality alone explains 3%. Although locus of causality has a small explanatory power on the expectation of service (or product) guarantee, it does have an impact. In addition, locus of attribution statistically significant and positively influences customer's expectation of service (or product) guarantee ($\beta = 0.20$, $t = 3.46$, $p < 0.001$). That is, when customers believe that the failure is caused by the hotel, they will expect the hotel to provide service (or product) guarantee. Callan and Moore (1998) propose that the guarantee offered by the organization will give consumers an expectation of a certain level of service, and when the service fails, the promise of a payout and/or that the service will strengthen their beliefs that their complaints will bring about a positive outcome for them (Robertson et al., 2012).

Table 7-45 The influence of locus of attribution on
the expectation of service (or product) guarantee

Variable name	Regression equation 1					Regression equation 2				
	B	SE	β	t	VIF	B	SE	β	t	VIF
Gender	0.08	0.16	0.03	0.49	1.05	0.09	0.15	0.03	0.59	1.05
Age	0.06	0.12	0.03	0.48	1.09	−0.08	0.12	−0.004	−0.06	1.12
Education	0.19	0.17	0.07	1.13	1.10	0.21	0.16	0.07	1.27	1.11
Occupation	−0.09	0.06	−0.09	−1.50	1.23	−0.09	0.06	−0.09	−1.54	1.23
Income	−0.02	0.08	−0.02	−0.28	1.34	−0.05	0.07	−0.04	−0.61	1.35
Locus of attribution						0.32	0.09	0.20	3.46***	1.05
R^2	0.02					0.05				
F	0.97					2.82*				

a. Dependent variable: the expectation of service (or product) guarantee.
Note: *$p < 0.05$; **$p < 0.01$; ***$p < 0.001$.

The explanatory power of customer locus attribution in immediate monetary compensation has the greatest explanatory power (5%), followed by psychological compensation (3%), service/product guarantee (3%), new/exchange service/product, and the smallest explanatory power lies in deferred monetary compensation (1%). The results indicate that customers who have encountered hotel-oriented service failures would like immediate monetary compensations, and sincere apologies and guarantees; they might want some new good or exchange good, also, deferred monetary compensations as supplementary.

Overall, it is indicated that the results of locus attribution influence the recovery type of customer expectation. Specifically, the independent variable (locus of attribution) is not influential in terms of free new/replicate service, yet influential in terms of the other five types of recovery. Thus, H2a—locus of attribution influences customer expectation (recovery magnitude of expectation, recovery type of expectation)— is supported. Locus of attribution is not statistically significant on influencing customer's expectation of free new/replicate service. It might because that the service process requires efforts put from both sides (hotels and customers), therefore it can be tiring to receive the service again as for customers.

7.2.2.2 The relationship between stability and customer recovery expectation

In this section, customer stability attribution is perceived as independent variable and recovery magnitude of expectation is perceived as dependent variable, and controlling variables for hierarchical regression are gender, age, education, profession, and income (See Table 7-46). As displayed in Table 7-46, in both of the regressions, $VIF < 1.5$, indicating a non-existence of sever collinearity. In regression 1, the involvement of five demographic factors has explained only 7% of the variation in recovery magnitude of expectation. By the minor account of variation, we can tell with quite confidence that demographic factors are not influential. In regression 2, five demographic factors and stability have explained 15% of the variation. That is, customer stability attribution alone explains 8%. Although stability has a small explanatory power on recovery magnitude of expectation, it does have an impact. In addition, the influence that customer stability attribution has over recovery magnitude of expectation is proved to be positive and statistically significant ($\beta = 0.29$, $t = 5.57$, $p < 0.001$). However, the influence that stability has over recovery types of expectation is proved to be statistically insignificant ($p > 0.05$). Therefore, H2b is only partially supported. This result means that customers' expectation of service recovery is raised when they determine the service failure to be a failure of stability.

Table 7-46 The influence of stability attribution on recovery magnitude of expectation

Variable name	Regression equation 1					Regression equation 2				
	B	SE	β	t	VIF	B	SE	β	t	VIF
Gender	0.28	0.13	0.12	2.21*	1.05	0.25	0.12	0.11	2.05*	1.05
Age	−0.01	0.10	−0.01	−0.12	1.09	−0.01	0.09	−0.01	−0.14	1.09
Education	0.28	0.14	0.12	2.06*	1.10	0.25	0.13	0.11	1.90	1.11
Occupation	−0.14	0.05	−0.18	−2.97**	1.23	−0.11	0.05	−0.14	−2.34*	1.25
Income	0.05	0.06	0.05	0.73	1.34	0.05	0.06	0.05	0.84	1.34
Customer stability attribution						0.77	0.14	0.29	5.57***	1.02

Continued

Variable name	Regression equation 1					Regression equation 2				
	B	SE	β	t	VIF	B	SE	β	t	VIF
R^2	0.07					0.15				
F	4.36**					9.15***				

a. Dependent variable: recovery magnitude of expectation.
Note: *$p < 0.05$; **$p < 0.01$; ***$p < 0.001$.

7.2.2.3   The relationship between controllability and customer recovery expectation

Regarding controllability's influences on customer expectation, it includes two aspects, namely, the impact on recovery magnitude of expectation and the impact on recovery types of expectation. On the one hand, regarding the relationship between controllability and recovery magnitude of expectation, as displayed in Table 7-47, controllability is perceived as independent variable and recovery magnitude of expectation is perceived as dependent variable, and controlling variables for hierarchical regression are gender, age, education, profession, and income. In both of the regressions, VIF < 1.5, indicating a non-existence of sever collinearity. In regression 1, the involvement of five demographic factors has explained only 7% of the variation in recovery magnitude of expectation. In regression 2, five demographic factors and controllability have explained 10% of the variation. That is, controllability attribution alone explains 3%. Although controllability has a small explanatory power on recovery magnitude of expectation, it does have an impact. In the light of above discussion, we find that the explanatory power of stability of service failure (8%) is greater than that of controllability (3%), meaning stability affects the magnitude of recovery expectation on a more significant level. In addition, the influence that customer controllability attribution has over recovery magnitude of expectation is proved to be positive and statistically significant ($\beta = 0.17$, $t = 3.18$, $p < 0.01$). The results show that when the customer thinks that the hotel can take measures to avoid the occurrence of failures, that is, the error can be avoided, the customer's expectation of service recovery will be higher.

Table 7-47   The influence of customer controllability attribution on recovery magnitude of expectation

Variable name	Regression equation 1					Regression equation 2				
	B	SE	β	t	VIF	B	SE	β	t	VIF
Gender	0.28	0.13	0.12	2.21*	1.05	0.29	0.13	0.12	2.26*	1.05
Age	−0.01	0.10	−0.01	−0.12	1.09	−0.01	0.10	−0.01	−0.12	1.09
Education	0.28	0.14	0.12	2.06*	1.10	0.27	0.14	0.12	2.03*	1.10
Occupation	−0.14	0.05	−0.18	−2.97**	1.23	−0.14	0.05	−0.18	−2.97**	1.23
Income	0.05	0.06	0.05	0.73	1.34	0.05	0.06	0.05	0.74	1.34
Customer controllability attribution						0.86	0.27	0.17	3.18**	1.00
R²	0.07					0.10				
F	4.36**					5.42***				

a. Dependent variable: recovery magnitude of expectation.
Note: *$p < 0.05$; **$p < 0.01$; ***$p < 0.001$.

On the other hand, regarding the relationship between controllability and recovery types of expectation, as displayed in Table 7-48, customer controllability attribution is perceived as independent variable and recovery types of expectation (overall) is perceived as dependent variable, and controlling variables for hierarchical regression are gender, age, education, profession, and income. In both of the regressions, VIF < 1.5, indicating a non-existence of sever collinearity. In regression 1, the involvement of five demographic factors has explained only 6% of the variation in recovery type of expectation. In regression 2, five demographic factors and controllability have explained 8% of the variation. That is, customer controllability attribution alone explains 2%. Although controllability has a very small explanatory power on recovery types of expectation, it does have an impact. In addition, the influence that customer controllability attribution has over recovery type of expectation is proved to be positive and statistically significant ($β = 0.16$, $t = 2.72$, $p < 0.01$). Specifically, the results indicate that controllability has statistically significant and positive influences on the expectation of service (or product) guarantee ($β = 0.17$, $t = 3.04$, $p < 0.01$). Yet controllability is not statistically significant when correlating to other types of recovery expectation ($p > 0.05$).

Table 7-48   The influence of customer controllability attribution on recovery type of expectation (overall)

Variable name	Regression equation 1					Regression equation 2				
	B	SE	β	t	VIF	B	SE	β	t	VIF
Gender	0.14	0.08	0.10	1.76	1.05	0.15	0.08	0.11	1.93	1.05
Age	0.05	0.06	0.06	0.92	1.08	0.05	0.06	0.05	0.90	1.08
Education	−0.02	0.08	−0.02	−0.25	1.11	−0.03	0.08	−0.02	−0.32	1.11
Occupation	−0.08	0.03	−0.18	−2.88***	1.21	−0.08	0.03	−0.18	−2.94**	1.21
Income	0.03	0.04	0.05	0.75	1.31	0.03	0.04	0.05	0.76	1.31
Customer controllability attribution						0.47	0.17	0.16	2.72**	1.00
R^2	0.06					0.08				
F	3.28**					4.03**				

a. Dependent variable: recovery types of expectation (overall).

Note: $*p < 0.05$; $**p < 0.01$; $***p < 0.001$.

In Table 7-49, customer controllability attribution is perceived as independent variable and the customer expectation of service (or product) guarantee is perceived as dependent variable, and controlling variables for hierarchical regression are gender, age, education, profession, income. In both of the regressions, $VIF < 1.5$, indicating a non-existence of severe collinearity. In regression 1, the involvement of five demographic factors has explained only 2% of the variation in the customer expectation of service (or product) guarantee. In regression 2, five demographic factors and controllability have explained 4% of the variation. That is, customer controllability attribution alone explains 2%. Although controllability has a very small explanatory power on the customer expectation of service (or product) guarantee, it does have an impact.

In summary, the customer controllability attribution does affect recovery magnitude of expectation, recovery type of expectation. Hence, H2c—customer controllability attribution influence customer expectation (recovery magnitude of expectation, recovery type of expectation—is supported.

Table 7-49 The influence of controllability on the expectation of customer
expectation of service (or product) guarantee

Variable name	Regressione quation 1					Regressione quation 2				
	B	SE	β	t	VIF	B	SE	β	t	VIF
Gender	0.08	0.16	0.03	0.49	1.05	0.08	0.15	0.03	0.51	1.05
Age	0.06	0.12	0.03	0.48	1.09	0.06	0.12	0.03	0.50	1.09
Education	0.19	0.17	0.07	1.13	1.10	0.18	0.16	0.06	1.09	1.10
Occupation	−0.09	0.06	−0.09	−1.50	1.23	−0.09	0.06	−0.09	−1.48	1.23
Income	−0.02	0.08	−0.02	−0.28	1.34	−0.02	0.07	−0.02	−0.28	1.34
controllability						1.00	0.33	0.17	3.04**	1.00
R^2	0.02					0.04				
F	0.97					2.38*				

a. Dependent variable: the expectation of service (or product) guarantee.
Note: *$p < 0.05$; **$p < 0.01$; ***$p < 0.001$.

With respect to the relationship between customer attribution and customer
recovery expectation, the results are summarized in Table 7-50. Customer
attribution (locus, stability, controllability) influences recovery magnitude of customer
expectation. Customer locus attribution and controllability also influence recovery
type of customer expectation. But the impact of stability on the recovery type
of customer expectation is not statistically significant. Hence Hypotheses 2 is
partially supported (See Table 7-51).

Table 7-50 The results of customer attribution influence recovery expectation

	Three dimensions of customer attribution		
Recovery expectation	locus	stability	controllability
Recovery magnitude of expectation	supported	supported	supported
Recovery type of expectation	supported		supported
A. Deferred monetary compensation	supported		
B. Immediate monetary compensation	supported		

Continued

	Three dimensions of customer attribution		
C. New/exchanged goods	supported		
D. Free new/replicate service			
E. Psychological compensation (apology)	supported		
F. Service (or product) guarantee	supported		supported

Table 7-51   The test results of Hypothesis 2

H2: Customer attribution (locus, stability, controllability) influences customer recovery expectation (recovery magnitude of expectation, recovery type of expectation)	Partially supported
H2a: Locus of attribution influences customer expectation (recovery magnitude of expectation, recovery type of expectation)	Supported
H2b: Stability of service failure influences customer expectation (recovery magnitude of expectation, recovery type of expectation)	Partially supported
H2c: Controllability of service failure influences customer expectation (recovery magnitude of expectation, recovery type of expectation)	Supported

7.2.3   Service failure influences customer recovery expectation

In this section, we need to testify the relationship between service failure that customer experienced and customer recovery expectation. It includes the relationship between the types of service failure and customer recovery expectation (magnitude and type), and the relationship between severity of service failure and customer recovery expectation (magnitude and type).

7.2.3.1   The relationship between type of service failure and customer recovery expectation (type and magnitude)

With respect to the relationship between type of service failure and type of recovery expectation, according to "matching hypothesis" (Smith et al., 1999), the researcher argues that if failures are related to monetary losses, monetary compensations are more favorable. When the problem is about respect, psychological compensations like apologies are more favorable (Worsfold et al., 2007; Roschk and Gelbrich, 2014). So, what about the influences that type of service failure has over recovery type of customer expectation?

As displayed from Table 7-52 to Table 7-59, we test the relationship between type of failure and type of expectation. Each type of service failure is perceived as independent variable separately and each recovery type of expectation is perceived as dependent variable respectively, and controlling variables for hierarchical regression are gender, age, education, profession, income. In both of the regressions, VIF < 1.5, indicating a non-existence of sever collinearity.

Firstly, there are three types of failure which statistically significant influence the expectation of deferred monetary compensation, they are: (1) unreasonable lagged service failure, (2) the failure due to customer preferences cannot be met, and (3) inventory loss due to customers' fault.

Table 7-52 shows the relationship between the failure due to unreasonable lagged service and the expectation of deferred monetary compensation. Unreasonable lagged service failure is perceived as independent variable, and the expectation of deferred monetary compensation is perceived as dependent variable. Controlling variables for hierarchical regression are gender, age, education, profession, and income. In regression 1, the involvement of five demographic factors has explained only 4% of the variation in expectation of deferred monetary compensation. Thus, demographic factors are not influential. In regression 2, five demographic factors and the failure due to unreasonable lagged service have explained 6% of the variation. That is, unreasonable lagged service failure alone explains 2%. Although unreasonable lagged service failure has a very small explanatory power on the expectation of deferred monetary compensation, it does have an impact. In addition, the influence that unreasonable lagged service failure has over the expectation of deferred monetary compensation is proved to be positive and statistically significant ($\beta = 0.15$, $t = 2.68$, $p < 0.01$). The result indicates that the customer who encounters unreasonable lagged service failure is expected to receive deferred monetary compensation.

Table 7-52 The influence of unreasonable lagged service on the expectation of deferred monetary compensation

Variable name	Regression equation 1					Regression equation 2				
	B	SE	β	t	VIF	B	SE	β	t	VIF
Gender	0.29	0.19	0.09	1.55	1.05	0.28	0.19	0.08	1.49	1.05
Age	0.26	0.14	0.11	1.81	1.09	0.25	0.14	0.10	1.76	1.09

Continued

Variable name	Regression equation 1					Regression equation 2				
	B	SE	β	t	VIF	B	SE	β	t	VIF
Education	−0.03	0.20	−0.01	−0.17	1.10	−0.02	0.20	0.01	−0.08	1.10
Occupation	−0.15	0.07	−0.13	−2.08*	1.23	−0.16	0.07	−0.14	−2.31*	1.24
Income	0.02	0.09	0.01	0.22	1.34	0.02	0.09	0.02	0.25	1.34
Unreasonable lagged service						0.50	0.19	0.15	2.68**	1.01
R^2	0.04					0.06				
F	2.41*					3.25**				

a. Dependent variable: the expectation of deferred monetary compensation.
Note: *$p < 0.05$; **$p < 0.01$; ***$p < 0.001$.

Table 7-53 shows the relationship between the failure due to customer preferences not met and the expectation of deferred monetary compensation. In the regression analysis, the failure due to customer preferences not met is perceived as independent variable, and the expectation of deferred monetary compensation is perceived as dependent variable. Controlling variables for hierarchical regression are gender, age, education, profession, and income. In regression 1, the involvement of five demographic factors has explained only 4% of the variation in expectation of deferred monetary compensation. Thus, demographic factors are not influential. In regression 2, five demographic factors and the failure due to customer preferences not met have explained 6% of the variation. That is, the failure due to customer preferences not met alone explains 2%. Although the failure due to customer preferences not met has a very small explanatory power on the expectation of deferred monetary compensation, it does have an impact. In addition, the influence that the failure due to customer preferences not met has over expectation of deferred monetary compensation is proved to be positive and statistically significant ($\beta = 0.15$, $t = 2.66$, $p < 0.01$). The results indicate that the customer who encounters the failure due to customer preferences not met is expected to receive deferred monetary compensation.

Table 7-53 The influence of the failure due to customer preferences
not met on expectation of deferred monetary compensation

Variable name	Regression equation 1					Regression equation 2				
	B	SE	β	t	VIF	B	SE	β	t	VIF
Gender	0.29	0.19	0.09	1.55	1.05	0.30	0.19	0.09	1.60	1.05
Age	0.26	0.15	0.11	1.81	1.09	0.29	0.14	0.12	2.03*	1.10
Education	−0.03	0.20	−0.01	−0.17	1.10	−0.001	0.20	0	−0.01	1.11
Occupation	−0.15	0.07	−0.13	−2.08*	1.23	−0.14	0.07	−0.12	−1.94	1.23
Income	0.02	0.09	0.01	0.22	1.34	0.03	0.09	0.02	0.31	1.34
customer preferences not met						0.77	0.29	0.15	2.66**	1.01
R^2	0.04					0.06				
F	2.41*					3.23**				

a. Dependent variable: the expectation of deferred monetary compensation.
Note: *$p < 0.05$; **$p < 0.01$; ***$p < 0.00$.

Table 7-54 shows the relationship between inventory loss due to admitted customers' fault and the expectation of deferred monetary compensation. In the regression analysis, inventory loss due to admitted customers' fault is perceived as independent variable, and the expectation of deferred monetary compensation is perceived as dependent variable. Controlling variables for hierarchical regression are gender, age, education, profession, and income. In regression 1, the involvement of five demographic factors has explained only 4% of the variation in expectation of deferred monetary compensation. Thus, demographic factors are not influential. In regression 2, five demographic factors and inventory loss due to admitted customers' fault have explained 6% of the variation. That is, inventory loss due to admitted customers' fault alone explains 2%. Although inventory loss due to admitted customers' fault has a very small explanatory power on the expectation of deferred monetary compensation, it does have an impact. In addition, the influence that inventory loss due to admitted customers' fault has over expectation of deferred monetary compensation is proved to be positive and statistically significant ($\beta = 0.14$, $t = 2.46$, $p < 0.05$). The results indicate that the customer who encounters inventory loss due to admitted customers' fault is expected to receive deferred monetary compensation, such as voucher, hotel credit.

Table 7-54 The influence of inventory loss due to customers' fault
on expectation of deferred monetary compensation

Variable name	Regression equation 1					Regression equation 2				
	B	SE	β	t	VIF	B	SE	β	t	VIF
Gender	0.29	0.19	0.09	1.55	1.05	0.33	0.19	0.10	1.76	1.05
Age	0.26	0.15	0.11	1.81	1.09	0.29	0.14	0.12	2.04*	1.10
Education	−0.03	0.20	−0.01	−0.17	1.10	−0.03	0.20	−0.01	−0.17	1.10
Occupation	−0.15	0.07	−0.13	−2.08*	1.23	−0.12	0.07	−0.10	−1.69	1.26
Income	0.02	0.09	0.01	0.22	1.34	0.02	0.09	0.02	0.27	1.34
inventory loss due to customers' fault						0.91	0.37	0.14	2.46*	1.04
R^2	0.04					0.06				
F	2.41*					3.05**				

a. Dependent variable: the expectation of deferred monetary compensation.
Note: *$p < 0.05$; **$p < 0.01$; ***$p < 0.001$.

Therefore, customers tend to accept deferred monetary compensation under three circumstances: unavailable service failure, customer's preference not met, and the service failure due to customer's faults. These three failure types include hotel-oriented failures and customer-oriented failures, yet they all have the same explanatory power (2%) in deferred monetary compensation. It reveals the fact that regardless of true responsibility for failures, customers would like compensations from hotels anyway, like vouchers, credit points which can be used in future purchase.

Secondly, regarding the relationship between types of service failure and the expectation of immediate monetary compensation, the results indicate only one of failure types, "the failure due to unreasonable lagged service" influences the expectation of immediate monetary compensation. As displayed in Table 7-55, the failure due to unreasonable lagged service is perceived as independent variable, and the expectation of immediate monetary compensation is perceived as dependent variable. Controlling variables for hierarchical regression are gender, age, education, profession, and income. In regression 1, the involvement of five demographic factors has explained only 4% of the variation in the expectation of immediate monetary compensation. Thus, demographic factors are not influential. In regression 2, five demographic factors and the failure due to unreasonable lagged service have explained 6% of the variation. That is, the failure due to unreasonable lagged service alone explains 2%. Although the failure due to unreasonable lagged service has a very small explanatory power on the expectation of immediate monetary compensation, it does have an impact. In addition, the results indicate only the influence that unreasonable lagged service has over expectation of immediate monetary compensation is proved to be positive and statistically significant ($\beta = 0.15$, $t = 2.72$, $p < 0.01$). The results indicate that the customer who encounters the failure due to unreasonable lagged service is expected to receive immediate monetary compensation, such as discount, refund.

Table 7-55   The influence of unreasonable lagged service failure on expectation of immediate monetary compensation tied to the current purchase

Variable name	Regression equation 1					Regression equation 2				
	B	SE	β	t	VIF	B	SE	β	t	VIF
Gender	0.18	0.16	0.06	1.12	1.05	0.17	0.16	0.06	1.05	1.05
Age	0.37	0.12	0.17	2.99**	1.09	0.36	0.12	0.17	2.95**	1.09
Education	−0.26	0.17	−0.09	−1.50	1.10	−0.24	0.17	−0.08	−1.43	1.11
Occupation	0.05	0.06	0.05	0.73	1.23	0.03	0.06	0.03	0.52	1.24
Income	0.004	0.08	0.003	0.05	1.34	0.01	0.08	0.001	0.07	1.34
Unreasonable lagged service						0.44	0.16	0.15	2.72**	1.01
R^2	0.04					0.06				
F	2.24					3.13**				

a. Dependent variable: the expectation of immediate monetary compensation.
Note: *$p < 0.05$; **$p < 0.01$; ***$p < 0.001$.

Thirdly, with respect to the relationship between types of service failure and the expectation of new/exchanged goods, the result indicates that there are two types of failure influence the expectation of new/exchanged goods. They are (1) the failure due to potential disruptive factors, and (2) inappropriate employee behavior related to cultural norms.

Table 7-56 shows the relationship between the failure due to potential disruptive factors and the expectation of new/exchanged goods. Potential disruptive factors are factors that may affect the customer's normal experience, which may cause some bad feelings to the guest. For example, the guests in the next room are gathered together for parties at 3 a.m., being very noisy, and the hotel staff could not handle it properly. The failure due to potential disruptive factors is perceived as independent variable, and the expectation of new/exchanged goods is perceived as dependent variable. Controlling variables for hierarchical regression are gender, age, education, profession, and income. In regression 1, the involvement of five demographic factors has explained only 2% of the variation in the expectation of new/exchanged goods. Thus, demographic factors are not of influential. In regression 2, five demographic factors and the failure due to potential disruptive factors have explained 4% of the variation. That is, the failure due to potential disruptive factors alone explains 2%. Although the failure due to potential disruptive factors has a very small explanatory power on the expectation of new/exchanged goods, it does have an impact. In addition, the influence that the failure due to potential disruptive factors has over the expectation of new/exchanged goods is proved to be positive and statistically significant ($\beta = 0.13$, $t = 2.25$, $p < 0.05$). The result indicates that the customer who encounters the failure due to potential disruptive factors expects receive new/exchanged goods.

Table 7-56 The influence of the failure due to potential disruptive factors on expectation of new/exchanged goods

Variable name	Regression equation 1					Regression equation 2				
	B	SE	β	t	VIF	B	SE	β	t	VIF
Gender	0.30	0.16	0.11	1.95	1.05	0.33	0.16	0.12	2.12*	1.05
Age	−0.04	0.12	−0.02	−0.37	1.09	−0.02	0.12	−0.01	−0.19	1.10
Education	0.07	0.17	0.02	0.40	1.10	0.07	0.17	0.02	0.40	1.10
Occupation	−0.02	0.06	−0.02	−0.38	1.23	−0.02	0.06	−0.02	−0.33	1.23
Income	0.14	0.08	0.12	1.83	1.34	0.15	0.08	0.13	2.01*	1.34

Continued

Variable name	Regression equation 1					Regression equation 2				
	B	SE	β	t	VIF	B	SE	β	t	VIF
Potential disruptive factors						0.43	0.19	0.13	2.25*	1.02
R²	0.02					0.04				
F	1.56					2.17*				

a. Dependent Variable: the expectation of new/ exchanged goods.
Note: *p < 0.05; **p < 0.01; ***p < 0.001.

Table 7-57 shows the relationship between the failure due to inappropriate employee behavior related to cultural norms and the expectation of new/exchanged goods. Inappropriate employee behavior related to cultural norms (Bitner et al., 1990), refers to the employee's behavior which is inappropriate, but may be related to its cultural traditions or norms. For example, the front desk staff priorities and serve those familiar customers to check-in. In regression analysis, the failure due to inappropriate employee behavior related to cultural norms is perceived as independent variable, and the expectation of new/exchanged goods is perceived as dependent variable. Controlling variables for hierarchical regression are gender, age, education, profession, and income. In regression 1, the involvement of five demographic factors has explained only 2% of the variation in the expectation of new/exchanged goods. Thus, demographic factors are not influential. In regression 2, five demographic factors and inappropriate employee behavior related to cultural norms have explained 4% of the variation. That is, inappropriate employee behavior related to cultural norms alone explains 2%. Although inappropriate employee behavior related to cultural norms has a very small explanatory power on the expectation of new/exchanged goods, it does have an impact. In addition, the influence that inappropriate employee behavior related to cultural norms has over the expectation of new/exchanged goods is proved to be positive and statistically significant ($\beta = 0.12$, $t = 2.20$, $p < 0.05$). The results indicate that the customer who encounters the failure due to inappropriate employee behavior related to cultural norms is expected to receive new/exchanged goods.

Table 7-57   The influence of inappropriate employee behavior related
to cultural norms on expectation of new/exchanged goods

Variable name	Regression equation 1					Regression equation 2				
	B	SE	β	t	VIF	B	SE	β	t	VIF
Gender	0.30	0.16	0.11	1.95	1.05	0.31	0.15	0.11	1.99*	1.05
Age	−0.04	0.12	−0.02	−0.37	1.09	−0.03	0.12	−0.01	−0.24	1.10
Education	0.07	0.17	0.02	0.40	1.10	0.07	0.17	0.02	0.40	1.10
Occupation	−0.02	0.06	−0.02	−0.38	1.23	−0.03	0.06	−0.03	−0.45	1.23
Income	0.14	0.08	0.12	1.83	1.34	0.14	0.08	0.12	1.88	1.34
Inappropriate employee behavior related to cultural norms						0.52	0.24	0.12	2.20*	1.01
R^2	0.02					0.04				
F	1.56					2.12				

a. Dependent variable: the expectation of new/exchanged goods.
Note: *$p < 0.05$; **$p < 0.01$; ***$p < 0.001$.

So, when the failure due to potential disruptive factors and inappropriate employee behavior related to cultural norms happens, customers would have expectation in new/exchanged goods, as they both have an explanatory power of 2%. While the explanatory power of these two types of failures is small, it is clear that the customer is most expected to solve their existing problems. That is, they expect service providers to give them the goods they can use.

Fourthly, as for the relationship between types of service failure and the expectation of psychological compensation (apology), the result indicates that there are two types of failure influencing the expectation of psychological compensation (apology). They are (1) unavailable service (invalid service), and (2) customer preferences not met.

Table 7-58 shows the relationship between the failure due to unavailable service and the expectation of psychological compensation (apology). The failure due to unavailable service (Bitner et al., 1990) refers to the hotel cannot provide service to customer for various reasons. For example, the hotel room is unavailable to book due to untraceable reservation information or overbooked situation; the reserved window table of the hotel restaurant is occupied by other customers. In regression analysis, the failure due to unavailable service is perceived as independent variable, and the expectation of psychological compensation (apology) is perceived as dependent variable. Controlling variables for hierarchical regression are gender, age, education, profession, and income. In regression 1, the involvement of five demographic factors has explained only 4% of the variation in the expectation of psychological compensation (apology). Thus, demographic factors are not influential. In regression 2, five demographic factors and unavailable service have explained 6% of the variation. That is, unavailable service alone explains 2%. Although unavailable service has a very small explanatory power on the expectation of psychological compensation (apology), it does have an impact. In addition, the influence that unavailable service or invalid service has over the expectation of psychological compensation (apology) is proved to be negative and statistically significant ($\beta = -0.15$, $t = -2.70$, $p < 0.01$). The results indicate that the customer who encounters the failure due to unavailable service does not expect to receive psychological compensation (apology).

Table 7-58   The influence of the failure due to unavailable service
on expectation of psychological compensation (apology)

Variable name	Regression equation 1					Regression equation 2				
	B	SE	β	t	VIF	B	SE	β	t	VIF
Gender	0.16	0.16	0.06	1.04	1.05	0.12	0.16	0.04	0.77	1.06
Age	0.08	0.12	0.04	0.61	1.09	0.07	0.12	0.03	0.58	1.09
Education	0.17	0.17	0.06	0.98	1.10	0.15	0.17	0.05	0.88	1.11
Occupation	0.15	0.06	0.16	2.51*	1.23	0.17	0.06	0.18	2.84**	1.25
Income	0.02	0.08	0.01	0.21	1.34	0.02	0.08	0.01	0.21	1.34
Unavailable service failure						0.51	0.19	0.15	2.70**	1.03
R²	0.04					0.06				
F	2.23					3.12				

a. Dependent variable: the expectation of psychological compensation (apology).
Note: *p < 0.05; **p < 0.01; ***p < 0.001.

Table 7-59 shows the relationship between the failure due to "customer preferences not met" and the expectation of psychological compensation (apology).

The failure due to "customer preferences not met" (Bitner et al., 1990) refers to the occasions that hotel does not meet the individualized needs of the guests. For example, pets are not allowed; accommodation types are not flexible to change like changing a mountain-view room to a sea-view room. In regression analysis, the failure due to "customer preferences not met" is perceived as independent variable, and the expectation of psychological compensation (apology) is perceived as dependent variable. Controlling variables for hierarchical regression are gender, age, education, profession, and income. In regression 1, the involvement of five demographic factors has explained only 4% of the variation in the expectation of psychological compensation (apology). Thus, demographic factors are not influential. In regression 2, five demographic factors and "customer preferences not met" have explained 5% of the variation. That is, "customer preferences not met" alone explains 1%. Although "customer preferences not met" has a very small explanatory power on the expectation of psychological compensation (apology), it does have an impact. In addition, the influence that unavailable service or invalid service has over the expectation of psychological compensation (apology) is proved to be negative and statistically significant ($\beta = -0.12$, $t = -2.15$, $p < 0.01$) The results indicate that the customer who encounters the failure due to "customer preferences cannot be met" is unexpected to receive psychological compensation (apology).

Table 7-59 The influence of the failure due to customer preferences not met on expectation of psychological compensation (apology)

Variable name	Regression equation 1					Regression equation 2				
	B	SE	β	t	VIF	B	SE	β	t	VIF
Gender	0.16	0.16	0.06	1.04	1.05	0.16	0.16	0.06	1.02	1.05
Age	0.08	0.12	0.04	0.61	1.09	0.05	0.12	0.03	0.45	1.10
Education	0.17	0.17	0.06	0.98	1.10	0.14	0.17	0.05	0.85	1.11
Occupation	−0.15	0.06	−0.16	−2.51*	1.23	−0.16	0.06	−0.16	−2.65**	1.23
Income	0.02	0.08	0.01	0.21	1.34	0.01	0.08	0.01	0.15	1.34
Customer preferences not met						−0.53	0.24	−0.12	−2.15*	1.01
R^2	0.04					0.05				

Continued

Variable name	Regression equation 1					Regression equation 2				
	B	SE	β	t	VIF	B	SE	β	t	VIF
F	2.23					2.65*				

a. Dependent variable: the expectation of psychological compensation (apology).
Note: *p < 0.05; **p < 0.01; ***p < 0.001.

In terms of explanatory power, unavailable service failure (2%) and failure due to customer's preference not met (1%) differs in affecting psychological compensation (apology). In comparison, unavailable service failure is of more explanatory power.

The results indicate that among all types of service failure, (1) "unreasonable lagged service", "customer preferences cannot be met" and "inventory loss due to customers' fault" are positively and statistically significant in influencing customer's expectation of deferred monetary compensation; (2) "unreasonable lagged service" statistically significantly influences customer expectation of immediate monetary compensation tied to the current purchase; (3) "the failure due to potential disruptive factors" and "inappropriate employee behavior related to cultural norms" are statistically significant in influencing expectation of "new/exchanged goods" both in a positive way; (4) the influence that unavailable service failure and the failure due to customer preferences not met have over the expectation of psychological compensation (apology) are both proved to be negative and statistically significant; and (5) all types of service failure are not statistically significant in influencing the expectation of free new / replicate service and service (product) guarantee. The above regressions conclude a result that in the Chinese hospitality industry, different failure types are influential with the types of customer recovery expectation. Such findings align with the "matching hypothesis" (Smith et al., 1999; Smith, Bolton and Wagner, 1999; Worsfold et al., 2007). And in future research, the relationship between variables can be further studied to see if there exists a one-to-one reflection.

After analyzing the relationship between types of service failure and types of recovery expectation, we analyze the impact of service failure types on magnitude of customer recovery expectation. However, the results indicate that the influence of failure type on recovery magnitude is not statistically significant at the level of 0.05.

Therefore, H3a—type of service failure that customer experienced in hotel influences customer recovery expectation (recovery magnitude of expectation, recovery type of expectation)—is partially supported. That type of service failure influences recovery type of expectation is statistically significant, though it is not a one-to-one corresponding relationship; that type of service failure influences recovery magnitude of expectation is not statistically significant at 0.05.

7.2.3.2   The relationship between severity of service failure and customer recovery expectation

As for the relationship between severity of service failure and customer recovery expectation (include types and magnitude of recovery expectation), the result indicates that the severity of service failure is statistically significant in influencing customer's expectation of "immediate monetary compensation tied to the current purchase" and "service (or product) guarantee".

As displayed in Table 7-60, it indicates the relationship between severity of service failure and customer's expectation of immediate monetary compensation, such as discount and refund. In this regression analysis, severity of service failure is perceived as independent variable, and customer's expectation of "immediate monetary compensation" is perceived as dependent variable. Controlling variables for hierarchical regression are gender, age, education, profession, and income. In regression 1, the involvement of five demographic factors has explained only 4% of the variation in the expectation of "immediate monetary compensation". Thus, demographic factors are not influential. In regression 2, five demographic factors and the severity of service failure have explained 6% of the variation. That is, the severity of service failure alone explains 2%. Although it has a very small explanatory power on the expectation of "immediate monetary compensation", it does have an impact. In addition, the severity of service failure statistically significant influences customer's "expectation of immediate monetary compensation tied to the current purchase" ($\beta = 0.16$, $t = 2.90$, $p < 0.01$). The result shows that the more serious the service failure is, the more customers tend to get immediate monetary compensation, including ways like discounts, monetary refunds.

Table 7-60   The influence of the severity of service failure
on the expectation of immediate monetary compensation

Variable name	Regression equation 1					Regression equation 2				
	B	SE	β	t	VIF	B	SE	β	t	VIF
Gender	0.18	0.16	0.06	1.12	1.05	0.17	0.16	0.06	1.06	1.05
Age	0.37	0.12	0.17	2.99**	1.09	0.40	0.12	0.19	3.27***	1.10
Education	−0.26	0.17	−0.09	−1.50	1.10	−0.25	0.17	−0.09	−1.47	1.10
Occupation	0.05	0.06	0.05	0.73	1.23	0.06	0.06	0.06	0.97	1.24
Income	0.004	0.08	0.003	0.05	1.34	−0.006	0.08	−0.01	−0.08	1.34
The severity of service failure						0.19	0.07	0.16	2.90**	1.02
R^2	0.04					0.06				
F	2.24*					3.31**				

a. Dependent variable: the expectation of immediate monetary compensation.
Note: *$p < 0.05$; **$p < 0.01$; ***$p < 0.001$.

Table 7-61 shows the relationship between severity of service failure and customer's expectation of "service (or product) guarantee". Service guarantee refers to the service provider's commitment and assurance to their future services (Callan and Moore, 1998; McDougall et al., 1998; Lee, 2000; Wirtz and Kum, 2001; Wirtz et al., 2009; Robertson et al., 2012). It can enhance the customer's confidence in continuing to receive services from this service provider. In this regression analysis, severity of service failure is perceived as independent variable, customer's expectation of "service (or product) guarantee" is perceived as dependent variable. Controlling variables for hierarchical regression are gender, age, education, profession, and income. In regression 1, the involvement of five demographic factors has explained only 2% of the variation in the expectation of "service (or product) guarantee". Thus, demographic factors are not influential. In regression 2, five demographic factors and the severity of service failure have explained 4% of the variation. That is, the severity of service failure alone explains 2%. Although it has a very small explanatory power on the expectation of "service (or product) guarantee", it does have an impact. In addition, the severity of service failure statistically significant influences customer's expectation of "expectation of service (or product) guarantee" (β = 0.16, t = 2.76, p < 0.01). The results show that the more serious the service failure is, the more customers expect the hotel to provide a commitment, guarantee for their service.

Table 7-61   The influence of the severity of service failure on the expectation of service (or product) guarantee

Variable name	Regression equation 1					Regression equation 2				
	B	SE	β	t	VIF	B	SE	β	t	VIF
Gender	0.08	0.16	0.03	0.49	1.05	0.07	0.15	0.02	0.43	1.05
Age	0.06	0.12	0.03	0.48	1.09	0.09	0.12	0.04	0.73	1.10
Education	0.19	0.17	0.07	1.13	1.10	0.20	0.16	0.07	1.19	1.10
Occupation	−0.09	0.06	−0.09	−1.50	1.23	−0.08	0.06	−0.08	−1.29	1.24
Income	−0.02	0.08	−0.02	−0.28	1.34	−0.03	0.08	−0.03	−0.40	1.34
The severity of service failure						0.18	0.06	0.16	2.76	1.02
R^2	0.02					0.04				
F	0.97*					2.09**				

a. Dependent variable: the expectation of service (or product) guarantee.
Note: *$p < 0.05$; **$p < 0.01$; ***$p < 0.001$.

In addition, regarding the relationship between severity of service failure and magnitude of recovery expectation, the results indicate that severity of failure does not have a statistically significant impact on recovery magnitude of customer expectation ($p > 0.05$). This result is kind of unexpected. It is suggesting that customers would not expect more compensation from the hotel because the more serious the failure is. This may be due to the impact of the customer attribution, if the attribution does not lead to hotel's fault, and even if the failure is serious, customers may not expect to be compensated by the hotel. Thus, the result seems reasonable.

Based on the above results, H3b—severity of service failure that customer experienced in hotel influences customer recovery expectation (recovery magnitude of expectation, recovery type of expectation)—is partially supported. Severity of service failure statistically significant influences customer recovery expectation about the type of recovery, instead of the magnitude of recovery. We conclude the results of Hypothesis 3 in Table 7-62.

Table 7-62 The test results of Hypothesis 3

H3: Service failure (type, severity) that customer experienced in hotel influences customer recovery expectation (recovery magnitude of expectation, recovery type of expectation)	Partially supported
H3a: Type of Service failure that customer experienced in hotel influences customer recovery expectation (recovery magnitude of expectation, recovery type of expectation)	Partial supported
H3b: Severity of Service failure that customer experienced in hotel influences customer recovery expectation (recovery magnitude of expectation, recovery type of expectation)	Partial supported

7.2.4 Disconfirmation influences satisfaction after recovery

According to expectation-disconfirmation paradigm (Churchill et al., 1982; Oliver, 1993; 1997; Parasuraman et al., 1994; Bolton et al., 1991; ZeithamI et al., 1993; Kim et al., 2012), whenever the obtained recovery does not meet customer recovery expectation, there would be a disconfirmation. If it is a surplus, the disconfirmation will be positive and will enhance customer satisfaction. Or on the contrary, if it is a shortage, negative disconfirmation would cause dissatisfaction. Customer satisfaction after recovery includes satisfaction with recovery and satisfaction with overall service process (including service and recovery) (Singh and Widing, 1991; Smith and Bolton, 1998; Mattila, 2001; Gruber et al., 2011). This section constructs a regression model to analyze the relationship between the disconfirmation (gap or discrepancy between customer recovery expectation and obtained recovery) and satisfaction after recovery.

As displayed in Table 7-63, as for the disconfirmation and customer recovery satisfaction, in this regression analysis, disconfirmation is perceived as independent variable, customer recovery satisfaction is perceived as dependent variable, and controlling variables for hierarchical regression are gender, age, education, profession, and income. In both of the regressions, VIF < 1.5, indicating a non-existence of sever collinearity. In regression 1, the involvement of five demographic factors has explained only 6% of the variation in customer recovery satisfaction. By the minor account of variation, we can tell that demographic factors are not influential. In regression 2, five demographic factors and disconfirmation have explained 57% of the variation. That is, the disconfirmation alone explains 51%. This shows that disconfirmation has a great explanatory power to the recovery satisfaction. In addition, the influence that disconfirmation has over customer recovery satisfaction is proved to be positive and statistically significant (β =

0.74, $t = 19.31$, $p < 0.001$). This means that the greater the gap between the customer's obtained recovery and the expected recovery is, the higher the customer's satisfaction with the recovery would be. Hence, H4a—the disconfirmation influences customer recovery satisfaction—is supported.

Table 7-63   The influence of disconfirmation on customer recovery satisfaction

Variable name	Regression equation 1					Regression equation 2				
	B	SE	β	t	VIF	B	SE	β	t	VIF
Gender	0.09	0.15	0.04	0.64	1.05	−0.07	0.10	−0.03	−0.65	1.05
Age	0.01	0.11	0.003	0.05	1.09	−0.01	0.08	−0.003	−0.08	1.09
Education	0.28	0.16	0.10	1.80	1.10	0.11	0.11	0.04	1.04	1.11
Occupation	−0.21	0.06	−0.23	−3.80***	1.23	−0.07	0.04	−0.07	−1.75	1.28
Income	−0.12	0.07	−0.10	−1.64	1.34	−0.08	0.05	−0.07	−1.66	1.34
Disconfirmation						0.78	0.04	0.74	19.31***	1.06
R²	0.06					0.57				
F	4.16**					69.72***				

a. Dependent variable: customer recovery satisfaction.
Note: *p < 0.05; **p < 0.01; ***p < 0.001.

As displayed in Table 7-64, with respect to disconfirmation and customer overall satisfaction, in this regression analysis, disconfirmation is perceived as independent variable, customer overall satisfaction is perceived as dependent variable, and controlling variables for hierarchical regression are gender, age, education, profession, and income. In both of the regressions, VIF < 1.5, indicating a non-existence of sever collinearity. In regression 1, the involvement of five demographic factors has explained only 6% of the variation in customer overall satisfaction. By the minor account of variation, we can tell that demographic factors are not influential. In regression 2, five demographic factors and disconfirmation have explained 44% of the variation. That is, the disconfirmation alone explains 38%. This shows that disconfirmation has a relatively large explanatory power to the overall satisfaction. In addition, the influence that disconfirmation has over customer overall satisfaction is proved to be positive and statistically significant (β = 0.64, $t = 14.61$, $p < 0.001$). That is, when customers find out that their recovery expectation is exceeded by obtained, the overall satisfaction rises accordingly; otherwise the overall satisfaction lowers down accordingly. Hence, H4b—the disconfirmation influences customer overall satisfaction—is supported.

Table 7-64 The influence of disconfirmation on customer overall satisfaction

Variable name	Regression equation 1					Regression equation 2				
	B	SE	β	t	VIF	B	SE	β	t	VIF
Gender	0.13	0.15	0.05	0.89	1.05	−0.01	0.12	−0.002	−0.05	1.05
Age	0.09	0.12	0.05	0.78	1.09	0.08	0.09	0.04	0.89	1.09
Education	0.04	0.16	0.02	0.27	1.10	−0.11	0.12	−0.04	−0.86	1.11
Occupation	−0.23	0.06	−0.24	−4.01***	1.23	−0.10	0.05	−0.11	−2.24*	1.28
Income	−0.14	0.07	−0.12	−1.90	1.34	−0.11	0.06	−0.09	−1.89	1.34
Disconfirmation						0.69	0.05	0.64	14.61***	1.06
R^2	0.06					0.44				
F	3.77**					40.83***				

a. Dependent variable: customer overall satisfaction.
Note: *p < 0.05; **p < 0.01; ***p < 0.001.

Then, we analyze the relationship between the disconfirmation and satisfaction after recovery. As displayed in Table 7-65, disconfirmation is perceived as independent variable and customer satisfaction after recovery is perceived as dependent variable, and controlling variables for hierarchical regression are gender, age, education, profession, and income. in both regressions, VIF < 1.5, indicating a non-existence of severe collinearity. In regression 1, the involvement of five demographic factors has explained only 7% of the variation in customer satisfaction after recovery. By the minor account of variation, we can say with certainty that explanatory power of five demographic factors are not influential. In regression 2, five demographic factors and disconfirmation have explained 58% of the variation. That is, the disconfirmation alone explains 51%. This shows that disconfirmation has a great explanatory power to the satisfaction after recovery. In addition, the influence that disconfirmation has over customer satisfaction after recovery is proved to be positive and statistically significant (β = 0.73, t = 19.30, p < 0.001). This means that the greater the gap between the customer's obtained recovery and the recovery expectation is, the higher the customer's satisfaction after recovery would be. Hence, Hypothesis 4—the disconfirmation between customer recovery expectation and obtained recovery has effects on customer satisfaction after recovery (include recovery satisfaction and overall satisfaction)—is supported (See Table 7-66).

Table 7-65   The influence of disconfirmation on customer satisfaction after recovery

Variable name	Regression equation 1					Regression equation 2				
	B	SE	β	t	VIF	B	SE	β	t	VIF
Gender	0.11	0.14	0.05	0.82	1.05	−0.04	0.09	−0.01	−0.38	1.05
Age	0.05	0.11	0.03	0.45	1.09	0.04	0.07	0.02	0.51	1.09
Education	0.16	0.15	0.06	1.10	1.10	0.00	0.10	0.00	0.02	1.11
Occupation	−0.22	0.05	−0.25	−4.19***	1.23	−0.08	0.04	−0.10	−2.31*	1.28
Income	−0.13	0.07	−0.12	−1.90	1.34	−0.09	0.05	−0.09	−2.05*	1.34
Disconfirmation						0.73	0.04	0.73	19.30***	1.06
R^2	0.07					0.58				
F	4.41**					70.13***				

a. Dependent variable: customer satisfaction after recovery.
Note: *$p < 0.05$; **$p < 0.01$; ***$p < 0.001$.

Table 7-66   The test results of Hypothesis 4

H4: The disconfirmation between customer recovery expectation and obtained recovery has effects on customer satisfaction after recovery (include recovery satisfaction and overall satisfaction)	Supported
H4a: The disconfirmation influences customer recovery satisfaction	Supported
H4b: The disconfirmation influences customer overall satisfaction	Supported

In addition, some researchers propose that customer satisfaction after recovery should include recovery satisfaction and overall satisfaction (Mattila, 2001; Gruber et al., 2011). It is determined not only by the disconfirmation of service performance (failure), but also by the disconfirmation of service recovery (Smith and Bolton, 1998). In this section, it examines the impact of recovery satisfaction on overall satisfaction.

As displayed in Table 7-67, recovery satisfaction is perceived as independent variable and customer overall satisfaction is perceived as dependent variable, and controlling variables for hierarchical regression are gender, age, education, profession, and income. In both regressions, VIF < 1.5, indicating a non-existence of sever collinearity. In regression 1, the involvement of five demographic factors has explained only 6% of the variation in customer overall satisfaction. By the minor account of variation, we can say with certainty that explanatory power of five demographic factors is not influential. In regression 2, five demographic factors and recovery satisfaction have explained 57% of the variation. That is, the recovery satisfaction alone explains 51%. This shows that recovery satisfaction has a very great explanatory power to the overall satisfaction. In addition, the influence that recovery satisfaction has over customer overall satisfaction is proved to be positive and statistically significant ($\beta = 0.74$, $t = 19.17$, $p < 0.001$). This means that the higher the recovery satisfaction is, the higher the customer's overall satisfaction would be.

Table 7-67   The influence of recovery satisfaction on overall satisfaction

Variable name	Regression equation 1					Regression equation 2				
	B	SE	β	t	VIF	B	SE	β	t	VIF
Gender	0.13	0.15	0.05	0.89	1.05	0.06	0.10	0.02	0.62	1.05
Age	0.09	0.12	0.05	0.78	1.09	0.09	0.08	0.04	1.09	1.09
Education	0.04	0.16	0.02	0.27	1.10	−0.17	0.11	−0.06	−1.54	1.12
Occupation	−0.23	0.06	−0.24	−4.01	1.23	−0.07	0.04	−0.07	−1.74	1.29
Income	−0.14	0.07	−0.12	−1.90	1.34	−0.05	0.05	−0.04	−1.02	1.35
Recovery Satisfaction						0.75	0.04	0.74	19.17	1.07
R²	0.06					0.57				
F	3.77**					68.10***				

a. Dependent variable: customer overall satisfaction.
Note: *p < 0.05; **p < 0.01; ***p < 0.001.

In brief, the explanatory power of disconfirmation in satisfaction after recovery (51%) is greater than it is in overall satisfaction (38%). Also, the explanatory power of satisfaction after recovery in overall recovery is 51%. Disconfirmation is highly influential in satisfaction after recovery.

7.2.5   Satisfaction after recovery influences customer behavioral intention

As discussed previously in literature, satisfaction after recovery can be divided into two sub-units: recovery satisfaction and overall satisfaction (Singh and Widing, 1991; Smith and Bolton, 1998; Mattila, 2001; Gruber et al., 2011). Most researchers believe that satisfaction after recovery helps explain and predict customer behavior in the future (Hirschman, 1970; Bearden and Teel, 1983; Richins, 1983; Singh, 1988; Fornell, 1992; Huang et al., 1996; Söderlund, 1998; Mattsson et al., 2004; Matzler et al., 2006; Hu et al., 2009; Casado-Díaz et al., 2009). In this section, we specifically analyze the impact of customer satisfaction after recovery on their behavioral intentions.

7.2.5.1   The relationship between customer satisfaction after recovery and repurchasing behavioral intention

Researchers have realized a relationship between satisfaction after recovery and repurchase intention (Yi, 1990; Halstead and Page, 1992; Spreng et al., 1995). We will individually verify the impact of the recovery satisfaction and overall satisfaction on customer purchase intentions.

As displayed in Table 7-68, as for the relationship between customer recovery satisfaction and repurchasing behavioral intention, in this regression analysis, customer recovery satisfaction (namely, customer satisfaction with recovery) is perceived as independent variable, customer repurchasing behavioral intention is perceived as dependent variable, and controlling variables for hierarchical regression are gender, age, education, profession, and income. In both regressions, $VIF < 1.5$, indicating a non-existence of severe collinearity. In regression 1, the involvement of five demographic factors has explained only 4% of the variation in repurchasing behavioral intention. By the minor account of variation, we can tell that demographic factors are not influential. In regression 2, five demographic factors and recovery satisfaction have explained 45% of the variation. That is, the recovery satisfaction alone explains 41%. This shows that recovery satisfaction has a great explanatory power to the customer repurchasing behavioral intention. In addition, the influence that customer recovery satisfaction has over repurchasing behavioral intention is proved to be positive and statistically significant $(\beta = 0.66, \ t = 15.26, \ p < 0.001)$. That is, the higher the customer's satisfaction with the recovery, the more likely they are to stay in the hotel again.

Table 7-68 The influence of recovery satisfaction on repurchasing
behavioral intention

Variable name	Regression equation 1					Regression equation 2				
	B	SE	β	t	VIF	B	SE	β	t	VIF
Gender	−0.06	0.17	−0.02	−0.36	1.05	−0.13	0.13	−0.04	−1.02	1.05
Age	0.21	0.13	0.09	1.60	1.09	0.20	0.10	0.09	2.06*	1.09
Education	−0.16	0.18	−0.05	−0.87	1.10	−0.37	0.14	−0.12	−2.68**	1.11
Occupation	−0.17	0.06	−0.16	−2.64**	1.23	−0.01	0.05	−0.01	−0.19	1.29
Income	−0.08	0.08	−0.06	−0.95	1.34	0.01	0.06	0.01	0.16	1.35
Recovery Satisfaction						0.74	0.05	0.66	15.26***	1.07
R²	0.04					0.45				
F	2.27*					42.13***				

a. Dependent variable: customer repurchasing behavioral intention.
Note: *p < 0.05; **p < 0.01; ***p < 0.001.

As displayed in Table 7-69, with respect to the relationship between customer overall satisfaction and repurchasing behavioral intention, in this regression analysis, customer overall satisfaction (include all processes, from service that customer experienced to recovery they obtained) is perceived as independent variable and customer repurchasing behavioral intention is perceived as dependent variable, and controlling variables for hierarchical regression are gender, age, education, profession, and income. in both regressions, VIF < 1.5, indicating a non-existence of sever collinearity. In regression 1, the involvement of five demographic factors has explained only 4% of the variation in repurchasing behavioral intention. It indicates that demographic factors are not influential. In regression 2, five demographic factors and overall satisfaction have explained 61% of the variation. That is, the overall satisfaction alone explains 57%. This shows that overall satisfaction has a very large explanatory power to the customer repurchasing behavioral intention. In addition, the influence that customer overall satisfaction has over repurchasing behavioral intention is proved to be positive and statistically significant ($\beta = 0.78$, $t = 21.53$, $p < 0.001$). This means that the higher the overall customer satisfaction is, the more likely it is to repurchase the hotel service would be.

Table 7-69 The influence of overall satisfaction on repurchasing behavioral intention

Variable name	Regression equation 1					Regression equation 2				
	B	SE	β	t	VIF	B	SE	β	t	VIF
Gender	−0.06	0.17	−0.02	−0.36	1.05	−0.18	0.11	−0.06	−1.64	1.05
Age	0.21	0.13	0.09	1.60	1.09	0.13	0.08	0.06	1.57	1.09
Education	−0.16	0.18	−0.05	−0.87	1.10	−0.19	0.11	−0.06	−1.70	1.10
Occupation	−0.17	0.06	−0.16	−2.64**	1.23	0.03	0.04	0.03	0.71	1.29
Income	−0.08	0.08	−0.06	−0.95	1.34	0.04	0.05	0.03	0.81	1.35
Overall satisfaction						0.86	0.04	0.78	21.53***	1.06
R^2	0.04					0.61				
F	2.27*					81.98***				

a. Dependent variable: customer repurchasing behavioral intention.
Note: *$p < 0.05$; **$p < 0.01$; ***$p < 0.001$.

In summary of Table 7-68 and Table 7-69, both of customer recovery satisfaction and overall satisfaction do affect repurchasing behavioral intention. Comparing the explanatory power of satisfaction after recovery and overall satisfaction in customer's repurchasing intention, we find that overall satisfaction (57%) is more explanatory than satisfaction after recovery (41%) in repurchasing, that they both have a large impact. Hence, H5a—customer satisfaction after recovery (include recovery satisfaction and overall satisfaction) positively influences the likelihood of repurchasing the services of this hotel in the future—is supported. The more satisfied customers are with the recovery process, the higher the likelihood of choosing the hotel again would be. Same principle applies to overall satisfaction. The higher the overall satisfaction is, the higher the likelihood will be.

7.2.5.2 The relationship between customer satisfaction after recovery and recommending behavioral intention

Most researchers suggest that if a service provider can perform an effectively recovery to satisfy the customer, it will increase the likelihood of a positive word of mouth, that is, it will increase the likelihood of customers recommending to their friends, relatives, and others (Blodgett et al., 1993, 1997;

Davidow, 2000; Maxham, 2001; Orsingher et al., 2009; Swanson and Hsu, 2011). In this section, we will examine the impact of the recovery satisfaction and overall satisfaction on customer's recommending behavioral intention separately.

As displayed in Table 7-70, we first examine the relationship between customer recovery satisfaction and customer's behavioral intention of recommending. In this case, customer recovery satisfaction is perceived as independent variable and recommending behavioral intention is perceived as dependent variable, and controlling variables for hierarchical regression are gender, age, education, profession, and income. in both regressions, VIF < 1.5, indicating a non-existence of sever collinearity. In regression 1, the involvement of five demographic factors has explained only 6% of the variation in recommending behavioral intention. By the minor account of variation, we can tell that demographic factors are not influential. In regression 2, five demographic factors and customer's recovery satisfaction have explained 46% of the variation. That is, customer recovery satisfaction alone explains 40%. This shows that customer recovery satisfaction has a great explanatory power to customer's recommending behavioral intention. In addition, the influence that customer recovery satisfaction has over recommending behavioral intention is proved to be positive and statistically significant ($\beta = 0.65$, $t = 15.02$, $p < 0.001$).

Table 7-70 The influence of recovery satisfaction on recommending behavior

Variable name	Regression equation 1					Regression equation 2				
	B	SE	β	t	VIF	B	SE	β	t	VIF
Gender	0.17	0.20	0.05	0.86	1.05	0.09	0.15	0.03	0.59	1.05
Age	0.30	0.15	0.11	1.98*	1.09	0.29	0.12	0.11	2.55	1.09
Education	0.02	0.21	0.01	0.08	1.10	−0.23	0.16	−0.06	−1.41*	1.12
Occupation	−0.27	0.07	−0.22	−3.63***	1.23	−0.09	0.06	−0.07	−1.49	1.29
Income	−0.17	0.10	−0.11	−1.76	1.34	−0.07	0.07	−0.04	−0.91	1.35
Recovery Satisfaction						0.86	0.06	0.65	15.02***	1.07
R²	0.06					0.46				
F	3.91**					43.22***				

a. Dependent variable: customer repurchasing behavioral intention.
Note: *p < 0.05; **p < 0.01; ***p < 0.001.

Next, we examine the relationship between overall satisfaction and customer's behavioral intention of recommending. In this case, customer overall satisfaction is perceived as independent variable and recommending behavioral intention is perceived as dependent variable, and controlling variables for hierarchical regression are gender, age, education, profession, income (Table 7-71). As displayed in Table 7-71, in both regressions, $VIF < 1.5$, indicating a non-existence of sever collinearity. In regression 1, the involvement of five demographic factors has explained only 6% of the variation in recommending behavioral intention. Demographic factors are not influential. In regression 2, five demographic factors and customer's overall satisfaction have explained 62% of the variation. That is, customer overall satisfaction alone explains 56%. This shows that customer recovery satisfaction has a very large explanatory power to customer's recommending behavioral intention. In addition, the influence that customer overall satisfaction has over recommending behavioral intention is proved to be positive and statistically significant ($\beta = 0.77$, $t = 21.22$, $p < 0.001$).

Table 7-71   The influence of overall satisfaction on recommending behavior

Variable name	Regression equation 1					Regression equation 2				
	B	SE	β	t	VIF	B	SE	β	t	VIF
Gender	0.17	0.20	0.05	0.86	1.05	0.04	0.13	0.01	0.28	1.05
Age	0.30	0.15	0.11	1.98*	1.09	0.21	0.10	0.08	2.15*	1.09
Education	0.02	0.21	0.01	0.08	1.10	−0.03	0.13	−0.01	−0.20	1.10
Occupation	−0.27	0.07	−0.22	−3.63***	1.23	−0.04	0.05	−0.03	−0.83	1.29
Income	−0.17	0.10	−0.11	−1.76	1.34	−0.03	0.06	−0.02	−0.46	1.35
Overall satisfaction						1.01	0.05	0.77	21.22***	1.06
R²	0.06					0.62				
F	3.91**					82.99***				

a. Dependent variable: customer repurchasing behavioral intention.
Note: *p < 0.05; **p < 0.01; ***p < 0.001.

In summary of Table 7-70 and Table 7-71, both of customer recovery satisfaction and overall satisfaction do affect recommending behavioral intention. Comparing the explanatory power of recovery satisfaction and overall satisfaction in customer's recommending intention, we find that overall satisfaction (56%) is more explanatory than recovery satisfaction (40%) in recommending, that they both have a large impact. Which indicates, the more satisfied customers are about the recovery and overall service process, the more likely they would recommend the hotel to others (relatives and friends), and spread positive WOM for example, actions that are favoured by hotels. So, satisfaction after recovery affect not only the repurchase intention of existing customers, but also of those potential guests. Hence, H5b—customer satisfaction after recovery (include recovery satisfaction and overall satisfaction) positively influences the likelihood of recommending this hotel to other people—is supported.

7.2.5.3   The relationship between customer satisfaction after recovery and discouraging behavioral intention

Researchers comprehend the NWOM as an alternative complaint response, a private complaint response to friends and family relative to a public complaint to the firm (Ashley and Varki, 2009). They suggest that NWOM is the intentions wherein dissatisfied customers discouraging others to purchase the goods or services from a service provider (Richins, 1983; Sabharwal et al., 2010). In this section, we propose that recovery satisfaction and overall satisfaction would have an impact on the behavioral intention of discouraging respectively.

As displayed in Table 7-72, we first examine the relationship between recovery satisfaction and discouraging others from buying. In this case, customer recovery satisfaction is perceived as independent variable and discouraging behavioral intention is perceived as dependent variable, and controlling variables for hierarchical regression are gender, age, education, profession, and income. In both regressions, VIF < 1.5, indicating a non-existence of sever collinearity. In regression 1, the involvement of five demographic factors has explained only 5% of the variation in discouraging behavioral intention. By the minor account of variation, we can tell that demographic factors are not influential. In regression 2, five demographic factors and customer's recovery satisfaction have explained 19% of the variation. That is, customer recovery satisfaction alone explains 14%. This suggests that the explanatory power of recovery satisfaction to discourage others from buying the service of the hotel is not too big, but it does have some explanatory power. In addition, the influence that customer recovery satisfaction has over discouraging behavioral intention is proved to be negative and statistically significant ($\beta = -0.40$, $t = -7.55$, $p < 0.001$). This means that when guests are less satisfied with the recovery, the more likely they would discourage others; conversely, the more they are satisfied with the recovery, the less likely they would discourage others from buying the hotel's services and products.

Table 7-72 The influence of recovery satisfaction on
discouraging behavioral intention

Variable name	Regression equation 1					Regression equation 2				
	B	SE	β	t	VIF	B	SE	β	t	VIF
Gender	−0.23	0.18	−0.07	−1.30	1.05	−0.19	0.16	−0.06	−1.14	1.05
Age	−0.04	0.14	−0.02	−0.32	1.09	−0.04	0.13	−0.02	−0.32	1.09
Education	−0.33	0.19	−0.10	−1.74	1.10	−0.20	0.18	−0.06	−1.12	1.11
Occupation	0.17	0.07	0.16	2.56*	1.23	0.07	0.06	0.07	1.13	1.29
Income	0.15	0.09	0.11	1.76	1.34	0.10	0.08	0.07	1.21	1.35
Recovery satisfaction						−0.47	0.06	−0.40	−7.55***	1.07
R^2	0.05					0.19				
F	3.05**					12.50***				

a. Dependent variable: customer discouraging behavioral intention.
Note: *$p < 0.05$; **$p < 0.01$; ***$p < 0.001$.

The next one is regarding the relationship between customer overall satisfaction and customer's discoursing behavioral intention. As displayed in Table 7-73, customer overall satisfaction is perceived as independent variable and discouraging behavioral intention is perceived as dependent variable, and controlling variables for hierarchical regression are gender, age, education, profession, and income. In both regressions, VIF < 1.5, indicating a non-existence of sever collinearity. In regression 1, the involvement of five demographic factors has explained only 5% of the variation in discouraging behavioral intention, demographic factors are not influential. In regression 2, five demographic factors and customer's overall satisfaction have explained 20% of the variation. That is, customer overall satisfaction alone explains 15%. The results show that the explanatory power of overall satisfaction to customer's discoursing behavioral intention is not too big, but it does have some explanatory power, similar with the results of recovery satisfaction. Moreover, the influence that customer overall satisfaction has over discouraging behavioral intention is proved to be negative and statistically significant ($\beta = -0.41$, $t = -7.84$, $p < 0.001$). This shows that the higher the overall customer satisfaction is, the less likely would customers discourage people from choosing this hotel; conversely, the lower the overall customer satisfaction is, the more likely would customers discourage others from choosing this hotel.

Table 7-73 The influence of overall satisfaction on discouraging behavioral intention

Variable name	Regression equation 1					Regression equation 2				
	B	SE	β	t	VIF	B	SE	β	t	VIF
Gender	−0.23	0.18	−0.07	−1.30	1.05	−0.17	0.16	−0.05	−1.03	1.05
Age	−0.04	0.14	−0.02	−0.32	1.09	0.00	0.12	0.00	−0.004	1.09
Education	−0.33	0.19	−0.10	−1.74	1.10	−0.31	0.17	−0.10	−1.78	1.10
Occupation	0.17	0.07	0.16	2.56*	1.23	0.06	0.06	0.06	0.99	1.29
Income	0.15	0.09	0.11	1.76	1.34	0.09	0.08	0.06	1.08	1.35
Overall satisfaction						−0.48	0.06	−0.41	−7.84***	1.06
R²	0.05					0.20				
F	3.05**					13.28***				

a. Dependent variable: customer discouraging behavioral intention.
Note: *p < 0.05; **p < 0.01; ***p < 0.001.

In summary, comparing the explanatory power of recovery satisfaction and overall satisfaction in customer's discouraging intention, we find that overall satisfaction (15%) is slightly more explanatory than recovery satisfaction (14%) in spreading negative word of mouth and discouraging, that they both have a considerable impact on such intention. In addition, both of customer recovery satisfaction and overall satisfaction do affect discouraging behavioral intention. The higher the satisfaction, the less dissuasion and negative word-of-mouth. Hence, H5c—customer satisfaction after recovery (include recovery satisfaction and overall satisfaction) negatively influences the likelihood of discouraging other people to use the hotel service—is supported.

7.2.5.4 The relationship between customer satisfaction after recovery and complaining (to hotel and manager) behavioral intention

In the study of customer satisfaction, most researchers believe that when a customer encounters a service failure and is dissatisfied with a hotel service, they tend to complain to the hotel or the manager (McColl et al., 2005; Ok et al., 2007; Ekiz and Arasli, 2007; Chan and Wan, 2008). However, there is little attention paid to the effect of customer satisfaction after recovery on the intention of complaint. In this section, we propose that recovery satisfaction and overall satisfaction have an impact on the behavioral intention of complaining (to hotel and manager) respectively.

As displayed in Table 7-74, we first examine the impact of the recovery satisfaction on customer complaints to service provider. In this case, customer recovery satisfaction is perceived as independent variable and complaining behavioral intention (to hotel and manager) is perceived as dependent variable, and controlling variables for hierarchical regression are gender, age, education, profession, and income. In both regressions, VIF < 1.5, indicating a non-existence of sever collinearity. In regression 1, the involvement of five demographic factors has explained only 3% of the variation in complaining behavioral intention (to hotel and manager). It indicates that demographic factors are not influential. In regression 2, five demographic factors and customer's recovery satisfaction have explained 18% of the variation. That is, customer recovery satisfaction alone explains 15%. This suggests that the explanatory power of recovery satisfaction to complaining behavioral intention (to hotel and manager) is not too big, but it does have some explanatory power. In addition, the influence that customer recovery satisfaction has over complaining behavioral intention (to hotel and manager) is proved to be negative and statistically significant ($\beta = -0.41$, $t = -7.73$, $p < 0.001$). The result shows that the higher the customer satisfaction with the recovery provided by hotel is, the less likely they would complain to the hotel and manager; conversely, the lower the recovery satisfaction is, the more likely would they complain to hotel and managers.

Table 7-74 The influence of recovery satisfaction on complaining
to the hotel and manager

Variable name	Regression equation 1					Regression equation 2				
	B	SE	β	t	VIF	B	SE	β	t	VIF
Gender	−0.45	0.17	−0.15	−2.68**	1.05	−0.41	0.16	−0.14	−2.64**	1.05
Age	−0.02	0.13	−0.01	−0.18	1.09	−0.02	0.12	−0.01	−0.18	1.09
Education	0.13	0.18	0.04	0.74	1.10	0.26	0.17	0.09	1.58	1.12
Occupation	0.06	0.06	0.06	0.94	1.23	−0.04	0.06	−0.04	−0.63	1.29
Income	0.07	0.08	0.05	0.80	1.34	0.01	0.08	0.01	0.16	1.35
Recovery satisfaction						−0.46	0.06	−0.41	−7.73***	1.07
R^2	0.03					0.18				
F	1.72					11.68***				

a. Dependent variable: customer complaining to hotel and manager intention.
Note: *$p < 0.05$; **$p < 0.01$; ***$p < 0.001$.

Next, as displayed in Table 7-75, as for the customer overall satisfaction and the behavioral intention of complaining to hotel and manager. In this case, customer overall satisfaction is perceived as independent variable and complaining behavioral intention (to hotel and manager) is perceived as dependent variable, and controlling variables for hierarchical regression are gender, age, education, profession, and income. In both regressions, VIF < 1.5, indicating a non-existence of sever collinearity. In regression 1, the involvement of five demographic factors has explained only 3% of the variation in complaining behavioral intention (to hotel and manager), demographic factors are not influential. In regression 2, five demographic factors and customer's overall satisfaction have explained 22% of the variation. That is, customer overall satisfaction alone explains 19%. The explanatory power of overall satisfaction to customer's discoursing behavioral intention is not too big, but it does have some explanatory power. In addition, the influence that customer overall satisfaction has over complaining behavioral intention (to hotel and manager) is proved to be negative and statistically significant ($β = −0.45$, $t = −8.77$, $p < 0.001$). It indicates that the higher the overall satisfaction is, the less likely customers would prefer to complain to service provider; conversely, the lower the overall level of satisfaction is, the more likely customers would complain to service provider.

Table 7-75   The influence of overall satisfaction after
recovery on complaining to the hotel and manager

Variable name	Regression equation 1					Regression equation 2				
	B	SE	β	t	VIF	B	SE	β	t	VIF
Gender	−0.45	0.17	−0.15	−2.68**	1.05	−0.39	0.15	−0.13	−2.54*	1.05
Age	−0.02	0.13	−0.01	−0.18	1.09	0.02	0.12	0.01	0.18	1.09
Education	0.13	0.18	0.04	0.74	1.10	0.16	0.16	0.05	0.96	1.10
Occupation	0.06	0.06	0.06	0.94	1.23	−0.05	0.06	−0.05	−0.92	1.29
Income	0.07	0.08	0.05	0.80	1.34	−0.004	0.07	−0.003	−0.05	1.35
Overall satisfaction						−0.50	0.06	−0.45	−8.77***	1.06
R^2	0.03					0.22				
F	1.72					14.60***				

a. Dependent variable: customer complaining to hotel and manager intention.
Note: *$p < 0.05$; **$p < 0.01$; ***$p < 0.001$.

In summary, the results show that the explanatory power of overall satisfaction (19%) is greater than the recovery satisfaction (15%) in the behavioral intention of complaining to hotel and manager. And they both have a considerable impact on customer complaining to the hotel. In addition, both of customer recovery satisfaction and overall satisfaction do affect complaining behavioral intention (to hotel and manager). The higher the satisfaction is, the smaller the tendency of complaint to the hotel and manager is. Hence, H5d—customer satisfaction after recovery (include recovery satisfaction and overall satisfaction) negatively influences the likelihood of complaining to the hotel and manager—is supported.

7.2.5.5   The relationship between customer satisfaction after recovery and complaining (to third parties) behavioral intention

Researchers have realized that dissatisfied customers tend to complain to a third party (Singh, 1988; De Matos and Leis, 2013). That is, the third party complaining is likely to increase when customer satisfaction levels decrease following a service failure (Bougie et al., 2003; Ramirez et al., 2008; Russell-Bennett et al., 2015). However, few researchers are concerned about the impact of service recovery satisfaction on customer complaints to third parties. In this section, we propose that recovery satisfaction and overall satisfaction have an impact on the behavioral intention of complaining (to third parties) respectively.

As displayed in Table 7-76, as for the relationship between recovery satisfaction and the intention of customer complaining to third parties, in this regression, customer recovery satisfaction is perceived as independent variable and complaining behavioral intention (to third parties) is perceived as dependent variable, and controlling variables for hierarchical regression are gender, age, education, profession, and income. In both regressions, VIF < 1.5, indicating a non-existence of sever collinearity. In regression 1, the involvement of five demographic factors has explained only 2% of the variation in complaining behavioral intention (to third parties), demographic factors are not influential. In regression 2, five demographic factors and customer's recovery satisfaction have explained 11% of the variation. That is, customer recovery satisfaction alone explains 9%. This suggests that the explanatory power of recovery satisfaction to complaining behavioral intention (to third parties) is relatively small, but it does have some explanatory power. In addition, the influence that customer recovery satisfaction has over complaining behavioral intention (to third parties) is proved to be negative and statistically significant ($\beta = -0.31$, $t = -5.65$, $p < 0.001$). The higher the recovery satisfaction is, the smaller the tendency of complaining to third parties would be.

Table 7-76 The influence of recovery satisfaction after recovery on complaining to the third parties

Variable name	Regression equation 1					Regression equation 2				
	B	SE	β	t	VIF	B	SE	β	t	VIF
Gender	−0.36	0.17	−0.12	−2.06*	1.05	−0.32	0.17	−0.11	−1.96	1.05
Age	−0.05	0.13	−0.02	−0.36	1.09	−0.05	0.13	−0.02	−0.36	1.09
Education	0.28	0.18	0.09	1.51	1.10	0.38	0.18	0.12	2.14*	1.11
Occupation	−0.01	0.07	−0.01	−0.15	1.23	−0.09	0.06	−0.08	−1.34	1.29
Income	−0.05	0.08	−0.04	−0.58	1.34	−0.09	0.08	−0.07	−1.13	1.35
Recovery satisfaction						−0.36	0.06	−0.31	−5.65***	1.07

Continued

Variable name	Regression equation 1					Regression equation 2				
	B	SE	β	t	VIF	B	SE	β	t	VIF
R^2	0.02					0.11				
F	1.33					6.54***				

a. Dependent variable: customer complaining intention to third parties.
Note: *$p < 0.05$; **$p < 0.01$; ***$p < 0.001$.

Next, with respect to the relationship between customer overall satisfaction and complaining behavioral intention (to third parties), as displayed in Table 7-77, customer overall satisfaction is perceived as independent variable and complaining behavioral intention (to third parties) is perceived as dependent variable, and controlling variables for hierarchical regression are gender, age, education, profession, and income. In both regressions, $VIF < 1.5$, indicating a non-existence of sever collinearity. In regression 1, the involvement of five demographic factors has explained only 2% of the variation in complaining behavioral intention (to third parties); demographic factors are not influential. In regression 2, five demographic factors and customer's overall satisfaction have explained 14% of the variation. That is, customer overall satisfaction alone explains 12%. The explanatory power of overall satisfaction to complaining behavioral intention (to third parties) is not big, but it does have some explanatory power. In addition, the influence that customer overall satisfaction has over complaining behavioral intention (to third parties) is proved to be negative and statistically significant ($\beta = -0.35$, $t = -6.43$, $p < 0.001$). The higher the overall satisfaction is, the smaller the tendency of complaining to third parties would be.

Table 7-77 The influence of overall satisfaction after
recovery on complaining to the third parties

Variable name	Regression equation 1					Regression equation 2				
	B	SE	β	t	VIF	B	SE	β	t	VIF
Gender	−0.36	0.17	−0.12	−2.06*	1.05	−0.30	0.16	−0.10	−1.86	1.05
Age	−0.05	0.13	−0.02	−0.36	1.09	−0.01	0.13	−0.01	−0.10	1.09
Education	0.28	0.18	0.09	1.51	1.10	0.29	0.17	0.09	1.70	1.10

Continued

Variable name	Regression equation 1					Regression equation 2				
	B	SE	β	t	VIF	B	SE	β	t	VIF
Occupation	−0.01	0.07	−0.01	−0.15	1.23	−0.10	0.06	−0.10	−1.58	1.29
Income	−0.05	0.08	−0.04	−0.58	1.34	−0.10	0.08	−0.08	−1.30	1.35
Overall satisfaction						−0.39	0.06	−0.35	−6.43***	1.06
R^2	0.02					0.14				
F	1.33					8.13***				

a. Dependent variable: customer complaining intention to third parties.
Note: *$p < 0.05$; **$p < 0.01$; ***$p < 0.001$.

In summary, the results show that the explanatory power of overall satisfaction is bigger than the recovery satisfaction in the behavioral intention of complaining to third parties. That is, comparing the explanatory power of recovery satisfaction and overall satisfaction in customer's complaining to third parties intention, we find that overall satisfaction (12%) is more explanatory than recovery satisfaction (9%), that they both have a considerable impact on complaining to third parties. In addition, both of customer recovery satisfaction and overall satisfaction do affect complaining behavioral intention (to third parties). Hence, H5e—customer satisfaction after recovery (include recovery satisfaction and overall satisfaction) negatively influences the likelihood of complaining to the third parties—is supported.

In all, the five regression models are proved to be meaningful and consistent with relevant analyses. The explanatory power of recovery satisfaction and overall satisfaction in "repurchasing intention" (41%, 57%), "recommending intention" (40%, 56%) are much greater than in "discouraging" (14%, 15%), and "complaining to hotel or third parties" (15%, 19%). whether it is the recovery satisfaction or overall satisfaction, they both have quite explanatory power in explaining customer behaviors. Hence, Hypothesis 5—customer satisfaction after recovery influences customer behavioral intention—is supported. We summarize the above conclusions as follows (See Table 7-78).

Table 7-78   The results of Hypothesis 5

H5: Customer satisfaction after recovery influences customer behavioral intention	Supported
H5a: Customer satisfaction after recovery (include recovery satisfaction and overall satisfaction) positively influences the likelihood of repurchasing the services of this hotel in the future	Supported
H5b: Customer satisfaction after recovery (include recovery satisfaction and overall satisfaction) positively influences the likelihood of recommending this hotel to other people	Supported
H5c: Customer satisfaction after recovery (include recovery satisfaction and overall satisfaction) negatively influences the likelihood of discouraging other people to use the hotel service	Supported
H5d: Customer satisfaction after recovery (include recovery satisfaction and overall satisfaction) negatively influences the likelihood of complaining to the hotel and manager	Supported
H5e: Customer satisfaction after recovery (include recovery satisfaction and overall satisfaction) negatively influences the likelihood of complaining to the third parties	Supported

Overall, the results show that (1) customer attribution has a statistically significant mediating function in lines between service failure and customer recovery expectation; (2) the discrepancy between recovery expectation and obtained recovery affects satisfaction after recovery (include recovery satisfaction and overall satisfaction); (3) customer satisfaction after recovery affects customer future behavioral intentions; (4) types of recovery expectation is influenced by types of service failure; and (5) obtained recovery is differentiated with recovery expectation to some extent, mainly because of "hotels not giving appropriate compensations" or "customers receiving undesired compensations"—such "mismatch" or "difference" affects the effectiveness of failure recovery and customer satisfaction after recovery.

The findings would provide insights for marketing academics and industry practitioners to better understand the role of customer attribution and recovery expectation in service failure and service recovery process (See Table 7-79). Therefore, more localized and more satisfying marketing strategies are to be expected in the Chinese market.

Table 7-79   The results of hypothesis tests

Hypothesis	Results
H1: Service failure that customer experienced in hotel influences customer attribution	Supported
H1a: Type of service failure that customer experienced in hotel influences customer attribution (to hotel, customer and environment)	Supported
H1b: Severity of service failure that customer experienced in hotel influences customer attribution (to hotel, customer and environment)	Supported
H1c: Stability and controllability of service failure influence customer attribution (to hotel, customer and environment)	Supported
H2: Customer attribution (locus, stability, controllability) influences customer recovery expectation (recovery magnitude of expectation, recovery type of expectation)	Supported
H2a: Locus of attribution influences customer expectation (recovery magnitude of expectation, recovery type of expectation)	Supported
H2b: Stability of service failure influences customer expectation (recovery magnitude of expectation, recovery type of expectation)	Partially Supported
H2c: Controllability of service failure influences customer expectation (recovery magnitude of expectation, recovery type of expectation)	Supported
H3: Service failure (type, severity) that customer experienced in hotel influences customer recovery expectation (recovery magnitude of expectation, recovery type of expectation)	Partially Supported
H3a: Type of Service failure that customer experienced in hotel influences customer recovery expectation (recovery magnitude of expectation, recovery type of expectation)	Partially supported
H3b: Severity of Service failure that customer experienced in hotel influences customer recovery expectation (recovery magnitude of expectation, recovery type of expectation)	Partially Supported
H4: The disconfirmation between customer recovery expectation and obtained recovery has effects on customer satisfaction after recovery (include recovery satisfaction and overall satisfaction)	Supported
H4a: The disconfirmation influences customer recovery satisfaction	Supported
H4b: The disconfirmation influences customer overall satisfaction	Supported
H5: Customer satisfaction after recovery influences customer behavioral intention	Supported
H5a: Customer satisfaction after recovery (include recovery satisfaction and overall satisfaction) positively influences the likelihood of repurchasing the services of this hotel in the future	Supported

Continued

H5b: Customer satisfaction after recovery (include recovery satisfaction and overall satisfaction) positively influences the likelihood of recommending this hotel to other people	Supported
H5c: Customer satisfaction after recovery (include recovery satisfaction and overall satisfaction) negatively influences the likelihood of discouraging other people to use the hotel service	Supported
H5d: Customer satisfaction after recovery (include recovery satisfaction and overall satisfaction) negatively influences the likelihood of complaining to the hotel and manager.	Supported
H5e: Customer satisfaction after recovery (include recovery satisfaction and overall satisfaction) negatively influences the likelihood of complaining to third parties	Supported

CHAPTER 8

DISCUSSION

For some time, researchers have studied service failure and failure recovery from different angles with hypotheses, frameworks and models of all sorts. However, a universally agreed conclusion or accepted methodology is still missing, not only in academic research but in practical context as well. It is confusing that although the service provider always puts customer as the starting point of its very being, it fails to satisfy customers sometimes and contain their loyalty. Meanwhile, recovery policies are not functional all along, and customers who encounter service failure and recovery afterwards might just walk away. In all, service failure and recovery require more research efforts.

As an attempt to answer the research question: in the hospitality industry of China, to what extent satisfaction recovery can be explained by customer attributions and expectations (dis)confirmation? Why do customers who accept service recovery still leave the service provider or do something that is not good for the service provider? This study proposes a conceptual model based on attribution theory (Weiner, 1979, 1980, 1985), expectation-disconfirmation paradigm (Oliver, 1980, 1997; Churchill et al., 1982; Parasuraman et al., 1985), justice theory (Adams, 1965; Greenberg, 1996; Tax et al., 1998; Lind et al., 1988; Thibaut et al., 1975; Bies et al., 1986). It relies on two key concepts (customer attribution and recovery expectation), and displays five hypotheses in three set of relationships: (1) the influences of service failure on customer attribution, the influences of customer attribution on recovery expectation, and the influences of service failure on recovery expectation; (2) the influences of the difference between customer recovery expectation and obtained recovery on customer satisfaction after recovery; and (3) the influences of customer satisfaction after recovery on behavioral intention. And then, according to "matching hypothesis" (Smith et al., 1999; Worsfold et al., 2007; Roschk et al., 2014), we explore the relationship between the categories of service failure (Bitner et al., 1990) and the type of customer recovery expectation (Roschk et al., 2014), and find some mismatch between recovery expectations and recovery obtained (Nyquist et al., 1985; Parasuraman et al., 1985; Kuenzel et al., 2011).

We have differentiated customers in Chinese hospitality industry from western hospitality customers by several unique characteristics. The historical Chinese culture is rooted so deeply in the country that it has become part of its people's sub-consciousness. Meanwhile, the dramatic changes occurred during the past few decades in both economic and social areas, which are still ongoing, also played a significant contribution to the formation of such unique customers. Literally, all human beings are influenced and shaped to some extent by the environment they live in, and the variation of those environmental factors as well. Therefore, no studies on customer behavior should ever ignore the social and cultural settings of customers (Li, 2007). When it comes to the case of Chinese market, such notice is especially important given the fact that in the past 100 years this country has gone through phenomenal and frequent social changes (Doctoroff, 2005). To take Chinese customers' individual perceived, cognitive and subsequent behavior into account, the study of the uniqueness of Chinese hospitality customer is the key for a comprehensive and contemporary understanding of the concept.

During the research, we have collected 318 effective responses by an online questionnaire software (http://www.wjx.cn) from respondents who claimed to have experienced service failure and complained to the service provider in the recent six months. The descriptive analysis identifies the socioeconomic and accommodation-related characteristics of Chinese hospitality customers which can reflect the general pattern of Chinese hospitality market. Generally, the majority of Chinese hospitality customers are the newly affluent middle class: they are well-educated white collars in the age group of 25—44. Nearly 50% of customers mark "pleasure" for travel purpose, followed by "business" (20%). Most customers (90%) choose 3 or 4 stars-rating hotels, suggesting those customers with decent education (about 90% has a bachelor degree or above) and fair income (85% is over ¥5,000). They tend to choose comfortable mid-range hotels rather than cheap or solely luxury one. In addition, hotel location is a very important factor for choosing hotels (35.4%), followed by online comments (e-WOM) (20%).

Such fact in a way shows the blooming growth of internet in China, and online platform becomes the main channel of hotel booking. Interestingly, in Chinese hospitality industry, compared to female customers, male customers are more sensitive to location and brand; women are more influenced by online information and word of mouth (See Table 7-3). Therefore, if the hotel is targeted at female customers, special attention should be paid to the issue of network evaluation and word of mouth communication.

To better discuss the results of data analysis, we organize the discussion along the three sets regarding service failure and recovery. Firstly, the relationship between service failure, customer attribution and recovery expectation; secondly, the relationship between recovery expectation, obtained recovery and satisfaction after recovery; thirdly, the relationship between satisfaction after recovery and customer behavioral intention.

8.1 The relationship between service failure, customer attribution and recovery expectation

To start off with, the service failures that Chinese hospitality customers encounter in hotels can be categorized into three types. They are unreasonably slow service (26.2%), invalid service and other core service failure (21.5%), lack of attention (12.5%). It is worth noting that 71.7% of customers have experienced more than one type of failures, and they perceive the severity of failure as over Mild. Failures are attributed largely to hotels (mean = 5.64) and external environments (mean = 5.43), instead of to customers (mean = 1.93). This result is consistent with Weiner's (1979) attribution theory that customer tends to attribute the cause of the failure to the service provider or external environment. That is, to protect their ego, consumers tend to perceive that they are not responsible for failures and they often attribute bad results to situational (or external) causes, while attribute good results to their own abilities (or internal causes) (Hui and Toffoli, 2002; Ye, 2005; Vázquez-Casielles et al., 2007). However, it is impossible to know from this result which specific type of failure or the severity of the failure affect the customer attribution.

In order to understand more specifically the impact of service failures on customer attribution, we use the method of hierarchical regression to analyze the impact of each type of failure on customer attribution. And the results indicate that different types of service failure lead to attribution differentiation. Six out of the twelve types of service failures significantly affect customer attribution (See Table 7-27 to Table 7-32). Among them, five out of the six types negatively influence customer attribution, which are the failure due to unavailable service, customers' special needs not satisfied, customer preferences not met, admitted customer error, and lack of the attention paid to customer are. Only one of them, and other core or main service failures positively influence customer attribution. It means that only with the appearance of core service failures like cleanness or security leak, would Chinese hospitality customers attribute to hotel and external causes, regardless of true allocation of responsibility. The statement aligns with Weiner's attribution theory that customers tend to attribute bad results to others instead of themselves. If the situations where hotels are unable to provide corresponding service, or individualized customer needs are not met, or inadequate attention is given to customers, or customers indeed make some mistakes occur, they might attribute causes to themselves instead of environments or hotels, considering themselves to be responsible. In this way, the attribution theory fails to function. Probably, it could be the idea of restraining oneself which originated from the traditional Chinese Confucianism that makes Chinese customers think in a more rational way while encountering service failure. Given the above facts, Heider (1958) proposed that people act based on their beliefs, no matter these beliefs are valid or not (Borkowski and Allen, 2003). Specifically, Kelley and Michela (1980) suggest that the attribution is affected by information, the perceiver's belief and motivation. Hence, cultural influence can be an important subject in future researches on customer attribution.

In addition, we noticed that there are also six types from Bitner et al. (1990)'s twelve types of failure that have no significant impacts on Chinese hospitality customer's attribution, such as unreasonably slow service, gestalt evaluation (societal/cultural insult). This may be because in the Chinese hotel industry, the content of customer concern is different, like low expectation on time-punctuality, and high tolerance on mistakes; it may also be because some types containing too much complexity, and it is difficult for customers to determine whom is to blame. Thus, the classification of service failure can be further studied and refined in the future. But with no doubt, the type of service failure does affect customer attribution in some ways.

Next is regarding the relationship between severity of service failure and customer attribution. Researchers defined failure severity as the customer's perceived magnitude of the problem (Smith and Bolton, 1998). Greater perceived severity of loss by customer not only leads to a lower satisfaction rate but also makes it more difficult to recover from service failure (e.g. Mattila, 1999; Harris et al., 2006). Some study finds that even the type of service failure perfectly matches the customer's mental account of the recovery effort when a serious service failure occurs, customers may remain dissatisfied because the perceived loss greatly outweighs the gain (Smith et al., 1999; Thaler, 1985). In this study, statistics also proves that the severity of service failure has a significantly positive influence on Chinese hospitality customer's attribution (to hotel, customer and environment). It means that the severity of service failure plays an important role in hospitality customer perceptions (Hoffman et al., 1995; Blodgett et al., 1995; Blodgett et al., 1997; Tax et al., 1998; Harris et al., 2006; Chuang et al., 2012). Hotels shall prevent failures that have already taken place from getting worse by, for example, authorizing front employees to do timely recovery.

The third relationship is between stability, controllability, and customer attribution. Weiner (1980, 1985a, 1985b) suggests that customer attribution based on three dimensions: locus of control, stability, and controllability. That is, individuals explain their performance decisions by cognitively constructing their reality in terms of internal-external, stable-unstable, and controllable-uncontrollable factors (Borkowski et al., 2003). Stability (stable-unstable) means the extent to which a cause is viewed as temporary or predictable and permanent, or whether the incident is likely to be repeated (Vázquez-Casielles et al., 2007; Akpoyomare Oghojafor, 2012; Anderson et al, 2009). Controllability (controllable-uncontrollable) refers to whether the person had the power to exert control over the events of the situation (Borkowski et al., 2003), researchers believe that control attribution involves the consumers' beliefs about whether the firm could avoid a failure from occurring, or alternatively it is the situation that forces the firm to follow a certain course of action (Weiner, 1985a, 2000; Hui et al., 2006; Vázquez-Casielles et al., 2007).

In Chinese hospitality industry, the results indicate that stability negatively significant influences customer attribution to hotel. Controllability positively influences customer attribution to hotel and external environment, negatively and significantly influences customer attribution to customer. That is, when failures are perceived as stable, customers would not attribute them to hotels; otherwise, when failures are perceived as unstable, customers would attribute them to hotels. From hotels' point of view, even customers do not blame stable failures to hotels, the consequences of those failures are not necessarily favorable by hotels. The reason is that customers will experience lower satisfaction when the cause of the service failure is perceived as stable (Casado and Mas, 2002; Tsiros and Mittal, 2000; Tsiros et al., 2004; O'Neill and Mattila, 2004). Besides, guests tend to avoid hotels with stable failures. Thus, an excellent service organization should have less tolerance for stable failures (Vázquez-Casielles et al., 2007).

As for controllability, the results indicate that when customers believe the service failure is controllable, the hotel can avoid it by taking measures in advance, they will attribute the service failure to the hotel and environment; when they consider the failure is uncontrollable, they will attribute the service failure to the themselves. Hence, hotels shall avoid controllable service failures, not only for the escape of customer attribution, but importantly, customers will experience lower satisfaction when the cause of the service failure is perceived as controllable (Oliver and DeSarbo, 1988; Vázquez-Casielles et al., 2007).

In this study, more than 50% of Chinese hospitality customers regard service failure as accidental and unstable events, while 94.7% of customers believe that failures can be controllable and preventable from happening if hotels take reasonable precautions. Thus, in Chinese hospitality industry, regardless of failure types, it is common for hotels to take most of blames. It is consistent with Weiner's attribution theory (1979, 1980, 1985). Notably, customers encountering multiple failures is a quite usual phenomenon, such circumstance might influence attribution process and then the future intentions.

The second relationship between customer attribution and recovery expectation. It is found that all the three dimensions (locus, controllability, stability) significantly influence recovery expectation (recovery magnitude of expectation, recovery type of expectation) in Chinese hospitality industry. Customer's recovery expectation is created in the pre-recovery phase and may last from a few seconds to several weeks or even months (Craighead et al., 2004). Attribution theory may also provide more understanding on consumer perceptions and intentions relative to service recovery experiences (Swanson and Kelley, 2001). Specifically, in terms of service failure, customers would have two aspects of expectation: magnitude of recovery and types of recovery.

With respect to magnitude of recovery expectation, Chinese hospitality customers want effective recoveries that help them solve the problem (mean = 5.09), make up loses (mean = 5.06), and get reasonable compensation (mean = 4.64). The results of our research indicate that when Chinese customers perceive the encountered failures as hotel-oriented and stable, or to be preventable by certain precautions (from hotels), they would expect higher in recovery, of both types and magnitude. That is, Chinese hospitality customer's recovery expectations would be impacted by their attribution of service failure (e.g. Hess et al., 2003; Ma, 2012).

As for recovery types of customer's expectation, the fact is that psychological compensation (apology) (mean = 5.44), replacing product or service (mean = 5.39), immediate monetary compensation(mean = 5.3), and service (or product) guarantee (mean = 5.20) are favorable in hospitality. Comparing to deferred monetary compensation (mean = 4.37), customers like immediate monetary compensation (mean = 5.3) more. Namely, comparing to deferred monetary compensations like voucher (mean = 4.3) and hotel or hotel chain credit received (mean = 4.25), customers would prefer immediate monetary compensations like refund (mean = 5.49), discount (mean = 5.44) and upgraded service (mean = 5.29). In Chinese hospitality industry, if service failures are attributed to hotels, customers prefer immediate monetary compensations like discount or refund, instead of deferred monetary compensations such as voucher or credit points. It implies an uncertainty for choosing the particular again in the future, hence, it would be less valuable for customers. Meanwhile, if it is the hotel who is held accountable, customers would like apology and service guarantee from the hotel to comfort their emotions and sense of security. Moreover, such compensation arguably raises customer expectation for new service/product and service/product replacement.

Nevertheless, when the blame goes to hotels and external causes (environments), the Chinese hospitality customers prefer immediate monetary compensation, apology, product/service replacement and service guarantee. Immediate monetary compensation shows a desire to recover financial loses; apology is a comfort to ego, dignity and emotion; product/service replacement means an expectation on ultimate solution. And they are likely to accept service/product guarantees to reduce risks of such failure happening again. The requests customers have for hotels are rational. If they prefer immediate compensation (monetary or other types), their loyalty is not ensured and they would very much hesitate to choose whether to purchase next time. Related to the traditional Confucianism philosophy, Chinese customers appear to care about psychological apologies remarkably. However, when Chinese customers attribute failures to hotels, they are less likely to be interested by a replicated service/product from hotels. It might be because that the service process requires efforts put from both sides (hotels and customers), it can be tiring to receive the service again as for customers. For example, when there is a water-leak problem in the room, to have a mechanician, most customers would prefer a direct room-switch as the prior option can be tiring.

In addition, when Chinese customers find the service failure can be avoided if hotels take certain actions, in other words, they appear to have very little interest in compensations except service guarantees. It in a way illustrates that Chinese customers do have faith in hotel's keeping promises and providing appropriate service recovery.

By the statistics analysis, we are able to conclude as follows. First of all, the more Chinese customers are convinced that the responsibility for failure goes to hotels, the higher their expectation on recovery (of both types and magnitude) would be. As Folkes (1988) states, problems arising from consumer actions should be solved by customers, whereas problems arising from service provider' actions should be solved by service provider. It also aligns with the "matching hypothesis" (Smith et al., 1999); that customers who experience service-failure and recovery encounters prefer to receive resources that match loss that they experienced in both types and severity (Smith et al., 1999). In other words, they choose to receive recovery resources that "match" the type of failure they experience in "amounts" that are commensurate with the magnitude of the failure (Smith et al., 1999; Worsfold et al., 2007). Next, when the service failure happened is perceived as stable (often taken place), customers would expect considerably higher in recovery magnitude, yet not necessarily in recovery type. According to Hess et al. (2003), customers tend to have high expectation of recovery on stable failures, yet have lower expectation of recovery on accidental failures. The results are in accordance with Hess et al.'s (2003) argument. Thus, hotels shall avoid stable failures from occurring, as such failures make the recovery process particularly difficult and then difficult to recover the satisfaction level as well. Anyway, appropriate policy and process to recover such failures is necessary for every hotel (Hess et al., 2003). Then, when the service failure happened is perceived as preventable if hotels had some precautions, customers would expect considerably highly in recovery magnitude, and in recovery type as well. It is consistent with the researches of Hess et al. (2003) and Folkes (1984). Hess et al. (2003) argue that when the cause of failure is considered as controllable, recovery expectations will be higher than when the cause of failure is considered as uncontrollable. The study of Folkes (1984) implicitly indicates the positive relationship between the controllability and recovery expectations. In the hotel industry, service providers need to pay more attention to those failures which are controllable and preventable. As discussed, those failures can make recovery particularly difficult, and are unfavorable in customer satisfaction. Hotels can perform certain guarantees or insurances to lift up the customer's confidence. Many researchers have now noticed the relationship between service guarantees and customer recovery expectation. Service guarantees have been identified as one of the antecedents of service recovery expectations in the studies of Craighead et al. (2004) and Miller et al. (2000). Although developing and implementing a guarantee will lead to high costs, it has been suggested that the benefits gained outweigh the costs in the long-term (Hart, 1988; Wirtz and Kum, 2001; Wong, Tsaur and Wang, 2009). When the service fails, the promise of a payout and/or the service will strengthen their beliefs that their complaints will bring about a positive outcome for them (Robertson et al., 2012).

The third relationship discussed is between service failure (types and severity) and customer recovery expectation (types and magnitude). According to equity theory (Adams, 1965) and "matching hypothesis" (Smith et al., 1999), customers would like to have compensation that matches their losses, and feel fairly treated. Thus, if it is a monetary loss, they would expect financial compensations; if it is related to emotion or esteem, they would naturally expect a decent apology, explaination and respect. Boulding et al. (1993) and Kelley et al., (1994) have as well studied relevant topics and consider service failure that can affect customer's recovery expectation.

For Chinese hospitality customers, the types of service failure would affect their expectation on recovery types, and they might expect more than one certain type of recovery for a particular failure type. In specific, among all types of service failure, when customers encounter failures caused by (1) "unreasonable lagged service", "customer preferences not met" and "inventory loss due to customers' fault", which would expect deferred monetary compensation, like voucher, credit points of hotel which can be used in their next stay; (2) "unreasonable lagged service", which would expect immediate monetary compensation tied to the current purchase, like discount or currency refund; (3) "potential disruptive factors" and "inappropriate employee behavior related to cultural norms", which would expect new/exchange product/service; and (4) "unavailable service failure" and "customer preferences not met", which would expect psychological compensations like apology. However, no types of service failure would affect customer expectation on new/replicate service and service/product guarantee.

In short, in the Chinese hospitality industry, the differentiation of failure types influences the types of customer recovery expectation. Such findings align with the "matching hypothesis" (Smith et al., 1999). Probably, too many variables are taken into consideration in this relationship (types of failure, types of recovery), so we failed to discover a one-to-one corresponding relationship. This could be a subject for future researches. That is, in the future research, the relationship between the variables can be further studied to see if there exists any one-to-one reflection.

For Chinese hospitality customers, the severity of failure hardly affects their expectation on recovery magnitude. It contradicts with the "matching hypothesis" (Smith et al., 1999). In other words, customers do not raise expectation just because of the severity of failure going up. It is an unexpected result, but understandable.

Combining the findings, we can see that customer attrition mediates the relationship between service failure and customer recovery expectation. When service failure occurs, customers would go for attribution first and according to the results of attribution, they would then form certain expectation of recovery. For example, rational customers would consider whom is to blame when failure occurs. If the answer is themselves, even the matter is severe, their expectation on recovery would not be high; if the answer is external causes, expectation is similar; but if the answer is hotels, then the expectation on recovery would increase according to the severity of failure. It is a result of seeking justice (Adams, 1965), and in the hope of getting corresponding compensation (Smith et al., 1999). Severity of failure influences the recovery types of customer expectation is consistent with "matching hypothesis" (Smith et al., 1999). It means that the higher the severity of failure is, the more customers would want hotels to provide matching compensations. Specifically, a more serious problem usually grows type of immediate monetary compensation and service/product guarantee compensation. It explains the fact that the higher the severity of failure is, the less confidence customers would have on the hotels, and they prefer immediate monetary compensations and service guarantees.

In all, the types and severity of service failure that customers encounter, do not significantly influence customer recovery magnitude, yet do affect types of recovery expectation. Service failure (type, severity) that customer experiences in hotel partially influences customer recovery expectation (magnitude, type). It suggests in the relationship between service failure and customer recovery expectation, service failure mainly affects types of recovery expectation. Hence, researchers aim to study the matching of the two variables (Roschk and Gelbrich, 2014). In practical context, service providers need to acquire more information about the matching relationships between types of service failure and types of customer recovery expectation to better recover customer satisfaction and save resources on "effective recovery".

8.2 The relationship between recovery expectation, obtained recovery, disconfirmation and customer satisfaction after recovery

The second set of relationship is between recovery expectation, obtained recovery, disconfirmation and customer satisfaction after recovery. According to the expectation-disconfirmation paradigm, there will be a positive-disconfirmation if obtained recovery exceeds expectation. And the greater the gap is, the more satisfied customers will be. In other words, positive-disconfirmation is positively correlated with customer satisfaction. In contrast, if expectation exceeds reality, negative-disconfirmation will dissatisfy customers and the greater the gap is, the more dissatisfied customers will be. That is, the expectation-disconfirmation model (Oliver, 1980, 1997) lies in the proposition that customer (dis)satisfaction is formed through (dis)confirmation, for instance, the gap between expectations and performance. Based on this model, one can assume that when a customer's perceived service/recovery performance is roughly matched by their expectations, the customer would be satisfied. In contrast, when the perceived service/recovery performance is far "better or worse" than expectations, the customer could possibly be delighted or dissatisfied (Kim et al., 2012).

In the analysis of data description, we can see most customers receive more than one type of recovery policies (See Table 7-13). Types of expectation often suit the types of actual gains (See Table 8-1).The three most wanted compensations are: "Psychological compensation (apology)", "New / exchanged goods", and "Immediate monetary compensation tied to the current purchase". The three most often given compensations are "Psychological compensation (apology)", "Immediate monetary compensation tied to the monetary purchase", and "Free product/service upgrade".

Table 8-1   Comparison between types of recovery
expectation and obtained recovery

Recovery expectation	Obtained recovery
1. Psychological compensation (apology)	1. Psychological compensation (apology)
2. New/exchanged goods	2. Immediate monetary compensation tied to the current purchase
3. Immediate monetary compensation tied to the current purchase	3. Free product/service upgrade
4. Free upgrade	4. Free new/replicate service

However, we find a mismatch in recovery type expectation and obtained recovery type (Table 7-18). There are two occasions: either hotels give customers unwanted recovery type; or hotels fail to give customers preferred recovery type. By looking into the sample details, the most unwanted but given compensation types are deferred monetary compensation, product/service replacement, psychological apology; the most preferred but not given compensation types are immediate monetary compensation including refund, discount, free upgrade and guarantee. Such mismatch is possibly the reason why customers only perceive recovery slightly better than expectation (See Table 7-22). This result is consistent with "matching hypotheses" (Smith et al., 1999). When the recovery type does not match customer expectation, the results would be less favorable and ineffective in terms of satisfying customers.

The customer recovery satisfaction and overall satisfaction both rise when obtained recovery exceeds expectation; recovery satisfaction and overall satisfaction both decrease when obtained recovery does not reach expectation. Thus, the results are consistent with the expectation-disconfirmation paradigm (Johnston, 1995; Kim et al., 2012; Churchill and Surprenant, 1982). Specifically, the concept of disconfirmation arises from discrepancies between prior expectations and actual performance (Churchill and Surprenant, 1982; Oliver, 1997). Positive disconfirmation occurs when performance surpasses expectations, which usually promotes the level of customer satisfaction. Negative disconfirmation occurs when performance is below expectations (Binter et al., 1990; Kelly and Davis, 1994), such a result usually leads to dissatisfaction (Oliver, 1997).

In Chinese hospitality industry, managers providing a service recovery that exceeds the customer's expectations is a prerequisite for satisfying customers who have suffered from service failures. The result also fits the matching hypothesis (Smith et al., 1999) that providing appropriate type of recovery is better in satisfying customers than valuable ones. For example, during the peak season of tourism, if customer reservation is canceled because of limited capacity, compensating exceedingly high money does not really help with recovering customer loyalty. This provides an inspiration that giving "matching" compensation is more appropriate.

8.3   The relationship between customer satisfaction after recovery and behavioral intention

The third set of relationships is between customer satisfaction after recovery and customer behavioral intention. As discussed previously in literature, satisfaction after recovery can be divided into two sub-units: recovery satisfaction and overall satisfaction (Singh and Widing, 1991; Smith and Bolton, 1998; Mattila, 2001; Gruber et al., 2011). Satisfied customers would be more likely to perform favorable actions in organization's perspective like re-purchase and positive WOM (Fornell, 1992; Hu et al., 2009; Matzler et al., 2006; Kandampully and Suhartanto, 2000; Dimitriades, 2006; Chi and Qu, 2008; Faullant et al., 2008). And dissatisfied customers would be more likely to perform unfavorable actions in organization's perspective, like exit, complaint, or NWOM (Bearden et al., 1983; Richins 1983; Singh, 1988; Huang et al., 1996). In an era of internet, any comments can be spread terribly quick and wide (Johnson, 2000; Chatterjee, 2001; Gelb et al., 2002; Hennig-Thurau et al, 2004; Godes et al., 2004).

Based on expectation-disconfirmation paradigm (Johnston, 1995; Kim et al., 2012; Churchill and Surprenant, 1982), the mismatching gap would affect customer satisfaction after recovery which consists of expectation on the magnitude and type of recovery, and overall satisfaction (whole process). In this study, after experiencing service failure and failure recovery, both customer recovery satisfaction and overall satisfaction are just above Mild (over 4 in 1—7 Likert Scale). It fits the conclusions generated from expectation-disconfirmation paradigm.

Customer satisfaction after recovery (recovery satisfaction and overall satisfaction) affects customer behavioral intentions. In Chinese hospitality industry, the intentions of Chinese customers tend to be rather restrained and uncertain, indicated by the means of behavior measure all around 4. To elaborate, the re-stay is slightly over 4, recommending or discouraging is slightly lower than 4. They prefer not to influences others' choice in their power. Also, Chinese customers are likely to complain to the service provider instead of external third parties because their main purpose is to solve the problem and help the provider improve service and prevent next failure. Complaining to a third party implies that the customer is more than dissatisfied and looking for revenge because it is an option with considerably bad consequences. So the likelihood for this option is low, given the cultural preference of Chinese customers (mean = 4.01).

Researchers believe that satisfaction after recovery helps explain and predict customer behavior in the future (Hirschman, 1970; Bearden and Teel, 1983; Richins, 1983; Singh, 1988; Fornell, 1992; Huang et al., 1996; Söderlund, 1998; Mattsson et al., 2004; Matzler et al., 2006; Hu et al., 2009; Casado-Díaz et al., 2009). The statistics shows that customer satisfaction after recovery has a significant impact on behavioral intention.

Specifically, in Chinese hospitality industry, the higher the customer's satisfaction after recovery (include recovery satisfaction and overall satisfaction), the more likely they are to stay in the hotel again. The results are consistent with the previous literature of customer behavioral research. Some of them have consistently found a relationship between satisfaction and repurchase intentions (Yi, 1990; Spreng et al., 1995). A higher customer satisfaction may imply a repurchase of the service or product (Hirschman, 1970; Stewart, 1998; McCollough et al., 2000; Colgate and Hedge, 2001; Malhotra et al., 2008; Sabharwal et al., 2010; Browning et al., 2013).

Next, in Chinese hospitality industry, the more satisfied customers are about the recovery and overall service process, the more likely they would recommend the hotel to others (relatives and friends), and spread positive WOM, for example, actions that are favorable by hotels. So, satisfaction after recovery affects not only the repurchase intention of existing customers, but also of those potential guests. Conversely, the higher the degree of satisfaction, the higher the satisfaction, the less dissuasion and negative word of mouth.

Results of these studies indicate that a positive correlation between satisfaction after recovery and word of mouth (e.g. Szymanski and Henard, 2001; Holloway, Wang, and Parish, 2005). Namely, less-satisfied customers are more likely to be pernickety and engage in negative word of mouth (e.g. Oliver, 1997; Anderson, 1998; Roos et al., 2004; Yanamandram and White, 2006; De Matos et al., 2012). Negative word of mouth is the intentions wherein customers recommend others not to purchase the goods or services from a particular firm or service provider (Richins, 1983; Sabharwal et al., 2010). The great majority of dissatisfied customers will participate in private word of mouth (Richins, 1983; Swanson and Kelley, 2001). They establish the importance of satisfaction and dissatisfaction as antecedents of word of mouth behavior (Richins, 1983; Yi, 1990; Spreng et al., 1995; Holloway et al., 2005).

Complaining behaviors include complaint to service provider and complaint to the third parties. Both of customer recovery satisfaction and overall satisfaction do affect complaining behavioral intention (to hotel and manager). The higher the satisfaction is, the smaller the tendency of complaint to the hotel and manager. The higher the satisfaction is, the smaller the tendency of complaining to third parties would be. Both of customer recovery satisfaction and overall satisfaction do affect complaining behavioral intention (to third parties). The results are consistent with most of the complaining behavioral researches. Empirical studies suggest that when customers feel dissatisfied, they tend to perform complaining behaviors (including to service provides or third parties). Some customers take actions to resolve the conflict, they often choose to complain to managers or employees (Ok et al., 2007; Ekiz and Arasli, 2007). Consumers may vent their frustration and, perhaps more importantly, get redress for their dissatisfaction (East, 2000; Jaccard, 1981).

Overall, in Chinese hospitality industry, the more satisfied customers are, the more likely they would re-stay in a particular hotel, or recommend it to others, and the less likely they would complain to hotel and third parties, or discourage others to stay with it. Interestingly, in the open question about other behavioral intentions, 43.6% of surveyed customers choose to make comments online. Also we find customers with higher satisfaction level show less intentions to do online comments—in all, the online comments are possibly negative.

The results of this study show that (1) in Chinese hospitality industry, customer attribution has a significant mediating function in lines between service failure and customer recovery expectation; (2) the discrepancy between customer recovery expectation and obtained recovery affects satisfaction after recovery (recovery satisfaction and overall satisfaction); (3) customer satisfaction after recovery affects customer future behavioral intentions; (4) types of recovery expectation is influenced by types of service failure customer experienced; (5) customer obtained recovery is differentiated with recovery expectation to some extent, mainly because of "hotels not giving appropriate compensations" or "customers receiving undesired compensations"—such "mismatch" or "difference" affects the effectiveness of failure recovery and customer satisfaction after recovery. The findings would provide insights for marketing academics and industry practitioners to better understand the role of customer attribution and recovery expectation in service failure and service recovery process. Therefore, more localized and more satisfying marketing strategies are to be expected in the Chinese market. In next chapter, we will describe the theoretical and managerial implications of this study, together with the limitations and future research recommendations.

CHAPTER 9

GENERAL CONCLUSION

The hotel industry is highly competitive, therefore in order to survive, organizations need to continuously improve competencies in service and other aspects. However, due to the complexity rooted in the nature of industry, service failure is almost unavoidable, hence must be dealt with (Bitner et al., 1990; McColl-Kennedy et al., 2003; Karatepe, 2006; Choi and Mattila, 2008). These service failures may negatively influence the reputation of the service providers, and even lead to the loss of customers, which makes recovery after failure a notably important subject in researching (Matos et al., 2012).

This book concentrates on the study of service failure and recovery. It elaborates a research model based on attribution theory (Heider, 1958; Weiner, 1979,1980, 1985a, 1985b), justice theory (Adams,1965; Greenberg 1996; Tax and Brown, 1998; Colquitt, 2001; Gonzalez et al., 2010), expectation-disconfirmation (e.g. Oliver, 1980, 1997; Oliver and Bearden, 1983; Churchill and Surprenant, 1982; Binter et al., 1990; Kelly and Davis, 1994), and matching hypothesis (e.g. Smith et al., 1999; Worsfold et al., 2007; Roschk and Gelbrich, 2014). It is a quite inclusive model that involves factors like service failure, customer attribution, customer expectation and obtained recovery, gap between recovery expectation and obtained recovery, satisfaction after recovery, and behavioral intention. Individual factors and relationships among them are analyzed respectively. The model has been empirically tested in the context of Chinese hospitality industry. This study mainly used the methods of descriptive statistics, multiple linear hierarchical regression and analysis of variance to analyze the basic characteristics of the sample and verify the model and hypotheses. In this chapter, the theoretical and practical contributions and implications are described;

the limitations of the study and future research recommendations are demonstrated.

9.1   Theoretical contributions

This research extends the body of knowledge on service failure and recovery. It introduces customer attribution as an important mediating variable between service failure and recovery expectation. It also proves that the types and severity of failure would influence customer attribution. In accordance with Weiner's attribution theory (1980, 1985a, 1985b), people tend to attribute bad results to external causes, and give credit to themselves for good results. Specifically, when there is a core service failure, such as the room is not clean, the food is not safe, customers tend to blame hotels (external causes) instead of themselves (internal causes). However, the model becomes less functional when dealing with the two failure types—unavailable service (invalid service) and lack of attention paid to customer. Unavailable service (invalid service) refers to the situation like the hotel room is unavailable to customer due to overbooked by hotel; the window table that customer reserved for the hotel restaurant is occupied by other customers, and so on. Lack of the attention paid to customer refers to some hotel staff at the front desk keep focusing on their mobile phone without, acting like those hotel guests are bothering them (Bitner et al., 1990). These types of service failures are obviously caused by the fault of the hotel or the staff, but the Chinese hospitality customers are more inclined to attribute the failure to themselves, rather than the hotel or environment. It is vital to realize the fact that Chinese hospitality customers may be different with western customers in cultural backgrounds. They do not always attribute bad results to hotels or the external environments, but are willing to take some responsibility and self-attribution. The reason may be that Chinese hotel customers have long been influenced by "self-denial" and "introspection" views (from *The Analects of Confucius*) in the traditional Chinese culture.

In the second place, empirical studies usually have considered failure recovery as a unique variable whereas in this book, it is divided into customer recovery expectation and obtained recovery. The reason for adding obtained recovery is to verify the effectiveness of recovery policies. According to expectation-disconfirmation paradigm (Oliver, 1997; Churchill et al., 1982; Binter et al., 1990; Kelly et al., 1994), strategic effectiveness depends on the gap between customer expectation and reality. The higher the customer's expectation of recovery is, the higher service recovery is needed for the service provider to create a positive disconfirmation. The results of this study indicate that disconfirmation between customer recovery expectation and obtained recovery positively influences customer satisfaction after recovery. That is, recovery expectation and obtained recovery (type and magnitude of recovery) together define customer satisfaction towards recovery. Therefore, the higher the magnitude of customer recovery expectation is, the harder it will be to satisfy customers, and the less effective the recovery is going to be (Yeop-Yunus, 2012; Kim et al., 2012).

Thirdly, based on the "matching hypothesis" (Smith et al., 1999; Worsfold et al., 2007; Roschk and Gelbrich, 2014), comparisons were made between the types of service failure and the types of expected recovery. Evidence shows that failure types affect types of recovery expectation. For example, when customers encounter the failure due to unreasonable lagged service, that is, the service provided by hotel is very slow, they prefer to get monetary compensations (including deferred monetary compensation tied to future purchase, such as voucher, hotel or hotel chain credit received, and immediate monetary compensation tied to the current purchase, such as discount, refund, and free upgrades). However, when it comes to the failure due to not achieved customer preferences, they prefer to psychological compensation (apology) and would stay confident with the service provider and accept deferred monetary compensations. When the failure occurs due to customers' faults, they also prefer to accept deferred monetary compensations. Our contribution is to advance Roschk and Gelbrich's (2014) research on matching types of service failure and types of recovery expectation by adopting Bittner's (1990) detailed classification of service failures. The classification covers various angles including failures caused by individualized customer needs, requests and preference, not all attributed to hotels or environments. Specifically, the failure types by Roschk and Gelbrich (2014) examined range from monetary harm like charges by the phone company for unsubscribed features (Liao, 2007), to flawed goods like shoes falling apart (Blodgett et al., 1997), to a failed service like an overcooked steak (Hess et al., 2003), or inattentive employees giving undue preference to other customers (Bonifield and Cole, 2008). The cause of service failure is mainly due to the fault of the service provider. In fact, the cause of service failures is very complicated and may be caused by the service provider, or caused by customers or external factors. Bitner et al.'s (1990) classification of service failure includes the failure due to service provider, customer, and environment, so it is more comprehensive. For example, unreasonably slow service due to hotel, admitted customer error due to customer, employee behavior in the context of cultural norms and gestalt evaluation (societal / cultural insult) may be due to environment, such as cultural environment. Therefore, we have chosen the Bitner et al.'s (1990) classification to fully understand the matching relationships between service failure types and types of customer recovery expectations. The results of this study indicate that even if the service failure is caused by the hotel, the customers may attribute it to themselves, such as unavailable service failure and the failure due to lack of attention paid to customer. On the contrary, even if the mistake is not necessarily caused by the hotel, the guest may also attribute the mistake to the hotel. For example, the failure is a core mistake, such as safety and health. These results in the Chinese hospitality are not completely consistent with the Weiner's attribution theory (1980, 1985a, 1985b), and it is worthwhile to continue exploring the reasons in the future researches. In addition, we can better understand that when a customer slips down in the hotel, they are more inclined to blame the hotel for not setting a safety sign, instead of their walking while watching the phone for instance. Overall, our contribution is to advance Roschk and Gelbrich's (2014) research on matching types of service failure and types of recovery expectation by adopting Bittner's (1990) detailed classification of service failures. Moreover, we find that customers who experienced core service failures, whether the failure is caused by hotel or not, may attribute causes to the hotel anyway.

Fourthly, in the light of expectation-disconfirmation paradigm, we for the first time look into the expected recovery and obtained recovery, and find out the disconfirmation lies in between. This could explain why customers choose to exit and why their loyalty remains low even after being provided with recoveries. This is because there is usually a standard procedure for recovery in hotel, and it is designed for general circumstances. In such ways, customers are likely to receive regular rather than customized compensations. For example, a customer who prefers apology gets monetary compensation. The ego might drive the customer to be more dissatisfied while hotels are paying extra expenditure. In addition, due to the cultural influences as discussed, Chinese customers tend to walk away without a sound under such circumstances. Overall, it is believed that there is a difference between customer expectations and customer expectations as perceived by the service provider (Kuenzel et al., 2011). But very few researchers have ever verified this problem. Thus, our contribution is for the first time to consider the expected recovery and obtained recovery, and have found out the disconfirmation lies in between.

Fifthly, it is a common practice to understand satisfaction after recovery as recovery satisfaction, yet we consider it as the combination of recovery satisfaction and overall satisfaction, and have proven it fruitful. It is found that customer's recovery satisfaction would strongly affect customer's overall satisfaction. According to previous literature, there are two sets of disconfirmations between expectation and actual performance in service failure and recovery encounter. Customers evaluate recovery efforts against their expectations, which results in a disconfirmation judgment between recovery expectation and obtained recovery. It is the recovery satisfaction (Oliver, 1981; Etzel and Silverman, 1981; Gilly, 1987; Westbrook, 1987). Overall satisfaction is the accumulation of satisfaction from pre-failure to post-recovery. That is, customer overall satisfaction is determined not only by the disconfirmation of service performance (failure), but also by the disconfirmation of service recovery (Smith and Bolton, 1998). Therefore, some researchers propose that customer satisfaction after recovery should include recovery satisfaction and overall satisfaction (Mattila, 2001; Gruber et al., 2011). But in the past, very few researchers have tried to verify this proposal. In this study, we separately verify the impact of differences between recovery expectations and obtained recovery on service recovery satisfaction and overall satisfaction. The effects of recovery satisfaction and overall satisfaction on customer behavioral intention were also verified. All of them have strong statistical significance.

Finally, most of empirical studies applied in this research is from western theorists and so are the researching scales. The success in applying those materials in the context of Chinese hospitality proves their reference value. Thus, in future researches addressing relevant issues or conducted in Chinese hospitality, it would be convenient to use mentioned materials and methodologies without specific verification.

9.2 Managerial implications

In this study, we tested the conceptual model in the Chinese hospitality industry. Hotels are quite typical in service industry for its high engagement with people, hence very suitable to be the research sample.

The study helps understand Chinese hospitality market and its customers.

For example, we can tell from the research that median-consumption and comfortable hotels are the most popular choices, so if someone attempts to set up hotel business in China, that would be a fair recommendation. In addition, we can better understand why the guest does not complain, but will not come to the hotel again. Because they tend to attribute the mistakes to themselves sometimes, they would not complain to the hotel, but they are likely to avoid the same mistake, that is, the possible action is to avoid choosing this hotel again. Therefore, the hotel should still invite customers to express dissatisfaction, and encourage unsatisfied customers to make complaints so that the hotel can get a second chance to recover losses. As an example of industrial practice, the Marriott Hotel that regulates its employees at front desk must enquire the feedback of stay to every customer is considered successful in retaining customer satisfaction. It is an opportunity to receive complaints and therefore a chance to recover customer satisfaction and loyalty.

Secondly, the results show that when core / main service failures occur, regardless of where responsibility truly lies, customers tend to attribute such failures to hotels and are likely to lose faith with that particular service provider, hence exit and cause losses for hotels. So, mangers must pay extra attention to core service failures (related to cleanness and safety for person and property) among other types, which includes exercising reasonable precautions, compensating customers who encounter these types of failure more carefully, constructing quality guarantee system and particular employee training.

Thirdly, hotels should provide individualized and matching recovery (type and magnitude) policies. This requires the awareness and right prediction of customer expectation. Our study can help with acquiring the type and magnitude that customers really encountered, customer preference about recovery, and suggesting desirable (by customers) and efficient (for hotels) recovery methods. For example, the research results show for customers who encountered a failure due to unreasonable lagged service, monetary compensations (including deferred monetary compensation tied to future purchase, such as voucher, hotel or hotel chain credit received, and immediate monetary compensation tied to the current purchase, such as discount, refund, and free upgrades) are more preferred. As for customers with failure due to unavailable service, a sincere apology is the best way to satisfy customers. Anyway, there exists a considerable expense for recovering service failures, and a mismatched compensation would be costly and ineffective; whereas a matched compensation, would receive customers' understanding and respect, and might be less expensive in terms of hotel's spending.

Fourthly, our study can help service providers to better understand the difference between, and relationships of satisfaction after recovery and overall satisfaction. Service failure recovery is usually an effective tool to recover losses, and if in best condition, there might be a "recovery paradox" (Hart et al., 1990; Ok et al., 2007; Krishna et al., 2011) where customers with service failure experience become more loyal than those without such experience. However, if the recovery went wrong, most customers would not give hotels a second chance and choose to exit rather than complain again. Therefore, hotels should have very reasonable recovery procedures and well-trained workforce to ensure the success of recovery.

Fifthly, a quality guarantee system is required from managers. Such system aims to ensure the stability of service quality and avoid unstable and controllable failures, because these two types of failure are perceived hotels' responsibility in most cases. The findings show that stability failure negatively influences customer attribution to hotel. That is, customers prefer hotels with a stable quality of service, rather than hotels with an unstable quality of service at any time. It means that hotels should maintain the stability of service quality and avoid the occurrence of unstable service failures. Also, the findings indicate that controllable failure positively influences customer attribution to hotel. Namely, when customers believe that the service failure they encountered could be avoided by the hotel through certain measures and procedures, they will consider that the hotel should be responsible for this failure, bear the losses caused by the mistakes, and give the guests a recovery (compensation). Therefore, the hotel should develop a sound quality inspection system to avoid the occurrence of controllable service failure.

9.3 Limitations and future research avenues

This study has several limitations that need to be addressed. We concluded it as follows, and looked forward to exploring them in the future research.

Firstly, the measurement of the service failure and recovery constructs was adapted from previous studies. All the scales were developed in the Western context. This might have led to a drop-off of some dimensions of certain factors due to a low reliability coefficient. For example, Chinese customers are likely to keep the extreme consequences away even for surveys because of the philosophy of *The Doctrine of the Mean* [《中庸》(Zhong Yong)]. It was composed by Zisi, a grandson of the Confucius'. *The Doctrine of the Mean* is indeed the highest principle of Confucianism regarding the ways of living. "Zhong" means neither too many nor too few, neither too much nor too little; and "Yong" means neither outstanding nor common. Therefore, according to the Confucian scholars, whatever they do and whomever they happen to deal with, people should always adhere to this principle. So that is why they prefer to tick options in the middle. To eliminate this issue, we may use a 9 or 10-Likert Scale to magnify the subtle difference and get to understand customers' true thinking. Also, Chinese customers do have some difficulty in understanding some items in Bitner et al.'s (1990) classification. For example, the types of inappropriate employee behavior related to cultural norms (Bitner, 1990), such as the front desk staff serving those familiar customers to check-in in a higher priority than others; or if someone asked for a double-bed room but was refused by the hotel staff due to lack of available rooms, yet, the next customer got one when he made the same request. Customers can not understand the situations where people with special needs are having better priorities (fast check-in or special rooms) to be a service failure. This calls for refine and well-designed scales that are rooted in the Chinese market. Also, controllability, stability in attribution, types of service failure, and types of obtained recovery are nominal or ordinal variables and hence cause difficulty in further statistical analysis. Such circumstance should be improved in the future.

Secondly, the sample of this study is unbalanced. It is concentrated mainly on customers who are aged 25—45 (87.1%) and well-educated (89.7% over bachelor degree). This may be due to the online data collection method. As for other customers who do not use internet much, or are elder and less-educated, the sample is not representative enough. Thus, future research should attempt to collect a larger and more representative sample.

Thirdly, there are big differences between the values of the Chinese traditional culture and Western cultures, but we did not address enough research attention to this issue. The preference on recovery expectation is inclined to apology which is a matter of attitude with involvement of cultural values. Some failures are caused by the hotel, but customers tend to attribute them to themselves. For example, unavailable service to customer due to hotel faults and lack of attention paid to customer by staff. The result is not completely consistent with Weiner's attribution theory (1980, 1985a, 1985b), but in line with

Confucius's beliefs of "self-denial" and "self-reflection" (*The Analects of Confucius*). It suggests that Chinese customers are extensively influenced by Confucianism even they are not all convinced to be Confucians, that they value ego, respect and emotion very much. Such facts are also reflected in behavioral intention analysis. For example, even for dissatisfied customers (after failure and corresponding recovery), the intention to complain again is not strong. Instead, they prefer to simply switch providers. In fact, it has become a consensus that Chinese customers are generally less loyal to a particular organization probably because of the massive amount of alternatives. In future research, cultural influences are worth noting and not limited in the Chinese or Asian context.

Finally, in dealing with the relationship between service failure type and recovery expectation type, some complicated failure type need to be noticed, like the "gestalt evaluation (societal / cultural insult)" (Bitner et al., 1990), which refers to the situation where customer perceived that "everything goes wrong". Such failure is a combination of the following types of behaviors: inefficient, unprepared, slow, inflexible or lacking of attention paid to customer, staff not being supportive by hotel manager, unprofessional staff, bad decor / atmosphere room or space, and so on. It is unconventional that this study fails to produce a strict one-to-one (from a failure type to a recovery expectation type) correlation. This can be improved in the future. That is, the classification of service failure by Bitner et al. (1990) can be further refined and continue to look for the corresponding relationships between failure type and recovery expectation type.

9.4   General conclusion

Despite the limitations, this study is among the first attempts to explore the behavioral profile of Chinese hospitality customers. A conceptual model is developed and empirically tested within the industry. Future studies may build on the present results and develop a more comprehensive understanding of Chinese hospitality customers.

In summary, this book enriches the study of service failure and failure recovery. It fills in some gaps in empirical researches, like the mediating function of customer attribution between service failure and failure recovery, the influence of service failure types on customer recovery expectation types, the matching issue of expected recovery and obtained recovery, and the differentiation between satisfaction after recovery and overall customer satisfaction. It clarifies the relationships among concepts, including: (1) customer attribution significantly mediates the effects of service failure on recovery expectation; (2) the difference between recovery expectation and obtained recovery affects satisfaction after recovery; (3) customer satisfaction after recovery affects behavioral intentions; (4) types of recovery expectation are influenced by types of service failure; (5) obtained recovery differs from recovery expectation to some extent, mainly because of "hotels not giving appropriate compensations" or "customers receiving undesired compensations" —such "mismatch" or "difference" affects the effectiveness of failure recovery and customer satisfaction after recovery. It has suggested a number of theoretical and managerial implications for the hotel industry, advancing key indicators in our time and avoiding less-effective expenditures.

Theoretical implications include: (1) for the first time to manifest the influence of service failure type on customer attribution; (2) for the first time to divide service recovery into expected recovery and obtained recovery in research; (3) for the first time to complete a matching test between variables (expected recovery type and obtained recovery type); (4) to divide satisfaction into satisfaction after recovery and overall satisfaction. Managerial implications include: (1) to help hotels better understand the Chinese market and customers, of their preference after experiencing service failures; (2) to verify the vital importance of core failures (like safety) for hotels; (3) to advise hotels to perform more individualized recovery polices that can increase customer overall satisfaction and reduce relevant costs; (4) to alarm the impact of satisfaction after recovery, and the necessity of providing matched recovery; (5) to propose a sustainable quality guarantee and inspection system which powerfully prevents unstable and controllable failures from happening.

In addition, this book specifies the influences of the explosion of internet and online reputation broadcast. Nearly 20% of customers select hotels in the light of comments on internet. And 43.6% customers choose "online comments" in measures of behavioral intentions. The online WOM has become a more important source of information than traditional WOM, spreading only in a small circle of population. Yet hotels seem to be slow on realizing such circumstance, hence deeply troubled by negative comments. It is argued that customers tend to believe negative comments and suspect positive comments. Empirical studies in this subject are inadequate thus they deserve research attention. Such themes are rarely seen in current literature, thus they are worth researching in a further research.

APPENDIX

Appendix 1: Questionnaire Regarding service failure, customer attribution, recovery expectation and obtained recovery, customer satisfaction after recovery, behavioral intention. (In English)

Dear Sir/Madame,

Hello, we invite you to participate in a study regarding service quality in China's hotel industry. Please kindly provide appropriate answers to the following questions. This survey does not require your name to be filled in. Your response is only for the academic research purposes. Your sincere cooperation and assistance will contribute to the research of China's hotel industry and worldwide hospitality industry.

We would like to hereby express to you our heartfelt thanks!

Part one: sample and filter condition

1. Did you stay in a hotel in the past six months?

A. Yes—continue.   B. NO—thank you and please leave the investigation.

2. Did you encounter any service failure (error) during you stay in the hotel?

A. Yes—continue.   B. NO—thank you and please leave the investigation.

3. Did you complain to the service provider or manager after experiencing the service failure?

A. Yes—continue.   B. NO—thank you and please leave the investigation.

Part two: types of service failure

From now on, we ask you to refer to the latest service failure problems you have experienced. Could you please choose the item(s) precisely from the following list that you consider matched in your mind.

4. Please list the type(s) of service problem(s) that you have experienced in the hotel(multiple choices available): _____.

(1)	Unavailable service (invalid service). For example, the hotel room is unavailable to book due to untraceable reservation information or overbooked situation; the window table you reserved for the hotel restaurant is occupied by other customers
(2)	Unreasonable lagged service. For example, when you are having meals in the hotel restaurant, dishes served are being delayed for almost one hour (usually dishes should be served within 15mins after order); you have to stay in hotel lobby, waiting 4 hours for an available room to check in due to inefficient house-keeping room services
(3)	Other core service failures. For example, the room you stayed is not clean; the food is expired or not safe; money is stolen during your stay
(4)	Customers' special requests cannot be satisfied. For example, the hotel cannot provide "extra-bed service" for kids; offering "nursery services" while occasionally leaving babies alone in the hotel room
(5)	Customer preferences cannot be met. For example, pets are not allowed; accommodation types are not flexible to change, e.g. changing a mountain-view room to a sea-view room
(6)	Admitted customer error. For example, you break the table lamp in the hotel room and being requested to reimburse for it; you lost personal items, e.g. glasses in the hotel lobby and unable to retrieve
(7)	Potential disruptive factors. For example, the guests in the next room are gathered together for parties at 3 a.m., very noisy, and the hotel staff could not handle it properly
(8)	Lack of attention. For example, some hotel staff at the front desk keep focusing on their mobile phone without, acting like those hotel guests are bothering them
(9)	Inappropriate and disruptive employee behavior. For example, when you are not ready to order and need some more time to decide on choosing meals, the waitress says, "If you would read the menu not the road tour map, you would know what you want to order"
(10)	Inappropriate employee behavior related to cultural norms. For example, the front desk staff prioritises and serve those familiar customers to check-in who are queued after you; you ask for a double-bed room when you check-in, and the hotel staff refuse to offer you due to no matched room available, however, the next customer after you get one when he makes the same request

continued

(11)	Gestalt evaluation (societal/ cultural insult): "Everything goes wrong". It refers to a combination of the following types of behaviors: inefficient, unprepared, slow, no flexibility or attention, not being supportive, unprofessional, bad decor/atmosphere, etc.
(12)	Exemplary performance under adverse / extra-ordinary circumstances. This category includes incidents in which the customer is particularly impressed / displeased with regard to the way the hotel employees handle an issue under stressful situation. This category emerges only for satisfactory encounters. Apparently, customers' empathy for contact employees and admiration for their "grace under pressure" leaves a statistically significant indelible impression to countervail customer discomfort with crowds, short-handedness, or "acts of God"
(13)	Others service failure, please describe it: _____

5. Based on your experience during your stay in the hotel, how would you describe the LATEST service problem?

Please indicate the extent of the service problem.

Severity of the service failure								
Mild	1	2	3	4	5	6	7	Severe
Major	1	2	3	4	5	6	7	Minor
Instatistically significant	1	2	3	4	5	6	7	Statistically significant

Part three: customer attribution

6. Regarding the service problems that you encountered, who should be responsible in your mind? Please choose from one of the seven numbers next to each statement. If you strongly disagree with the meaning of the statement, please circle 1, and if you strongly agree, circle 7. If your feelings are not strong, circle one of the numbers in the middle.

	1	2	3	4	5	6	7
The service problem that I encountered was totally the hotel's fault	○	○	○	○	○	○	○
The service problem that I encountered was my fault	○	○	○	○	○	○	○
The service problem that I encountered was due to the external environment, not my fault	○	○	○	○	○	○	○

7. The perceived cause of an event that you experience is:

Consumer(yourself)						External environmental factors
1	2	3	4	5	6	7

8. Do you think the service failure that you experienced in this hotel happens frequently?

A. Yes, it happens frequently in this hotel.

B. No, it rarely happens in this hotel.

9. Do you think the reason for the service failure that you experienced in this hotel is likely to be a permanent problem?

A. Yes, it is a permanent problem (stable).

B. No, it varies over time and context (unstable).

10. Do you think the service failure that you experienced in this hotel could be avoided?

A. Yes, it could be avoided by taking precaution actions.

B. No, it cannot be avoided.

Part Four: recovery expectation and obtained recovery

11. Given the problem you encountered in the hotel, how do you expect the hotel to respond? (Choose from 1 to 7 to represent your expectation, 1 = strongly disagree, 7 = strongly agree)

Recovery expectation	1	2	3	4	5	6	7
I expect the hotel to do everything they can to solve the problem I encountered.	O	O	O	O	O	O	O
I don't expect the hotel to exert much effort to solve the problem. (R)	O	O	O	O	O	O	O
I expect the hotel to try to make up for the service failure.	O	O	O	O	O	O	O
I expect the hotel to compensate me to some extent.	O	O	O	O	O	O	O

12. Regarding the service problems that you encountered, how would you like to be compensated? Please choose from one of the seven numbers next to each statement. If you strongly disagree with the meaning of the statement and

don't desire the following compensation, please circle 1, and if you strongly agree and expect the following compensation, circle 7. If your feelings are not strong, circle one of the numbers in the middle.

Please choose the level of compensation that you expected in response to the service failure that you experienced.

List of the compensation you expected	1	2	3	4	5	6	7
A. Deferred monetary compensation tied to future purchase	O	O	O	O	O	O	O
(1) Voucher (coupon for a price reduction for the next purchase)	O	O	O	O	O	O	O
(2) Hotel or hotel chain credit received (which could be spent as an amount of money for next purchase)	O	O	O	O	O	O	O
B. Immediate monetary compensation tied to the current purchase	O	O	O	O	O	O	O
(1) Discount (a price reduction < 100% of the purchase price)	O	O	O	O	O	O	O
(2) Refund (100% price reduction), e.g. providing a free hotel room or dinner during stay	O	O	O	O	O	O	O
(3) Free upgrades	O	O	O	O	O	O	O
C. New/exchanged goods, such as changed a new room for you	O	O	O	O	O	O	O
D. Free new/replicate service, e. g. house-keeping service	O	O	O	O	O	O	O
E. Psychological compensation (apology)	O	O	O	O	O	O	O
F. Service (or product) guarantee	O	O	O	O	O	O	O
G. Other compensation	O	O	O	O	O	O	O

If you choose the answer "other compensation" in question 12, please describe it in detail: _____.

13. Please list the type of compensation that you obtained from the hotel after you experienced the service failure. Can you choose the item(s) precisely from the following list that matched you?

A. Deferred monetary compensation (including voucher, hotel or hotel chain credit), that is tied to future purchase.

(1) Voucher (coupon for a price reduction on the next purchase)

(2) Hotel or hotel chain credit received (which could be spent as an amount of money for next purchase)

(3) Others

B. Immediate monetary compensation (including discount, refund) tied to the current purchase

(1) Discount (a price reduction < 100% of the purchase price)

(2) Refund (100% price reduction), e. g. providing a free hotel room or dinner during stay

(3) Free product/service upgrade

(4) Others

C. Free product/services upgrade, e.g. upgrading a new room for guests

D. Free new/replicate service, e.g. house-keeping service

E. Psychological compensation (apology)

F. Product/service guarantee

G. Others compensation:_____

H. No compensation/ no respondent (the hotel does not respond to your complaint)

14. What is your opinion of the hotel's response to your complaint about the service problem or compensation provided?

	Disconfirmation							
Better than my expectation	1	2	3	4	5	6	7	Worse than my expectation (R)
Beyond my expectation	1	2	3	4	5	6	7	Lower than my expectation

Part Five: customer satisfaction after recovery

Regarding the following descriptions, please choose from one of the seven numbers to express your satisfactory level of service recovery the hotel provided. If you strongly disagree with the meaning of the statement, please circle 1, and if you strongly agree, please circle 7. If your feelings are not strong, please circle one of the numbers in the middle.

15. Please indicate your satisfaction with the service recovery provided by

the hotel.

Satisfaction to the service recovery	1	2	3	4	5	6	7
I am happy with the way that the hotel handled my complaint.	O	O	O	O	O	O	O
I am satisfied with the attitude and manner in which the complaint was dealt with.	O	O	O	O	O	O	O
Overall I am not satisfied with the way the complaint was handled by the hotel.	O	O	O	O	O	O	O

16. Please indicate the level of your overall satisfaction (including the procedure between pre-failure and post-recovery process).

Overall satisfaction	1	2	3	4	5	6	7
I am satisfied with my overall experience with the hotel.	O	O	O	O	O	O	O
Overall, I am satisfied with the hotel.	O	O	O	O	O	O	O
To sum up, I am pleased with the service experienced in this hotel.	O	O	O	O	O	O	O

Part Six: Customers' behavioral intention after service recovery

17. After experiencing service failure and service recovery provided by this hotel, please read the following descriptions, and choose from one of the seven numbers to express your extent of the intention to the following behaviors / actions. If you strongly disagree, please circle 1, and if you strongly agree, please circle 7. If you are not sure about your intention, please circle one of the numbers in between. 1 = highly unlikely(defection); 7 = highly likely(loyalty).

	1	2	3	4	5	6	7
Indicate your likelihood of staying this hotel again in the future	O	O	O	O	O	O	O
Indicate your likelihood of recommending this hotel to others	O	O	O	O	O	O	O

continued

Indicate your likelihood of discouraging other people to choose this hotel	○	○	○	○	○	○	○
Indicate your likelihood of complaining to the hotel and manager	○	○	○	○	○	○	○
Indicate your likelihood of complaining to third parties, e.g., customer association, etc	○	○	○	○	○	○	○
Other behavior intention	○	○	○	○	○	○	○

If you choose the answer "Other behavioral intention" in question 17, please describe it in detail: _____

Part Seven: others

18. Please specify the purpose of your trip.

A. Pleasure   B. Business   C. Visiting   D. Meeting/Conference

E. Friends/Relatives   F. Others, please describe it:_____

19. How long have you been staying in the hotel?

A. 1 night   B. 2—3 nights   C. 4—5 nights   D. 6 nights or more

20. Please specify the hotel star-rating that you stayed in and experienced service failure.

A. 1 star hotel

B. 2 star hotel

C. 3-star hotel

D. 4-star hotel

E. 5-star hotel

F. others, please describe it:_____

21. Why did you choose this hotel? (multiple choices available)

A. Location of the hotel

B. Brand

C. Recommended by other people or travel agency

D. Online Information

E. Recommended by friends/relatives

F. Included in the package

G. Others

22. Attention please: If you do not chose this hotel in the future, you do not have to answer this question. If you will choose this hotel again in the future, please answer this question.

Do this by picking one of the seven numbers next to each statement. After experiencing service failure in your chosen hotel during your stay, why would you choose this hotel in the future? Regarding the reasons listed below, if you strongly disagree, please circle 1, and if you strongly agree, please circle 7. If your feelings are not strong, please circle one of the numbers in the middle.

	1	2	3	4	5	6	7
I cannot change the hotel because my company have an agreement with this hotel.	○	○	○	○	○	○	○
There is no other choice available in the surrounded area, and thus the hotel is the only option.	○	○	○	○	○	○	○
Other reasons.	○	○	○	○	○	○	○

If you choose the answer "Other reasons" in question 22, please describe it in details: _____

Part Eight: demographic characteristics

23. Please specify your gender.
   A. Male   B. Female
24. Please specify your age group.
   A. 18—24   B. 25—34   C. 35—44
   D. 45—54   E. 55 and above
25. Please specify your educational level.
   A. Doctorate   B. Master's Degree   C. Bachelor's Degree
   D. College Degree   E. High School Level   F. Others
26. Please specify your occupation.
   A. Manager of enterprise   B. Civil servants
   C. Businessman (including service staff, sales)
   D. Professionals & technical workers   E. Worker   F. Farmer
   G. Soldier/Policemen   H. Students   I. Freelancer
   J. Retiree   K. Homemaker
   L. Others, please describe it in detail: _____

27. Please specify your region of residency: _____

28. Please specify your average monthly income?

A. Less than RMB 2,999   B. RMB 3,000—4,999

C. RMB 5,000—7,999   D. RMB 8,000—9,999

E. RMB 10,000—30,000   F. More than RMB 30,000

Thank you for your participation again!

Appendix 2: Questionnaire Regarding service failure, customer attribution, recovery expectation and obtained recovery, customer satisfaction after recovery, behavioral intention. (In Chinese)

尊敬的朋友：

您好!我们邀请您参加一项中国饭店业服务质量的调查研究,请您对以下问题给出相应的答案。本调查不要求填写姓名,您所填写的内容仅被用于学术研究。您的真诚配合和协助,将会对中国乃至世界饭店业研究贡献一份力量。

我们对您表示由衷的感谢!

第一部分:样本过滤条件

1. 您在最近六个月内是否入住过饭店？

A. 是;继续。　　　　　B. 否;感谢您的参与,请您退出调查。

2. 在您入住饭店期间是否遇到过服务失误(差错)?

A. 是;继续。　　　　　B. 否;感谢您的参与,请您退出调查。

3.在遇到服务失误之后,您是否向提供服务的员工或饭店管理者投诉?

A. 是;继续。　　　　　B. 否;感谢您的参与,请您退出调查。

第二部分:服务失误的类型

从这里开始,我们问您的关于服务失误的问题是指您最近一次在饭店中遇到的问题,请您在下列清单中精确地选择您认为正确的选项。

4. 请列出您在饭店中经历的服务失误问题的类型(可多选):_____

(1)	不能提供服务(无效服务)。例如,因为"找不到"预订信息或超额预订使得饭店不能提供房间给您,您预订的餐厅窗边的位置被其他客人占用了。
(2)	不合情理的服务滞后。例如,您在饭店餐厅用餐时,延迟近一个小时才上菜(一般应15分钟后开始上菜);由于饭店客房来不及清扫,您不得不待在饭店大厅等待4个小时才入住一间干净的房间。
(3)	其他一些核心服务失误。例如,您入住的房间不干净,食品坏掉了或者食用不安全,在饭店客房里钱被偷了。
(4)	不能满足顾客的"特殊需求"。例如,饭店不能为您的孩子提供额外的加床服务,提供"婴儿看护服务"的饭店员工将幼小的孩子独自留在了房间里。
(5)	不能满足顾客的偏好。例如,饭店员工不允许您将狗／猫带进房间,饭店员工拒绝将您的房间从山景房换到海景房。

续　表

(6)	公认的顾客差错造成的失误。例如,你打破了房间里的台灯并被要求赔偿,你在饭店大厅丢失了眼镜而饭店员工没能帮您找到。
(7)	其他潜在的破坏性因素造成的失误。例如,隔壁房间客人聚会开派对直至夜里三点,非常喧闹,而饭店员工无法妥善处理。
(8)	不够关注顾客。例如,饭店前台员工一直在玩手机,比起饭店客人,她似乎更加关注手机,而客人好像打扰了她一样。
(9)	员工行为确实有些超乎常规。例如,在饭店餐厅用餐时,您需要多点时间来确定点什么菜肴,服务员说:"如果你刚才是在看菜单而不是在研究地图,就知道自己想点什么了。"
(10)	在一定文化规范背景下的员工行为。例如;饭店员工优先给他熟悉的、排在您后面的客人办理入住登记手续;您在办理入住登记手续时想要一个大床间,饭店员工告诉你没有此类房间了,但是您后面的客人提出同样要求时则得到了一个大床间。
(11)	格式塔评价(社会/文化损害):"一切都出错了"。指的是以下各种行为类型的组合:低效率、无准备、缓慢、不肯通融或不细心、不能提供帮助、不专业、糟糕的装修/氛围等。
(12)	在困境下的典型表现。就是在有压力的环境下,诸如顾客在遇到印象特别深刻或者不开心的事情时,对所接触的员工如何处理这些问题的看法。这种类型一般只出现在最终令人满意的遭遇中。显然,员工的同理心和对他们在"压力下的优雅表现",会让所接触的顾客深感钦佩,进而留下不可磨灭的印象,最终抵消顾客对拥挤、人手不足,或不可抗力造成的不舒服感。
(13)	其他服务失误,请具体描述:

5. 依据您的饭店入住经验,您会如何描述您最近一次遇到的服务问题?
请您指出您所遇到的服务失误问题的严重程度。

服务失误的严重程度							
轻微的	1	2	3	4	5	6	7	严重的
主要的	1	2	3	4	5	6	7	次要的
无关紧要的	1	2	3	4	5	6	7	重要的

第三部分:顾客归因

6. 针对您所遭遇的服务失误问题,您认为谁应负责? 从1—7中选择一个合适的数字说明您的观点,如果您完全反对下面的表述,请选择1;如果您非常赞同下面的表述,请选择7;如果您感觉并不强烈,请选择中间适当的数字。

	1	2	3	4	5	6	7
(1)我所遇到的服务失误问题完全是饭店的过错。	○	○	○	○	○	○	○
(2)我在饭店中所遇到的麻烦(服务问题)都是我自己的过错造成的。							
(3)我在饭店中所遇到的服务问题主要是外部环境因素造成的,不是我的原因造成的。							

7. 对于您在饭店中所遭遇的服务问题的责任,您的看法是什么?

您认为造成您在饭店遭遇的服务失误问题的原因是什么?								
消费者(您自己)	1	2	3	4	5	6	7	外部环境因素

8. 您认为在这个饭店中经常发生您所遭遇的这类服务失误问题吗?

A. 是的,这个饭店中经常发生这类服务问题。

B. 不,这个饭店极少发生这类服务问题。

9. 您认为在这个饭店中所遇到的服务问题很可能是长期存在的问题吗?

A. 是的,是长期性的(是稳定的)。

B. 不是,是随时间和环境而变化的(是不稳定的)。

10. 您认为您所遭遇到的这类服务问题是可以避免的吗?

A. 是的,饭店采取防范措施很可能是可以避免此类服务问题的发生的。

B. 不,饭店根本无法避免这类服务问题的发生。

第四部分:补偿(补救)期望与实际获得的补救

11. 针对您在饭店中所遇到的问题,您期待饭店如何做出反应? (从1—7中选择一个合适的数字说明您的预期,如果您完全反对下面的表述,请选择1;如果您非常赞同下面的表述,请选择7;如果您感觉并不强烈,请选择中间适当的数字。)

补救预期	1	2	3	4	5	6	7
我期望饭店尽其所能解决我遇到的问题	○	○	○	○	○	○	○
我并不指望饭店会花费很多精力来解决我遇到的问题(R)	○	○	○	○	○	○	○
我期望饭店能够尽力对我所遇到的服务问题做出弥补	○	○	○	○	○	○	○
我期望饭店给我一定程度的补偿	○	○	○	○	○	○	○

12. 为了回应您在饭店中遇到的服务问题,饭店可能进行相应的补偿或采取补救措施,请选择您对饭店可能提供的补偿或补救措施的期待程度。从1—7中选择一个合适的数字说明您对饭店补偿的预期,如果您"非常不期望"得到下面的表述中的补偿,请选择1;如果您"非常期望"得到下面的表述中的补偿,请选择7;如果您感觉并不强烈,请选择中间适当的数字。

您期望从饭店得到下列补偿的程度:	1	2	3	4	5	6	7
A. 与未来购买相关的延迟性货币类补偿	○	○	○	○	○	○	○
(1)代金券(下次购买时可以用来抵扣费用的优惠券)	○	○	○	○	○	○	○
(2)饭店或饭店连锁的信用积分(饭店提供一定的信用积分可以用于客人的下次购买时使用,抵用一定金额的消费)	○	○	○	○	○	○	○
B. 与当前购买相关的即时性货币类补偿	○	○	○	○	○	○	○
(1)折扣(价格降低<购买价格的100%)	○	○	○	○	○	○	○
(2)退款(100%价格减少),例如饭店为您提供免费客房或晚餐	○	○	○	○	○	○	○
(3)免费进行产品或服务升级	○	○	○	○	○	○	○
C. 提供新的商品或更换商品,例如为您更换一个新的客房	○	○	○	○	○	○	○
D. 提供新的服务或再次提供服务,例如给您客房重新清扫一次	○	○	○	○	○	○	○
E. 进行心理上的补偿(道歉)	○	○	○	○	○	○	○
F. 提供服务(或产品)保证	○	○	○	○	○	○	○
G. 其他补偿	○	○	○	○	○	○	○

如果您在问题12选择的答案是"其他补偿",请具体描述:＿＿＿＿＿＿＿＿＿

13. 请列举当您遭遇服务问题后,饭店实际给予您的补偿的类型。请您在下列项目中准确地选择一个或多个正确的答案来描述这些补偿。

A. 与未来购买相关的延迟的货币类补偿(包括优惠券,饭店或饭店连锁的信用积分)

(1)代金券(下次购买时可以用来抵扣费用的优惠券)

(2)饭店或饭店连锁的信用积分(饭店提供一定的信用积分可以用于客人的下次购买时使用,抵用一定金额的消费)

B. 与当前购买相关的即时性货币类补偿(包括折扣、退款)

(1)折扣(价格降低 < 购买价格的100%)

(2)退款(100%价格减少),例如饭店为您提供免费客房或晚餐

(3)免费进行产品或服务升级

(4)其他

C. 提供新的商品或更换商品,例如为您更换一个新的客房

D. 提供新的服务或再次提供服务,例如给您客房重新清扫一次

E. 进行心理上的补偿(道歉)

F. 提供服务(或产品)保证

G. 其他补偿:_____

H. 没有补偿或没有回应(饭店对于您的投诉没有任何回应)

14. 针对您在饭店中所遭遇的服务问题,您对饭店进行的回应(或补偿措施)有什么看法?

比我预想的要好	1	2	3	4	5	6	7	比我预想的要差(R)
超出我的预期	1	2	3	4	5	6	7	低于我的预期

第五部分:顾客补救后的满意度

15. 针对下面的描述,请选择一个合适的数字说明您对饭店所提供的服务补偿和/或补救措施的满意程度。如果您"非常反对"这个描述,请选择1;如果"非常赞同"这个描述,请选择7;如果您感觉不强烈,请选择中间的数字。

服务补救的满意程度	1	2	3	4	5	6	7
对于饭店处理我的投诉的那些措施,我感到很欣喜。	○	○	○	○	○	○	○
我很满意饭店处理我的投诉的那些举措和态度。	○	○	○	○	○	○	○
总体而言,对于饭店处理我的投诉的那些措施,我不是很满意。	○	○	○	○	○	○	○

16. 针对下面的描述,请选择一个合适的数字说明您对饭店所提供的服务的总体满意度(包含从服务失误前到服务补救后的整个过程之后)。如果您非常不满意,请选择1;如果非常满意,请选择7;如果您的满意程度不强烈,请选择中间的数字。

总体满意度	1	2	3	4	5	6	7
我很满意在饭店中所经历的总体体验	○	○	○	○	○	○	○
整体而言,我对饭店很满意	○	○	○	○	○	○	○
总之,对于在这家饭店的服务体验,我感到很满意	○	○	○	○	○	○	○

第六部分:服务补救后的顾客行为或行为意图

17. 您在这家饭店中经历了服务失误和饭店提供的服务补救或补偿措施之后,针对下面的描述,请选择一个合适的数字说明您进行如下行为的可能性程度。如果您极不可能进行如下描述的行为,请选择1;如果非常可能选择进行如下的行为,请选择7;如果您并不是很确定,可能性在上述两者之间,请选择中间的数字。

	1	2	3	4	5	6	7
说明您将来再次选择这家饭店的可能性	○	○	○	○	○	○	○
说明您向其他人推荐这家饭店的可能性	○	○	○	○	○	○	○
说明您劝阻其他人选择这家饭店的可能性	○	○	○	○	○	○	○
说明您向这家饭店和管理者投诉的可能性	○	○	○	○	○	○	○
说明您向第三方机构投诉的可能性,比如消费者协会	○	○	○	○	○	○	○
说明选择其他行为的可能性	○	○	○	○	○	○	○

如果您在问题17中选择说明其他行为的可能性,请详细描述这个可能的行为:_____

第七部分:其他

18. 请说明您旅行的目的
A. 休闲娱乐   B. 商务活动
C. 访问   D. 会议
E. 走亲访友
F. 其他,请具体描述:_____

19. 你在这家饭店中住了多久?

A. 1晚　　　B. 2—3晚　　　C. 4—5晚　　　D. 6晚以上

20. 请注明您所入住并经历了服务失误的这家饭店的星级:

A. 一星级　　B. 二星级　　　C. 三星级

D. 四星级　　E. 五星级

F. 其他,请详细描述饭店的具体等级状况:＿＿＿＿＿＿＿＿＿＿＿＿＿

21. 你为什么选择这家饭店(多项选择)?

A. 地理位置

B. 品牌

C. 其他人或旅行社的推荐

D. 在线信息(网络信息)

E. 亲朋好友的推荐

F. 被包含在套餐中

G. 其他

22. 请注意,如果你未来再也不会选择入住此饭店,您不必回答这个问题;如果您未来还是会再次选择这家饭店,请回答下面这个问题。

当您在所入住的饭店遭遇过服务问题之后,您依然会选择再次入住此饭店的原因是什么? 针对下列原因,如果"完全不是"这个原因,请选择1;如果"完全是"这个原因,请选择7;如果您并不是很确定,可能性在上述两者之间,请选择中间的数字。

	1	2	3	4	5	6	7
我无法更换饭店,因为我的公司与这家饭店有协议	○	○	○	○	○	○	○
在这个地方没有其他的选择,这家饭店是唯一的选择	○	○	○	○	○	○	○
其他原因	○	○	○	○	○	○	○

如果您在问题22中选择的答案是"其他原因",请具体描述:＿＿＿＿＿＿＿＿＿

第八部分:人口统计特征

23. 请说明您的性别。

A. 男　　　　B. 女

24. 请说明您的年龄段。

A. 18—24岁　　B. 25—34岁　　C. 35—44岁

D. 45—54岁　　E. 55岁以上

25. 请说明您的教育程度。

A. 博士   B. 硕士   C. 本科

D. 大专   E. 高中   F. 其他

26. 请说明您的职业。

A. 企业的管理者   B. 公务员

C. 商界人士(包括服务性行业员工,销售人员等)

D. 专业技术人员   E. 工人   F. 农民

G. 士兵/警察   H. 学生   I. 自由职业者

J. 退休人员   K. 家庭主妇

L. 其他,请具体描述您的职业:_____

27. 请说明您的居住地(您来自哪个省份和城市):_____

28. 请说明您的平均月收入?

A. 少于 RMB 2,999   B. RMB 3,000—4,999

C. RMB 5,000—7,999   D. RMB 8,000—9,999

E. RMB 10,000—30,000   F. 高于 RMB 30,000

非常感谢您的参与!

BIBLIOGRAPHY

A

ABBASI A S, KHALID W, AZAM M, et al., 2010. Determinants of customer satisfaction in hotel industry of Pakistan [J]. European journal of scientific research, 8(1): 97-105.

ABDULLAH D N M A, ROZARIO F, 2009. Influences of service and product quality towards customer satisfaction: a case study at the staff cafeteria in the hotel industry [J]. International scholarly and scientific research and innovation, 3(5): 346-351.

ABDULLAH F, 2006. Measuring service quality in higher education: HEDPERF versus SERVPERF [J]. Marketing intelligence and planning, 24(1): 31-47.

ABRAMSON L Y, SELIGMAN M E, TEASDALE J D, 1978. Learned helplessness in humans: critique and reformulation [J]. Journal of abnormal psychology, 87 (1): 49-74.

ADAMS J S, 1963. Toward an understanding of inequity [J]. Journal of abnormal and social psychology, 67(5): 422-436.

ADAMS J S, 1965. Inequality in social exchange [G]//BERKOWITZ L. Advances in experimental psychology. New York: Academic Press: 267-299.

AKBABA A, 2006. Measuring service quality in the hotel industry: a study in a business hotel in Turkey [J]. International journal of hospitality management, 25 (2): 170-192.

AKPOYOMARE-OGHOJAFOR B E, OLAYEMI O O, OLUWATULA O O, et al., 2012. Attribution theory and strategic decisions on organizational success factors[J]. Journal of management and strategy, 3(1): 32-39.

AL-ALAK B A, 2011. An assessment of guest perceptions of service quality in luxury hotels in Kuala Lumpur, Malaysia[J]. Global management journal, 3 (1/2): 5-16.

ALBRECHT K, 1988. At America's service[M]. Homewood, IL: Dow-Jones-Irwin.

ALEGRE J, GARAU J, 2010. Tourist satisfaction and dissatisfaction[J]. Annals of tourism research, 37(1): 52-73.

AMIN M, YAHYA Z, ISMAYATIM W F A, NASHARUDDIN S Z, et al., 2013. Service quality dimension and customer satisfaction: an empirical study in the Malaysian hotel industry[J]. Services marketing quarterly, 34(2): 115-125.

ANDALEEP S S, BASU A K, 1994. Technical complexity and consumer knowledge as moderators of service quality evaluation in the automobile service industry [J]. Journal of retailing, 70(4): 367-381.

ANDERSON E W, FORNELL C, LEHMANN D R, 1994. Customer satisfaction, market share, and profitability: findings from Sweden[J]. Journal of marketing, 58 (3): 53-66.

ANDERSON E W, 1998. Customer satisfaction and word-of-mouth[J]. Journal of service research, 1(1): 5-17.

ANDERSON J C, GERBING D W, 1988. Structural equation modeling in practice: a review and recommended Two-Step Approach [J]. Psychological bulletin, 103(3): 411-423.

ANDERSON J C, GERBING D W, 1991. Predicting the performance of measures in a confirmatory factor analysis with a pretest assessment of their substantive validities[J]. Journal of applied psychology, 76(5): 732-740.

ANDERSON R E, 1973. Consumer dissatisfaction: the effect of disconfirmed expectancy on perceived product performance [J]. Journal of marketing research, 10(1): 38-44.

ANDERSON R E, BUSH A J, HAIR J F, 1992. Professional sales management [M]. 2nd ed. New York: McGraw Hill.

ANDERSON S W, BAGGETT L S, WIDENER S K, 2009. The impact of service operations failures on customer satisfaction: evidence on how failures and their source affect what matters to customers [J]. Manufacturing and service operations management, 11(1): 52-69.

ANDREASSEN T W, 1999. What drives customer loyalty with complaint resolution?[J]. Journal of service research, 1(4): 324-332.

ANDREASSEN T W, 2000. Antecedents to satisfaction with service recovery[J]. European journal of marketing, 34(1/2): 156-175.

ANDREASSEN T W, 2001. From disgust to delight: Do customers hold a grudge? Journal of Services Research, 4(1): 39-49.

ANTÓN C, CAMARERO C, CARRERO M, 2007. Analysing firms' failures as determinants of consumer switching intentions: the effect of moderating factors [J]. European journal of marketing, 41(1/2): 135-158.

ANTONY J, ANTONY F J, GHOSH S, 2004. Evaluating service quality in a UK hotel chain: a case study [J]. International journal of contemporary hospitality management, 16(6): 380-384.

ARMISTEAD C G, CLARK G, STANLEY P, 1995. Managing service recovery [M]. Cranfield School of Management: Cranfield.

B

BAGOZZI R P, HEATHERTON T F, 2009. A general approach to representing multifaceted personality constructs: application to state self-esteem [J]. Structural equation modeling, 1(1): 35-67.

BAGOZZI R P, GURHAN-CANLI Z, PRIESTER J R, 2002. The social psychology of consumer behavior[M]. Buckingham: Open University Press.

BAILEY D,1994. Service recovery: a ten-stage approach in the training of front-line staff[J]. Training and management development methods, 8(4): 17-21.

BAKER T, COLLIER D A, 2005. The economic payout model for service guarantees[J]. Decision sciences, 36(2): 197-220.

BARON R M, KENNY D A, 1986. The moderator-mediator variable distinction in social psychological research: conceptual, strategic, and statistical considerations [J]. Journal of personality and social psychology, 51(6): 1173-1182.

BEARDEN W O, TEEL J E, 1983. Selected determinants of consumer satisfaction and complaint reports. Journal of marketing research, 20(1): 21-28.

BEBKO C P, 2000. Service intangibility and its impact on consumer expectations of service quality[J]. Journal of service marketing, 14(1): 9-26.

BEJOU D, PALMER A, 1998. Service failure and loyalty: an exploratory empirical study of airline customers[J]. Journal of service marketing, 12(1): 7-22.

BELK R, PAINTER J, 1983. Effects of causal attributions on pollution and litter control attitudes[G]//KELLY S F, PETER R. Non-profit marketing: conceptual and empirical research. Tempe, AZ: Arizona State University.

BELK R, PAINTER J, SEMENIK R, 1981. Preferred solutions to the energy crisis as a function of causal attributions[J]. Journal of consumer research, 8 (3): 306-312.

BELL C, RIDGE K, 1992. Service recovery for trainers[J]. Training and development, 46(5): 58-63.

BELL C R, ZEMKE R E, 1987. Service breakdown: the road to recovery[J]. Management review, 76(10): 32-35.

BEM D J, 1965. An experimental analysis of self-persuasion[J]. Journal of experimental social psychology, 1(3): 199-218.

BEM D J, 1967. Self-perception: an alternative interpretation of cognitive dissonance phenomena[J]. Psychological review, 74(3):183-200.

BEM D J, 1972. Self-perception theory[M]//BERKOWITZ L. Advances in experimental social psychology(6). New York: Academic Press:1-62.

BEMMELS B, 1991. Attribution theory and discipline arbitration[J]. Industrial and labor relations review, 44(3): 548-562.

BERRY L, PARASURAMAN A, 1991. Marketing services: competing through quality[M]. New York, Free Press.

BEST A, ANDREASEN A R, 1977. Consumer response to unsatisfactory purchases: a survey of perceiving defects, voicing complaints, and obtaining redress[J]. Law and society review, 11(4): 701-742.

BEUGRE C, VISWANATHAN N K, 2006. Perceptions of fairness and customer satisfaction following service failure and recovery[J]. Latin american advances in consumer research(1): 10-14.

BIERHOFF H-W, 1989. Person perception and attribution[M]. Berlin: Springer-Verlag.

BIES R J, MOAG J S, 1986. Interactional communication criteria of fairness, research in org[M]. Behavior, Greenwich, CT: JAI Press.

BITNER M J, 1990. Evaluating the service encounters: the effects of physical surroundings and employee responses[J]. Journal of marketing, 54(2): 69-82.

BITNER M J, 1992. Services capes: the impact of physical surroundings on customers and employees[J]. Journal of Marketing, 56(2): 57-71.

BITNER M J, BOOMS B H, TETREAULT M S, 1990. The service encounter: diagnosing favorable and unfavorable incidents[J]. Journal of marketing, 54(4): 95-105.

BITNER M J, BOOMS B H, MOHR L A,1994. Critical service encounters: the employee's viewpoint[J]. Journal of marketing, 58(4): 95-106.

BITNER M J, BOOMS B H, TETREAULT M S, 1990. The service encounter: diagnosing favorable and unfavorable incidents[J]. Journal of marketing, 54(4): 95-105.

BITNER M J, HUBBERT A R, 1994. Encounter satisfaction versus overall satisfaction versus quality: the customer voice[G]//RUST R T, OLIVER R L. Service quality: new direction in theory and practice. Thousand Oaks, CA: Sage: 72-94.

BLEŠIÆ I, TEŠANOVIÆ D, AND PSODOROV D, 2011. Consumer satisfaction and quality management in the hospitality industry in South-East Europe[J]. African journal of business management, 5(4): 1388-1396.

BLEUEL B, 1990. Commentary: customer dissatisfaction and the zone of uncertainty [J]. The journal of services marketing, 4(1): 49-52.

BLODGET J, ANDERSON R D, 2000. A Bayesian network model of the consumer complaint process[J]. Journal of service research, 2(4): 321-338.

BLODGETT J G, GRANBOIS D H, WALTERS R G, 1993. The effects of perceived justice on complainants ' negative word-of-mouth behavior and repatronage intentions[J]. Journal of retailing, 69(4): 399-428.

BLODGETT J G, HILL D J, TAX S S, 1997. The effect of distributive, procedural and interactional justice on postcomplaint behavior[J]. Journal of retailing, 73(2): 185-210.

BLODGETT J, GRANBOIS D, 1992. Toward an integrated conceptual model of consumer complaining behavior[J]. Journal of consumer satisfaction, dissatisfaction, and complaining behavior(5): 93-103.

BLODGETT J G, WAKEFIELD K L, BARNES J H, 1995. The effects of customer service on consumer complaining behavior[J]. Journal of services marketing, 9(4): 31-42.

BODEY K, GRACE D, 2006. Segmenting service "complainers" and "non-complainers" on the basis of consumer characteristics[J]. Journal of services marketing, 20(3): 178-187.

BODEY K, GRACE D, 2007. Contrasting "complainers" with "non-complainers" on attitude toward complaining, propensity
to complain, and key personality characteristics: a nomological look [J]. Psychology and marketing, 24(7): 579-594.

BOLTON R N, DREW J H, 1991a. A longitudinal analysis of the impact of service changes on customer attitudes[J]. Journal of marketing, 55(1): 1-9.

BOLTON R N, DREW J H, 1991b. A multistage model of customers' assessments of service quality and value[J]. Journal of consumer research, 17 (4): 375-384.

BONIFIELD C, COLE C, 2008. Better him than me: social comparison theory and service recovery[J]. Journal of the academy of marketing science, 36(4): 565-577.

BONO J E, JUDGE T A, 2001. Relationship of core self-evaluation traits–self-esteem, generalized self-efficacy, locus control and emotional stability–with job satisfaction and job performance: a meta-analysis [J]. Journal of applied psychology, 86(1): 80-93.

BOONE C, BRABANDER B D, HELLEMANS J, 2000. Research note: CEO locus of control and small firm performance[J]. Organization studies, 21(3): 641-647.

BORKOWSKI N M, ALLEN W R, 2003. Does attribution theory explain physicians' nonacceptance of clinical practice guidelines?[J]. Hospital topics: research and perspectives on healthcare, 81(2): 9-21.

BOSHOFF C, 1997. An experimental study of service recovery options [J]. International journal of service industry management, 8(2): 110-130.

BOSHOFF C, 1999. RECOVSAT: an instrument to measure satisfaction with transaction-specific service recovery[J]. Journal of service research, 1(3): 236-249.

BOSHOFF C, 2005. A re-assessment and refinement of RECOVSAT—an instrument to measure satisfaction with transaction-specific service recovery[J]. Managing service quality, 15(5): 410-425.

BOSHOFF C, 2007. Understanding service recovery satisfaction from a service encounter perspective: a pilot study[J]. South African journal of business and management, 38(2): 41-51.

BOSHOFF C, 2012. Can service firms overdo service recovery? an assessment of non-linearity in service recovery satisfaction[J]. South African journal of business management, 43(3): 1-12.

BOSHOFF C, LEONG J, 1998. Empowerment, attribution and apologising as dimensions of service recovery [J]. International journal of service industry management, 9(1): 24-47.

BOSHOFF C, STAUDE G, 2003. Satisfaction with service recovery: its measurement and its outcomes[J]. South African journal of business and management, 34

(3): 9-16.

BOUGIE R, PIETERS R, ZEELENBERG M, 2003. Angry customers don't come back, they get back: the experience and behavioral implications of anger and dissatisfaction in services[J]. Journal of the academy of marketing science, 31 (4): 377-393.

BOULDING W, KALRA A, STAELIN R, et al., 1993. A dynamic process model of service quality: from expectations to behavioral intentions[J]. Journal of marketing research, 30(1): 7-27.

BOWEN D E, GILLILAND S W, FOLGER R, 1999. HRM and service fairness: how being fair with employees spills over to customers [J]. Organizational dynamics, 27(3), 7-23.

Brady D, 2000. Why service stinks: a critical view and interpretation [J]. Business Week, (10. 23rd), 118-128.

BRIGGS S, SUTHERLAND J, DRUMMOND S, 2007. Are hotels serving quality? An exploratory study of service quality in the Scottish hotel sector [J]. Tourism management, 28(4): 1006-1019.

BROWN J J, REINGEN P H, 1987. Social ties and word-of-mouth referral behavior[J]. Journal of consumer research, 14(3): 350-360.

BROWN S W, FISK R P, BITNER M J, 1994. The development and emergence of service marketing thought [J]. International journal of service industry management, 5(1): 21-48.

BUNKER M P, BRADLEY M S, 2007. Toward understanding customer powerlessness: analysis of an internet complaint site[J]. Journal of consumer satisfaction, dissatisfaction and complaining behavior(20): 54-71.

BUTTLE F, 1996. SERVQUAL: review, critique, research agenda[J]. European journal of marketing, 30(1): 8-32.

C

CADOTTE E R, WOODRUFF R B, JENKINS R L, 1987. Expectations and norms in models of consumer satisfaction[J]. Journal of marketing research, 24 (3): 305-304.

CADOTTE E R, TURGEON N, 1988. Dissatisfiers and satisfiers: suggestions for consumer complaints and compliments [J]. Journal of consumer satisfaction, dissatisfaction and complaining behavior(1): 74-79.

CALLAN R J, MOORE J, 1998. Service guarantee: a strategy for service recovery[J]. Journal of hospitality and tourism research, 22(1): 56-71.

CALLAN R J, BOWMAN L, 2000. Selecting a hotel and determining salient quality attributes: a preliminary study of mature British travelers[J]. International journal of tourism research, 2(2): 97-118.

CARDOZO R N, 1965. An experimental study of customer effort, expectation and satisfaction[J]. Journal of marketing research, 2(3): 244-249.

CAMBRA-FIERRO J, BERBEL-PINEDA, J M, RUIZ-BENÍTEZ R, 2011. Managing service recovery processes: the role of customers' age[J]. Journal of business economics and management, 12(3): 503-528.

CARLZON J, 1987. Moments of truth[M]. New York: Bellinger Publishing Company.

CARMAN J M, 1990. Consumer perceptions of service quality: an assessment of the SERVQUAL dimensions[J]. Journal of retailing, 66(1): 33-55.

CARO L M, GARCÍA J A M, 2007. Consumer satisfaction with a periodic reoccurring sport event and the moderating effect of motivations[J]. Sport marketing quarterly, 16(2): 70-81.

CARR C L, 2007. The FAIRSERV model: consumer reactions to services based on a multidimensional evaluation of service fairness[J]. Decision sciences, 38 (1): 107-130.

CARVALHO C, BRITO C, 2012. Assessing users' perceptions how to improve public services quality. Public management review, 14(4): 451-472.

CASADO A B, MAS F J, 2002. The consumer's reaction to delays in service [J]. International journal of service industry management, 13(2): 118-140.

CASADO-DÍAZ A B, NICOLAU-GONZÁLBEZ J L, 2009. Explaining consumer complaining behavior in double deviation scenarios: the banking services[J]. The service industries journal, 29(12): 1659-1668.

CHAN H, WAN L C, 2008. Consumer responses to service failures: a resource preference model of cultural influences, Journal of international marketing, 16 (1): 72-97.

CHAN H C Y, NGAI E W T, 2010. What makes customers discontent with service providers? An empirical analysis of complaint handling in information and communication technology services[J]. Journal of business ethics, 91(1): 73-110.

CHANG H S, HSIAO H L, 2008. Examining the causal relationship among service recovery, perceived justice, perceived risk, and customer value in the hotel industry[J]. The service industries journal, 28(4): 513-528.

CHANG J, KHAN M A, TSAI C-T, 2012. Dining occasions, service failures and customer complaint behaviors: an empirical assessment [J]. International journal of tourism research, 14(6): 601-615.

CHASE R B, 1978. Where does the customer fit in a service operation? [J]. Harvard business review, 56(6): 137-142.

CHEBAT J-C, DAVIDOW M, CODJOVI I, et al., 2005. Silent voices: why some dissatisfied consumers fail to complain[J]. Journal of service research, 7 (4): 328-342.

CHENG B L, RASHID M Z A, 2013. Service quality and the mediating effect of corporate image on the relationship between customer satisfaction and customer loyalty in the Malaysian hotel industry [J]. Gadjah Mada international journal of business, 15(2): 99-112.

CHENG S, LAM T, 2008. The role of the customer—seller relationship in the intention of the customer to complain: a study of Chinese restaurateurs [J]. International journal of hospitality management, 27(4): 552-562.

CHATTERJEE P, 2001. Online reviews—do consumers use them?[C]//GILLY M C, MYERS-LEVY, P J. ACR 2001 proceeding. UT: Association for Consumer Research: 129-134.

CHI C G Q, QU H, 2008. Examining the structural relationships of destination image, tourist satisfaction and destination loyalty: an integrated approach[J]. Tourism management, 29(4): 624-636.

CHOI S, MATTILA A S. (2008). Perceived controllability and service expectation: Influences on customer reactions following service failure [J]. Journal of business research, 61(1): 24-30.

CHOI T Y, CHU R, 2001. Determinants of hotel guests' satisfaction and repeat patronage in the Hong Kong hotel industry [J]. International journal of hospitality management, 20(3): 277-297.

CHOU C, HSU Y H, GOO Y J, 2009. Service failures and recovery strategies from the service provider perspective[J]. Asia Pacific management review, 14 (2): 237-249.

CHUANG S C, CHENG Y H, CHANG C J, et al., 2012. The effect of service failure types and service recovery on customer satisfaction: a mental accounting perspective[J]. The service industries journal, 32 (2): 257-271.

CHUNG-HERRERA B G, GOLDSCHMIDT N, DOUG H K, 2004. Customer and employee views of critical service incidents [J]. Journal of services marketing, 18(4): 241-254.

CHURCHILL G A, 1979. A paradigm for developing better measures of marketing constructs, Journal of marketing research, 16(1): 64-73.

CHURCHILL G A, SURPRENANT C, 1982. An investigation into the determinants of customer satisfaction[J]. Journal of marketing research, 19(4): 491-504.

CHURCHILL G A, FORD N M, WALKER O C, 1997. Sales force management [M]. 5th ed. Chicago, IL: Irwin.

CLARK G L, KAMINSKI P F, RINK D R, 1992. Consumer complaints: advice on how companies should respond based on an empirical study[J]. Journal of services marketing, 6(1): 41-50.

CLAVER E, TARI J J, PEREIRA J, 2006. Does quality impact on hotel performance? [J]. International journal of contemporary hospitality management, 18 (4): 350-358.

CLEMMER E C, 1993. An investigation into the relationship of fairness and customer satisfaction with services [G]//CROPANZANO R. Justice in the workforce: approaching fairness in human resource management. Hillsdales, NJ: Lawrence Eribaum Associates.

CLEMMER E C, SCHNEIDER B, 1996. Fair service [G]//SWARTZ T A, BOWEN D E, BROWN S W. Advances in services marketing and management (5). Greenwich, CT: JAI Press: 109-126.

COLGATE M, HEDGE R, 2001. An investigation into the switching process in retail banking services[J]. International journal of bank marketing, 19(5): 201-212.

COLGATE M, NORRIS M, 2001. Developing a comprehensive picture of service failure[J]. International journal of service industry management, 12(3): 215-235.

COLQUITT J A, 2001. On the dimensionality of organizational justice: a construct validation of a measure [J]. Journal of applied psychology, 86(3): 386-400.

CONLON D E, MURRAY N M, 1996. Customer perceptions of corporate responses to product complaints: the role of explanations [J]. Academy of management journal, 39(4): 1040-1056.

COOKE A J, MEYVIS T, SCHWARTZ A, 2001. Avoiding future regret in purchase-timing decisions[J]. Journal of consumer research, 27(4): 447-459.

CORTINA J M, 1993. What is coefficient alpha? An examination of theory and applications[J]. Journal of applied psychology, 78(1): 98-104.

COTTE J, AOULTER R, MOORE M, 2005. Enhancing or disrupting guilt: the role of ad credibility and perceived manipulative intent[J]. Journal of business research, 58(3): 361-368.

CRAIGHEAD C W, KARWAN K R, MILLER J L, 2004. The effects of severity of failure and customer loyalty on service recovery strategies [J]. Production and operations management,13(4): 307-321.

CRIÉ D, 2003. Consumers' complaint behavior. Taxonomy, typology and determinants: towards a unified ontology [J]. Journal of database marketing and customer strategy management, 11(1): 60-79.

CRONBACH L J, 1951. Coefficient alpha and the internal structure of tests[J]. Psychometrika, 16(3): 297-334.

CRONIN J J, TAYLOR S A, 1994. SERVPERF versus SERVQUAL: reconciling performance based and perceptions-minus-expectations measurement of service quality[J]. Journal of marketing, 58(1): 125-131.

CRONIN J J, TAYLO S A, 1992. Measuring service quality: a reexamination and extension[J]. Journal of marketing, 56(3): 55-68.

CRONIN J J, BRADY M K, HULT G T M, 2000. Assessing the effects of quality, value, and customer satisfaction on consumer behavioral intentions in service environments[J]. Journal of retailing, 76(2): 193-218.

CURREN M T, FOLKES V S, 1987. Attributional influences on consumers' desires to communicate about products[J]. Psychology and marketing, 4(1): 31-45.

D

D'ANDRADE R, 1992a. Cognitive anthropology[G]//THEODORE S, GEOFFREY W, CATHERINE L. New directions in psychological anthropology. New York: Cambridge University Press: 47-58.

D'ANDRADE R, 1992b. Schemas and motivation[M]//D'ANDRADE R, STRAUSS C. Human motives and cultural models. New York: Cambridge University Press: 23-44.

DABHOLKAR P A, SHEPHERD C D, THORPE D I, 2000. A comprehensive framework for service quality: an investigation of critical conceptual and measurement issues[J]. Journal of retailing, 76(2): 139-173.

DABHOLKAR P A, 1993. Consumer satisfaction and service quality: two construct or one? [G]//Peter D W. Enhancing knowledge development in marketing[J]. Chicago, IL: American Marketing Association.

DANAHER P J, MATTSSON J, 1994. Customer satisfaction during the service delivery process[J]. European journal of marketing, 28(5): 5-16.

DAVIDOW M, 2000. The bottom-line impact of organizational responses to customer complaints[J]. Journal of hospitality and tourism research, 24 (4): 473-490.

DAVIDOW M, 2003. Organizational responses to customer complaints: what works and what doesn't[J]. Journal of service research, 5(3): 225-251.

DAWES J, ROWLEY J, 1999. Negative evaluations of service quality—a framework for identification and response[J]. Journal of marketing practice: applied marketing science, 5(2): 46-55.

DAY R L, 1980. Research perspectives on consumer complaining behavior[G]// LAMB C W, DUNNE P M. Theoretical developments in marketing. Chicago, IL : American Marketing Association: 211-215.

DAY R L, 1984. Modeling choices among alternative responses to dissatisfaction [G]//KINNEAR T C. Advances in consumer research (2). Provo, UT: Association for Consumer Research.

DAY R L, LANDON E L, 1977. Towards a theory of consumer complaining behavior [G]//LAMB C W, DUNN P M. Theoretical developments in marketing. Chicago, IL: American Marketing Association.

DAY R L, SCHAETZLE T, GRABICKE K, et al., 1981. The hidden agenda of consumer complaining[J]. Journal of retailing, 57(3): 86-106.

DE MATOS C A, LEIS R P, 2013. The antecedents of complaint behavior for Brazilian and French consumers of services [J]. International journal of consumer studies, 37(3): 327-336.

DE MATOS C A, FERNANDES D, LEIS R P, et al., 2011. A cross-cultural investigation of customer reactions to service failure and recovery[J]. Journal of international consumer marketing, 23(3-4): 211-228.

DE MATOS C A, VIEIRA V A, VEIGA R T, 2012. Behavioural responses to service encounter involving failure and recovery: the influences of contextual factors[J]. Service industries journal, 32(14): 2203-2217.

DE MATOS C A, HENRIQUE J L, VARGAS C A, 2007. Service recovery paradox: a meta-analysis[J]. Journal of service research, 10(1): 60-77.

DE MATOS C A, ROSSI C A V, VEIGA R T, et al., 2009. Consumer reaction to service failure and recovery: the moderating role of attitude toward complaining[J]. Journal of service marketing, 23(7): 462-475.

DE RUYTER K, BLOEMER J, PEETERS P, 1997. Merging service quality and service satisfaction an empirical test of an integrative model[J]. Journal of economic psychology, 18(4): 387-406.

DEAUX K, 1976. Sex: a perspective on the attribution process[G]//HARVEY J H, ICKES W J, KIDD R F. New directions in attribution research. Hillsdale, NJ: Erlbaum.

DEBASISH S S, DEY S, 2015. Customer perceptions of service quality towards luxury hotels in Odisha using servqual model[J]. International journal of research in business studies and management, 2(8): 1-9.

DEL RÍO LANZA A B, VA ZQUEZ CASIELLES R, DÍAZ MARTÍN A M, 2009. Satisfaction with service recovery: perceived justice and emotional responses[J]. Journal of business research, 62(8): 775-781.

DELLANDE S, 1995. Consumer response to dissatisfaction: an overview[D]. California: University of California.

DENG W J., YEH, M. L., AND SUNG, M. L. (2013). A customer satisfaction index model for international tourist hotels: integrating consumption emotions into the American customer satisfaction index[J]. International journal of hospitality management, 35(12): 133-140.

DEV C S, BUSCHMAN J D, BOWEN J T, 2010. Hospitality marketing: a retrospective analysis (1960—2010) and predictions (2010—2020)[J]. Cornell hospitality quarterly, 51 (4): 459-469.

DEVELLIS R F, 1991. Scale development: theory and application[M]. Newbury Park, CA: Sage.

DEWITT T, BRADY M K, 2003. Rethinking service recovery strategies: the effect of rapport on consumer responses to service failure[J]. Journal of service research, 6(2): 193-207.

DEWITT T, NGUYEN D, MARSHALL R, 2008. Exploring customer loyalty following service recovery[J]. Journal of service research, 10(3): 269-281.

DIMITRIADES Z S, 2006. Customer satisfaction, loyalty and commitment in service organizations—some evidence from Greece[J]. Management research news, 29(12): 782-800.

DOLNICAR S, OTTER T, 2003. Which hotel attributes matter? A review of previous and a framework for future research[C]//GRIFFIN, HARRIS R. Proceedings of the 9th annual conference of the Asia Pacific Tourism Association (APTA). Sydney: University of Technology Sydney: 176-188.

DONG B, EVANS K R, ZOU S, 2008. The effects of customer participation in co-created service recovery[J]. Journal of the academy of marketing science,

36(1): 123-137.

DOS SANTOS C P, FERNANDES D V DER H, 2007. The impact of service recovery processes on consumer trust and loyalty in car repair services[J]. Latin American business review, 8(2): 89-113.

DOS SANTOS C P, FERNANDES D V DER H, 2011. Perceptions of justice after recovery efforts in internet purchasing: the impact on consumer trust and loyalty toward retailing sites and online shopping in general [J]. Brazilian administration review, 8(3): 225-246.

DRACH-ZAHAVY A, SOMECH A, 2006. Professionalism and helping: harmonious or discordant concepts? An attribution theory perspective [J]. Journal of applied social psychology, 36(8): 1892-1923.

DUBINSKY A J, SKINNER S J, WHITTLER T E, 1989. Evaluating sales personnel: an attribution theory perspective[J]. Journal of personal selling and sales management, 9 (1): 9-21.

DUFFY J, MILLER J, BEXLEY J, 2006. Banking customers' varied reactions to service recovery strategies[J]. The international journal of bank marketing, 24 (2): 112-132.

DWYER F, SCHURR P, OH S, 1987. Developing buyer-seller relationships[J]. Journal of marketing, 51(2): 11-27.

E

EBERLY M B, HOLLEY E C, JOHNSON M D, et al., 2011. Beyond internal and external: a dyadic theory of relational attribution[J]. Academy of management review, 36(4): 731-753.

EKINCI Y, DAWES P L, MASSEY G R, 2008. An extended model of the antecedents and consequences of consumer satisfaction for hospitality services [J]. European journal of marketing[J], 42(1/2):35-68.

EKINCI Y, RILEY M, FIFE-SCHAW C, 1998. Which school of thought? The dimensions of resort hotel quality [J]. International journal of contemporary hospitality management, 10(2): 63-67.

EMARI H, IRANZADEH S, BAKHSHAYESH S, 2011. Determining the dimensions of service quality in banking industry: examining the Grönroos's model in Iran [J]. Trends in applied sciences research, 6(1): 57-64.

ENIS B M, ROERING K J, 1980. Product classification taxonomies: synthesis and consumer implications, theoretical development in marketing [G]//LAMB

C, DUNNE P. Theoretical development in marketing. Chicago: American Marketing Association: 186-189.

ENNEW C, SCOEFER K, 2003. Service failure and service recovery in tourism: A review[G]//RAJ A. The Tourist: A psychological perspective. New Delhi: Kanishka Publications.

EPSTUDE K, ROESE N J, 2008. The functional theory of counterfactual thinking[J]. Personality and social psychology review, 12(2): 168-192.

EREVELLES S, LEAVITT C, 1992. A comparison of current models of consumer satisfaction / dissatisfaction [J]. Journal of consumer satisfaction, dissatisfaction, and complaining behavior(5): 104-114.

ETZEL M J, SILVERMAN B I, 1981. A managerial perspective on directions for retail customer dissatisfaction research[J]. Journal of retailing, 57(3): 124-136.

F

FAN Y W, MIAO Y F, WU S C, 2013. Customer complaints and service policy in electronic commerce[J]. South African journal of business management, 44 (3): 15-19.

FARRELL D, 1983. Exit, voice, loyalty, and neglect as responses to job dissatisfaction: a multidimensional scaling study [J]. The academy of management journal, 26(4): 596-607.

FAULLANT R, MATZLER K, FÜLLER J, 2008. The impact of satisfaction and image on loyalty: the case of Alpine ski resorts[J]. Managing service quality, 18(2): 163-178.

FELDMAN J M, 1981. Beyond attribution theory: cognitive processes in performance appraisal[J]. Journal of applied psychology, 66(2):127-148.

FINKEL E J, RUSBULT C E, KUMASHIRO M, et al., 2002. Dealing with betrayal in close relationships: does commitment promote forgiveness? [J]. Journal of personality and social psychology, 82 (6): 956-974.

FINN D W, LAMB C W, 1991. An evaluation of the servqual scale in a retailing setting [G]//HOLMAN R, SOLOMON M R. Advances in consumer research. Provo, UT: Association for Consumer Research.

FISK R P, BROWN S W, BITNER M J, 1993. Tracking the evolution of the services marketing literature[J]. Journal of retailing, 69(1): 61-103.

FISK R P, YOUNG C, 1985. Disconfirmation of equity expectations: effects on consumer satisfaction with services [G]//HIRSCHMAN E, HOLBROOK H. Advances in consumer research. Provo, UT: Association for Consumer Research.

FISK R P, BROWN S W, BITNER M J, 1995. Tracking the evolution of the service marketing literature[J]. Journal of retailing, 69(1): 61-103.

FOLKES V S, 1984. Consumer reactions to product failure: an attributional approach[J]. Journal of consumer research, 10(4): 398-409.

FOLKES V S, KOTSOS B, 1986. Buyers' and sellers' explanations for product failure: Who done It?[J]. Journal of marketing, 50(2): 74-80.

FOLKES V S, KOLETSKY S, GRAHAM J L, 1987. A field study of causal inferences and consumer reaction: the view from the airport[J]. Journal of consumer research, 13(4): 534-539.

FOLKES V S, 1988. Recent attribution research in consumer behavior: a review and new directions[J]. Journal of consumer research, 14(4): 548-565.

FOLKES V S, KOLETSKY S, GRAHAM J L, 1987. A field study of causal inferences and consumer reaction: the view from the airport[J]. Journal of consumer research, 13(3): 534-539.

FORNELL C, 1992. A national customer satisfaction barometer: the Swedish experience[J]. Journal of marketing, 56(1): 6-21.

FORNELL C, WERNERFELT B, 1987. Defensive marketing strategy by customer complaint management: a theoretical analysis[J]. Journal of marketing research, 24(4): 337-346.

FORNELL C, WERNERFELT B, 1988. A model for customer complaint management [J]. Journal of marketing science, 7(3): 287-298.

FORNELL C, JOHNSON M D, ANDERSON E W, et al., 1996. The American customer satisfaction index: nature, purpose, and findings [J]. Journal of marketing, 60(4): 7-18.

FOURNIER S, MICK D G, 1999. Rediscovering satisfaction [J]. Journal of marketing, 63(4): 5-23.

FRIEZE I, WEINER B, 1971. Cue utilization and attribution judgment for success and failure[J]. Journal of personality, 39(4): 591-605.

G

GELB B D, SUNDARAM S, 2002. Adapting to word of mouse[J]. Business horizon, 45(4): 21-25.

GELBRICH K, 2010. Anger, frustration, and helplessness after service failure: coping strategies and effective informational support [J]. Journal of the academy of marketing science, 38(5): 567-585.

GELBRICH K, GÄTHKE J, GRÉGOIRE Y, 2015. How much compensation should a firm offer for a flawed service? An examination of the non-linear effects of compensation on satisfaction [J]. Journal of service research, 18(1): 107-123.

GELBRICH K, ROSCHK H, 2011. A meta-analysis of organizational complaint handling and customer responses[J]. Journal of service research, 14(1): 24-43.

GERBING D W, ANDERSON J C, 1988. An updated paradigm for scale development incorporating unidimensionality and its assessment [J]. Journal of marketing research, 25(2): 186-192.

GETTY J, THOMOPSON K, 1994. A procedure for scaling perceptions of lodging quality[J]. Hospitality research journal, 18(2): 75-96.

GETTY J M, GETTY R L, 2003. Lodging quality index (LQI): assessing customers' perceptions of quality delivery [J]. International journal of contemporary hospitality management, 15(2): 94-104.

GIESE J L, COTE J A, 2000. Defining consumer satisfaction[J]. Academy of marketing science review(1): 1-24.

GILLY M C, 1987. Post complaint processes: from organizational responses to responses to repurchase behavior [J]. The journal of consumer affairs, 21(2): 293-313.

GODES D, MAYZLIN D, 2004. Using online conversations to study word-of-mouth communication. Marketing science, 23(4): 545-560.

GOLDBERG L R, 1981. Unconfounding situational attributions from uncertain, neutral, and ambiguous ones: a psychometric analysis of descriptions of oneself and various types of others [J]. Journal of personality and social psychology, 41(3): 517-552.

GONZALEZ G R, HOFFMAN K D, INGRAM T N, et al., 2010. Sales organization recovery management and relationship selling: a conceptual model and empirical test[J]. Journal of personal selling and sales management, 30 (3): 223-237.

GOODING R Z, KINICKI A J, 1995. Interpreting event causes: the complementary role of categorization and attribution processes [J]. Journal of management studies, 32(1): 1-22.

GOODWIN C, ROSS I, 1990. Consumer evaluations of responses to complaints:

What's fair and why?[J]. The journal of consumer marketing, 7(2): 39-47.

GOODWIN C, ROSS I, 1992. Consumer responses to service failures: influences of procedural and interactional fairness perceptions [J]. Journal of business research, 25(2): 149-163.

GORDON M, BOWLBY R L, 1989. Reactance and intentionality attributions as determinants of the intent to file a grievance[J]. Personnel psychology, 42(2): 309-329.

GREENBERG J, 1996. The quest for justice on the job: essays and experiments [M]. Thousand Oaks, CA: Sage Publications.

GREENBERG J, 1990. Organizational justice: yesterday, today, and tomorrow[J]. Journal of management, 16(2): 399-432.

GREGOIRE Y, TRIPP T M, LEGOUX R, 2013. When customer love turns into lasting hate: the effects of relationship strength and time on customer revenge and avoidance[J]. Journal of marketing, 73(6): 18-32.

GRÖNROOS C, 1982. Strategic management and marketing in the service sector [M]. Sweden: Helsingfors.

GRÖNROOS C, 1988. Service quality: the six criteria of good perceived service [J]. Review of business, 9(3): 10-13.

GRÖNROOS C, 1990. Relationship approach to marketing in service contexts: the marketing and organizational behavior interface [J]. Journal of business research, 20(1): 3-11.

GRUBER T, CHOWDHURY I N, REPPEL A E, 2011. Service recovery in higher education: does national culture play a role?[J]. Journal of marketing management, 27(11-12): 1261-1293.

GRŽINIĆ J, 2007. Concepts of service quality measurement in hotel industry[J]. Economic thought and practice, 110 (1): 81-98.

GUNDERSEN M G, HEIDE M, OLSSON U H, 1996. Hotel guest satisfaction among business travellers: what are the important factors? [J]. The Cornell hotel and restaurant administration quarterly, 37(2): 72-81.

GUSTAFSON A, 2009. Customer satisfaction with service recovery[J]. Journal of business research, 62(11): 1220-1223.

GUSTAFSON A, JOHNSON M D, ROOS I, 2005. The effects of customer satisfaction, relationship commitment dimensions, and triggers on customer retention[J]. Journal of marketing, 69(4): 210-218.

H

HA H Y, 2006. An integrative model of consumer satisfaction in the context of e-services[J]. International journal of consumer studies, 30(2): 137-149.

HA J, JANG S, 2009. Perceived justice in service recovery and behavioral intentions: the role of relationship quality [J]. International journal of hospitality management, 28(3): 319-327.

HAIR J F, ANDERSON R E, TATHAM R L, et al., 1998. Multivariate data analysis[m]. Upper Saddle River, NJ: Prentice Hall.

HAIR J F, BLACK B, BABIN B, et al., 2006. Multivariate data analysis[M]. 6th ed. Upper Saddle River, NJ: Prentice Hall.

HALSTEAD D, PAGE T J, 1992. The effects of satisfaction and complaining behavior on consumer repurchase intentions[J]. Journal of consumer satisfaction, dissatisfaction, and complaining behavior(5): 1-11.

HALSTEAD D, HARTMAN D, SCHMIDT S L, 1994. Multisource effects on the satisfaction formation process[M]. Journal of the academy of marketing science, 22(2): 114-129.

HAMILTON D L, 1998. Dispositional and attributional inferences in person perception[G]//DARLEY J M, COOPER J. Attribution and social interaction: the legacy of Edward E. Jones. Washington, DC: American Psychological Association.

HAMILTON V L, 1980. Intuitive psychologist or intuitive lawyer? Alternative models of the attribution process [J]. Journal of personality and social psychology, 39(5): 767-772.

HARRIS K E, GREWAL D, MOHR L A, et al., 2006. Consumer responses to service recovery strategies: the moderating role of online versus offline environment[J]. Journal of business research, 59(4): 425-431.

HARRIS K E, MOHR L A, BERNHARDT K L, 2006. Online service failure, consumer attributions and expectations[J]. Journal of services marketing, 20 (7): 453-458.

HART C W L, 1988. The power of unconditional service guarantees[J]. Harvard business review, 66(4): 54-62.

HART C W L, HESKETT J L, SASSER W E, 1990. The profitable art of service recovery[J]. Harvard business review, 68(4): 148-156.

HART C W L, SCHLESINGER L A, MAHER D, 1992. Guarantees come to professional service firms[J]. Sloan management review, 33(3): 19-29.

HARVEY J M, WEARY G, 1984. Current issues in attribution theory and research[J]. Annual review of psychology, 35(1): 427-459.

HATTIE J, 1985. Methodology review: assessing unidimensionality of tests and ltenls[J]. Applied psychological measurement, 9(2): 139-164.

HAYS J M, HILL A, V, 2001. A longitudinal study of the effect of a service guarantee on service quality[J]. Production and operations management, 10(4): 405-423.

HEIDER F, 1944. Social perception and phenomenal causality[J]. Psychological review, 51(6): 358-374.

HEIDER F, 1958. The psychology of interpersonal relations[M]. New York: John Wiley and Sons, Inc.

HENNIG-THURAU F T, GWINNER K P, WALSH G, et al., 2004. Electronic word-of-mouth via consumer opinion platforms: what motivates consumers to articulate themselves on the internet?[J]. Journal of interactive marketing, 18 (1): 38-52.

HEMMASI M, GRAF L, WILLIAMS M, 1997. Strategic planning in health care: merging two methodologies[J]. Competitiveness review, 7(2): 38-58.

HESKETT J L, JONES T O, LOVEMAN G W, et al., 1994. Putting the service-profit chain to work[J]. Harvard business review, 72(2): 164-174.

HESKETT J L, SASSER W E, HART C W L, 1990. Service breakthroughs: changing the rules of the game[M]. New York: The Free Press.

HESS R L, GANESAN S, KLEIN N M, 2003. Service failure and recovery: the impact of relationship factors on customer satisfaction[J]. Journal of the academy of marketing science, 31(2): 127-145.

HIBBERT S A, PIACENTINI M G, HOGG M K, 2012. Service recovery following dysfunctional consumer participation[J]. Journal of consumer behavior, journal of consumer behavior, 11(4): 329-338.

HILTON D J, SMITH R H, KIN S H, 1995. Processes of causal explanation and dispositional attribution[J]. Journal of personality and social psychology, 68(3): 377-387.

HIRSCHMAN A O, 1970. Exit, voice, and loyalty-responses to decline in firms, organizations, and states[J]. Cambridge, MA: Harvard University Press.

HIRSCHMAN A O, 1970. Exit, voice, and loyalty: responses to decline in firms, organizations, and states[J]. Journal of Finance, 25(5): 1194-1195.

HOCUTT M A, CHAKRABORTY G, MOWEN J C, 1997. The impact of perceived justice on customer satisfaction and intention to complain in a service recovery[J]. Advances in consumer research(24): 457-463.

HOFFMAN K D, BATESON E G, 2005. Services marketing: concepts, strategies, and cases[M]. 3rd ed. Florence, KY: Cengage Learning.

HOFFMAN K D, KELLEY S W, 1996. Guidelines for developing retail recovery strategies [G]//WILSON E J, JR HAIR J F. Developments in marketing science. Phoenix: Academy of Marketing Science:123.

HOFFMAN K D, KELLEY S W, ROTALSKY H M, 1995. Tracking service failures and employee recovery efforts[J]. Journal of services marketing, 9(2): 49-61.

HOFFMAN K D, KELLEY S W, 2000. Perceived justice needs and recovery evaluation: a contingency approach. European journal of marketing, 34(3/4), 418-432.

HOFFMAN K D, KELLEY S W, CHUNG B C, 2003. A CIT investigation of servicescape failure and associated recovery strategies [J]. The journal of service marketing, 17(5): 322-345.

HOLLAND D, 1992. How cultural systems become desire: a case study of American romance[G]//D'ANDRADE R, STRAUSS C. Human motives and cultural models. New York: Cambridge University Press: 61-89.

HOLLOWAY B B, WANG S J, PARISH J T, 2005. The role of cumulative online purchasing experience in service recovery management[J]. Journal of interactive marketing, 19(3): 54-66.

HOMANS G C, 1961. Social behavior: its elementary gorms[M]. New York: Harcourt, Brace and World.

HOWARD J A, SHETH J N, 1969. The theory of buyer behavior[M]. New York: John Wiley and Sons.

HU H, KANDAMPULLY J, JUWAHEER T D, 2009. Relationships and impacts of service quality, perceived value, customer satisfaction, and image: an empirical study[J]. The service industries journal, 29(2): 111-125.

HU L, BENTLER P M, 1998. Fit indices in covariance structure modeling: sensitivity to underparameterized model misspecification [J]. Psychological methods, 3(4): 424-453.

HUANG J H, CHANG C C, 2008. The role of personality traits in online consumer complaint behavior and service recovery expectation [J]. Social behavior and personality, 36(9): 1223-1232.

HUANG J H, HUANG C T, WU S, 1996. National character and response to unsatisfactory hotel service[J]. International journal of hospitality management,

15(3): 299-243.

HUI M K, HO C K Y, WAN L C, 2011. Prior relationships and consumer responses to service failures: a cross-cultural study[J]. Journal of international marketing, 19(1): 59-81.

HUI M K, TSE A C, ZHOU L, 2006. Interaction between two types of information on reactions to delays[J]. Marketing letters, 17(2): 151-162.

HUI M, TOFFOLI R, 2002. Perceived control and the effects of crowding and consumer choice on the service experience[J]. Applied social psychology, 32 (9): 1825-1844.

HUI T L, CHERN B H, OTHMAN M, 2011. Development of service quality dimensions in Malaysia: the case of multicultural society[J]. SEGi Review, 4 (1): 93-108.

HUNING T M, THOMSON N F, 2011. Escalation of commitment: an attribution theory perspective[J]. Allied academies international conference: proceedings of the academy of organizational culture, communications and conflict, 16(1): 13-18.

HUNT H K, 1977. CS/D overview and future research directions[M]// Conceptualization and measurement of consumer satisfaction and dissatisfaction. Cambridge: Marketing Science Institute: 455-488.

HUPPERTZ J W, 2003. An effort model of first-stage complaining behavior[J]. Journal of consumer satisfaction, dissatisfaction and complaining behavior(16): 132-144.

HUPPERTZ J W, ARENSON S J, EVANS, R W, 1978. An application of equity theory to buyer-seller exchange situations[J]. Journal of marketing research, 15 (5): 250-260.

HWANG S N, LEE C, CHEN H J, 2005. The relationship among tourists' involvement, place attachment and interpretation satisfaction in Taiwan's parks [J]. Tourism management, 26(2): 143-156.

I

IACOBUCCI D, OSTROM A, GRAYSON K, 1995. Distinguishing service quality and customer satisfaction: the voice of the consumer[J]. Journal of consumer psychology, 4(3): 277-303.

ISPAS A, CONSTANTIN C, CANDREA A N, 2010. Evaluating customer satisfaction with Brasov accommodation services[J]. Tourism and hospitality management, conference proceedings(2): 373-387.

J

JACOBY J, JARRARD J J, 1981. The sources, meaning and validity of consumer complaint behavior: a psychological analysis[J]. Journal of retailing, 57(3): 4-24.

JAHANDIDEH S, ASEFZADEH S, JAHANDIDEH M, et al., 2013. The comparison of methods for measuring quality of hospital services by using neural networks: a case study in Iran (2012) [J]. International journal of healthcare management, 6(1): 45-50.

JAIN S K, GUPTA G, 2004. Measuring service quality: SERVQUAL vs. SERVPERF scales[J]. Vikalpa: the journal for decision makers, 29(2): 25-37.

JIANG J J, KLEIN G, PAROLIA N, et al., 2012. An analysis of three SERVQUAL variations in measuring information system service quality [J]. The electronic journal information systems evaluation, 15(2): 149-162.

JOHNS N, HOWARD A, 1998. Customer expectations versus perceptions of service performance in foodservice industry[J]. International journal of service industry management, 9(3): 248-265.

JOHNS N, TYAS P, 1996. Use of service quality gap theory to differentiate between foodservice outlets[J]. Service industries journal, 16(3): 321-346.

JOHNSON D, 2000. Anonymity and the internet[J]. The futurist, 34(4): 12.

JOHNSON M D, FORNELL C, 1991. A framework for comparing customer satisfaction across individuals and product categories[J]. Journal of economic psychology, 12(2): 267-286.

JOHNSON M S, 2006. A bibliometric review of the contribution of attribution theory to sales management [J]. Journal of personal selling and sales management, 26(2): 181-195.

JOHNSON T C, HEWA M A, 1997. Fixing service failures [J]. Industrial marketing management, 26(5): 467-473.

JOHNSTON R, 1995a. The zone of tolerance: exploring the relationship between service transactions and satisfaction with the overall service [J]. International journal of service industry management, 6(2): 46-61.

JOHNSTON R, 1995b. Service failure and recovery: impact, attributes, and process [G]//SWARTZ T A, BOWEN D E, BROWN S W. Advances in services marketing and management(4). Greenwich, CT: 211-228.

JOHNSTON R. The effect of intensity of dissatisfaction on complaining behavior [J]. Journal of consumer satisfaction, dissatisfaction and complaining behavior (11): 69-77.

JOHNSTON R, FERN A, 1999. Service recovery strategies for single and double deviation scenarios[J]. The service industries journal, 19(2): 69-82.

JONES E E, DAVIS K, 1965. From acts to dispositions: the attribution process in person perception//BERKOWITZ L. Advances in experimental social psychology. New York: Academic Press: 219-266.

JONES E E, 1971. Attribution: perceiving the causes of behavior [M]. Morristown, N.J.: General Learning Press.

JONES E E, MCGILLIS D, 1976. Correspondent Inferences and the attribution cube: a comparative reappraisal [G]//HARVEY J, ICKES W, KIDD R. New directions in attribution research(1). Hillsdale, NJ: Lawrence Erlbaum: 389-420.

JONES E E, DAVIS K E, 1965. From acts to dispositions: the attributions process in person perception[J]. Advances in experimental social psychology, 2 (4): 219-266.

JONES M, MOTHERSBAUGH D, BEATTY S, 2000. Switching barriers and repurchase intentions in services[J]. Journal of retailing, 76(2): 259-274.

JORESKOG K G, SORBOM D, 1993. LISREL 8: structural equation modeling with the simplis command language[M]. Lincolnwood, IL: Scientific Software International, Inc.

JUSTICE-TILLMAN C, LAWRENCE E R, DASPIT J J, 2014. A tale of perception: the role of perceived intent on OCBs and interpersonal relationships [J]. Journal of Behavioral and Applied Management, 15(4): 77-86.

JUWAHEER T D, 2004. Exploring international tourists' perceptions of hotel operations by using a modified SERVQUAL approach—a case study of Mauritius[J]. Managing service quality, 14(5): 350-364.

K

KAHNEMAN D, TVERSKY A, 1979. Prospect theory: an analysis of decisions under risk[J]. Econometrica, 47(2): 263-291.

KAHNEMAN D, TVERKSY A, 1984. Choices, values, and frames[J]. American Psychologist. 39(4): 341-350.

KANDAMPULLY J, SUHARTANTO D, 2000. Customer loyalty in the hotel industry: the role of customer satisfaction and image[J]. International journal of contemporary hospitality management, 12(6): 346-351.

KARATEPE O M, 2006. Customer complaints and organizational responses: the effects of complainants' perceptions of justice on satisfaction and loyalty[J]. International journal of hospitality management, 25(1): 69-90.

KARATEPE O M, 2006. The effects of selected antecedents on the service recovery performance of frontline employees[J]. The service industries journal, 26(1): 39-57.

KASHYAP R, 2001. The effect of service guarantees on external and internal markets[J]. Academy of marketing science review, 1(10): 1-19.

KAU A, LOH E W, 2006. The effects of service recovery on consumer satisfaction: a comparison between complainants and non-complainants [J]. Journal of services marketing, 20(2): 101-111.

KEAVENEY S M, 1995. Customer switching behavior in services industries: an exploratory study[J]. Journal of marketing, 59(2): 71-82.

KEITH N K, SIMMERS C S, 2013. Measuring hotel service quality perceptions: the disparity between comment cards and LODGSERV [J]. Academy of marketing studies journal, 17(2): 119-132.

KELLEY H H, 1967. Attribution theory in social psychology[G]//LEVINE D. Nebraska Symposium on Motivation[M]. Lincoln, NB: University of Nebraska Press: 192-238.

KELLEY H H, 1971. Attribution in social interaction [G]//JONES E E. Attribution: Perceiving the Causes of Behavior. Morristown, NJ: General Learning Press.

KELLEY H H, 1972. Causal schemata and the attribution process [M]. Morristown: General Learning Press.

KELLEY H H, 1973. The processes of causal attribution [J]. American psychologist, 28(2): 107-128.

KELLEY H H, MICHELA J L, 1980. Attribution theory and research [J]. Annual review of psychology(31): 457-501.

KELLEY S W, HOFFMAN K D, DAVIS M A, 1993. A typology of retail failures and recoveries[J]. Journal of retailing, 69(4): 429-452.

KELLEY S W, DAVIS M A, 1994. Antecedents to customer expectations for service recovery[J]. Journal of the academy of marketing science, 22(1): 52-61.

KELLOWAY E K, 1998. Using LISREL for structural equation modeling[M]. Thousand Oaks, California: Sage Publications.

KETTINGER W J, LEE C C, 2005. Zones of tolerance: alternative scales for measuring information systems service quality[J]. MIS quarterly, 29(4): 607-618.

KHAN M, 2003. ECOSERV – Ecotourists' quality expectations[J]. Annals of tourism research, 30(1): 109-124.

KILIBARDA M, ZEC ˘ EVIC' S, VIDOVIC M, 2012. Measuring the quality of logistic service as an element of the logistics provider offering[J]. Total quality management, 23 (12): 1345-1361.

KIM J W, MAGNUSEN M, KIM Y K, 2014. A critical review of theoretical and methodological issues in consumer satisfaction research and recommendations for future sport marketing scholarship[J]. Journal of sport management, 28 (3): 338-355.

KIM S H, CHA J, SINGH A J, KNUTSON B, 2013. A longitudinal investigation to test the validity of the American customer satisfaction model in the U.S. hotel industry[J]. International journal of hospitality management(35): 193-202.

KIM W, OK C, CANTER D D, 2012. Moderating role of a priori customer-firm relationship in service recovery situations[J]. Service industries journal, 32 (1): 59-82.

KNOUSE S B, 1989. The role of attribution theory in personnel employment selection: a review of the recent literature [J]. The journal of general psychology, 116(2): 183-196.

KNUTSON B J, BECK J A, KIM S H, et al., 2009. Identifying the dimensions of the guest's hotel experience[J]. Cornell hospitality quarterly, 50(1): 44-55.

KNUTSON B J, STEVENS P, PATTON M, et al., 1992. Consumers' expectations for service quality in economy, mid-price and luxury hotels[J]. Journal of hospitality and leisure marketing, 1(2): 27-43.

KNUTSON B J, STEVENS P, WULLAERT C, et al., 1990. LODGSERV: a service quality index for the lodging industry[J]. Journal of hospitality and tourism research, 14(2): 277-284.

KONOVSKY M A, 2000. Understanding procedural justice and its impact on business organization[J]. Journal of management, 26(3): 489-511.

KOTLER P, 1997. Marketing management: analysis, planning, implementation and control[M]. 9th ed. Engelwood Cliffs, New York: Prentice Hall Inc.

KRISHNA A, DANGAYACH G S, JAIN R, 2011. A conceptual framework for the service recovery paradox[J]. The marketing review, 11(1): 41-56.

KRISHNAN S, VALLE V A, 1979. Dissatisfaction attributions and consumer complaint behavior [G]//WILKIE W L. Advances in consumer research(6).

Miami: Association for Consumer Research: 445-449.

KRUGLANSKI A W, 1970. Attributing trustworthiness in supervisor-worker relations[J]. Journal of experimental social psychology, 6(2): 214-232.

KUENZEL S, KATSARIS N, 2011. Discrepancies between tourists ' and managers' perceptions of service failures and service recoveries in hotels[J]. International journal of business research, 11(5): 16-25.

L

LABARBERA P A, MAZURSKY D, 1983. a longitudinal assessment of consumer satisfaction/dissatisfaction: the dynamic aspect of the cognitive process[J]. Journal of marketing research, 20(4): 393-404.

LACZNIAK R N, DECARLO T E, RAMASWAMI S N, 2001. Consumers' responses to negative word-of-mouth communication: an attribution theory perspective[J]. Journal of consumer psychology, 11(1): 57-73.

LADHARI R, 2008. Alternative measures of service quality: a review [J]. Managing service quality, 18(1): 65-86.

LADHARI R, 2009. A review of twenty years of SERVQUAL research [J]. International journal of quality and service sciences, 1(2): 172-198.

LAPIERRE L, 1996. Service quality: the construct, its dimensionality and its measurement[J]. Advances in service marketing and management (JAI Press) (5): 45-70.

LATOUR S A, PEAT N C, 1979. Conceptual and methodological issues in consumer satisfaction[J]. Advances in consumer research, 6(1): 31-37.

LAU M P, AKBAR A K, YONG D Y G, 2006. Measuring service quality and customer satisfaction of the hotels in Malaysia: Malaysian, Asian and non-Asian hotel guests[J]. Journal of hospitality and tourism management, 13(2): 144-160.

LAU M P, AKBAR A K, YONG D Y G, 2005. Service quality: a study of the luxury hotels in Malaysia[J]. The journal of american academy of business, 7 (2): 46-55.

LEVESQUE T J, MCDOUGALL G H G, 2000. Service problems and recovery strategies: an experiment[J]. Canadian journal of administrative sciences, 17 (1): 20-37.

LEVESQUE T J, MCDOUGALL G H G, 1993. Managing customer satisfaction: the nature of service problems and customer exit, voice and loyalty[J]. Asia

Pacific journal of quality management, 2(2): 40-58.

LEWIS B R, SYPRAKOPOULOS R, 2001a. Transaction or relationship marketing: determinants of strategic choices[J]. Journal of marketing management, 17(4): 449-464.

LEWIS B R, MCCANN P, 2004. Service failure and recovery: evidence for the hotel industry[J]. International journal of contemporary hospitality management, 6 (1): 6-17.

LEWIS B R, SYPRAKOPOULOS R, 2001b. Service failures and recovery in retail banking: the customers' perspective[J]. The international journal of bank marketing, 19(1): 37-48.

LEWIS F M, DALTROY L H, 1990. How causal explanations influences health behavior: Attribution theory [G]//GLANZ K, LEWIS F M, RIMER B K. Health education and health behavior: theory, research, and practice. San Francisco, CA: Jossey-Bass Publishers, Inc.

LI C, FOCK H, MATTILA A S, 2012. The role of cultural tightness-looseness in the ethics of service recovery[J]. Journal of global marketing, 25(1): 3-16.

LI M M, 2007. Modeling the travel motivation of mainland Chinese outbound tourists[D]. West Lafayette, Indiana: Purdue University.

LIANG P, 2013. Exit and voice: a game-theoretic analysis of customer complaint management[J]. Pacific economic review, 18(2): 177-207.

LIAO H, 2007. Do it right this time: the role of employee service recovery performance in customer-perceived justice and customer loyalty after service failures[J]. Journal of applied psychology, 92(2): 475-489.

LICHTENSTEIN D R, BEARDEN W O, 1986. Measurement and structure of Kelley's covariance theory[J]. Journal of consumer research, 13(2): 290-296.

LIDEN S B, SKALEN P, 2003. The effect of service guarantees on service recovery[J]. International journal of service industry management, 14(1): 36-58.

LII Y S, CHIEN C S, PANT A, LEE M, 2013. The challenges of long-distance relationships: the effects of psychological distance between service provider and consumer on the efforts to recover from service failure[J]. Journal of applied social psychology, 43(6): 1121-1135.

LII Y S, PANT A, LEE M, 2012. Balancing the scales: recovering from service failures depends on the psychological distance of consumers[J]. The service industries journal, 32(11): 1775-1790.

LILJANDE V, STRANVIK T, 1995. The nature of customer relationships in services [G]//SWARTZ T A, BOWEN D E, BROWN S W. Advances in services marketing and management (JAI Press) (14): 141-167.

LILJANDE V, 1999. Customer satisfaction with complaint handling following a dissatisfactory experience with car repair[J]. European advances in consumer research(4): 270-275.

LILJANDE V, STRANVIK T, 1997. Emotions in service satisfaction [J]. International journal of service industry management, 8(2): 148-169.

LIM J, 2012. Attribution of service failure with sst (self-service technology), does it matter?[J]. Review of business research, 12(1): 80-89.

LIN W B, 2010a. Relevant factors that affect service recovery performance[J]. The service industries journal, 30(6): 891-910.

LIN W B, 2010b. Service recovery expectation model–from the perspectives of consumers[J]. The service industries journal, 30(6): 873-889.

LIN W B, 2006. Correlation between personality characteristics, situations of service failure, customer relation strength and remedial recovery strategy [J]. Services marketing quarterly, 28(1): 55-88.

LIND A E, TOM R, 1988. The social psychology of procedural justice. New York: Plenum Press.

LOUDON D, BITTA D, ALBERT J, 1993. Consumer behavior[M]. Singapore: McGraw-Hill.

LOVELOCK C, WRIGHT L, 1998. Principles of service marketing and management[J]. Upper saddle River, NJ: Prentice Hall.

LOVELOCK C, 1994.Product plus[M]. New York: McGraw-Hill.

LUK S T-K, LAYTON R, 2004. Managing both outcome and process quality is critical to quality of hotel service[J]. Total quality management and business excellence, 15(3): 259-278.

LURIA G, GAL I, YAGIL D, 2009. Employees willingness to report service complaints[J]. Journal of service research, 12(2): 156-174.

M

MA J, 2012. Does the customer-firm relationship affect consumer recovery expectations?[J]. Academy of marketing studies journal, 16(2): 17-29.

MAGNINI V P, FORD J B, MARKOWSKI E P, et al., 2007. The service recovery paradox: justifiable theory or smoldering myth? [J]. Journal of services marketing, 21(3): 213-225.

MALLE B F, 2011. Attribution theories: how people make sense of behavior [G]// CHADEE D. Theories in social psychology. New York: Wiley-Blackwell: 72-95.

MANGOLD W G, BABAKUS E, 1991. Service quality: the front stage versus the back-stage perspective[J]. Journal of services marketing, 5(4):59-70.

MANIU LC, MARIN-PANTELESCU A, 2012. Managing the hotels service products and e-services [J]//Case study: researching tourists ' satisfaction regarding the hotels' services. Romania, Journal of Knowledge Management, Economics and Information Technology(8): 1-14.

MANO H, OLIVER R L, 1993. Assessing the dimensionality and structure of the consumption experience: evaluation, feeling, and satisfaction[J]. Journal of Consumer Research, 20(3): 451-466.

MARKOVI S, RASPOR S, 2010. Measuring perceived service quality using servqual: a case study of the Croatian hotel industry[J]. Management, 5(3): 195-209.

MARTIN D, O'NEILL M, HUBBARD S, et al., 2008. The role of emotion in explaining consumer satisfaction and future behavioral intention[J]. Journal of services marketing, 22(3): 224-236.

MARTINKO M J, HARVEY P, DOUGLAS S C, 2007. The role, function, and contribution of attribution theory to leadership: a review [J]. Leadership quarterly, 18(6): 561-585.

MATOS C A, HENRIQUE J L, VARGAS C A, 2007. Service recovery paradox: a meta-analysis[J]. Journal of service research, 10(1): 60-77.

MATOS C A, VIEIRA V A, VEIGA R T, 2012. Behavioural responses to service encounter involving failure and recovery: the influences of contextual factors[J]. The service industries journal, 32(14): 2203-2217.

MATTILA A S, 2001. The impact of relationship type on customer loyalty in a context of service failures[J]. Journal of service research, 4(2): 91-101.

MATTILA A S, 1999. An examination of factors affecting service recovery in a restaurant setting[J]. Journal of hospitality and tourism research, 23(3): 284-298.

MATTILA A S, 2001a. The effectiveness of service recovery in a multi-industry setting[J]. Journal of services marketing, 15(7): 583-596.

MATTILA A S, 2001b. The impact of relationship type on customer loyalty in a context of service failures[J]. Journal of service research, 4(2): 91-101.

MATTILA A S, CRANAGE D, 2005. The impact of choice on fairness in the context of service recovery[J]. Journal of services marketing, 19(5): 271-279.

MATTSSON J, LEMMINK J, ANDMCCOLL R, 2004. The effect of verbalized emotions on loyalty in written complaints[J]. Total quality management, 15(7): 941-958.

MATZLER K, RENZL B, ROTHENBERGER S, 2006. Measuring the relative importance of service dimensions in the formation of price satisfaction and service satisfaction: a case study in the hotel industry[J]. Scandinavian journal of hospitality and tourism, 6(3): 179-196.

MAXHAM J G, NETEMEYER R G, 2003. Firms reap what they sow: the effects of shared values and perceived organizational justice on customers' evaluations of complaint handling[J]. Journal of marketing, 67(1): 46-62.

MAXHAM J G III, 2001. Service recovery's influences on consumer satisfaction, positive word-of-mouth, and purchase intentions [J]. Journal of business research, 54(1): 11-24.

MAXHAM J G III, NETEMEYER R G, 2002a. A longitudinal study of complaining customers' evaluations of multiple service failures and recovery efforts[J]. Journal of marketing, 66(4): 57-71.

MAXHAM J G III, NETEMEYER R G, 2002b. Modeling customer perceptions of complaint handling over time: the effects of perceived justice on satisfaction and intent[J]. Journal of retailing, 78(4): 239-252.

MAZUMDER S, HASAN A B M R, 2014. Measuring service quality and customer satisfaction of the hotels in Bangladesh: a study on national and international hotel guest[J]. Journal of tourism and hospitality management, 2 (1): 95-111.

MCARTHUR L Z, 1972. The how and what of why: some determinants and consequences of causal attribution [J]. Journal of personality and social psychology, 22(2): 171-193.

MCCOLL R, MATTSSON J, MORLEY C, 2005. The effects of service guarantee on service evaluations during a voiced complaint and service recovery[J]. Journal of consumer satisfaction, dissatisfaction and complaining behavior, 18(1): 32-50.

MCCOLL-KENNEDY J R, SPARKS B A, 2003. Application of fairness theory to service failures and service recovery[J]. Journal of service research, 5(3): 251-266.

MCCOLL-KENNEDY J R, DAUS C S, SPARKS B A, 2003. The role of gender in reactions to service failure and recovery [J]. Journal of service research, 6(1): 66-82.

MCCOLLOUGH M A, GREMLER D, 2004. A conceptual model and empirical examination of the effect of service guarantees on post-purchase consumption evaluations[J]. Managing service quality, 14(1): 58-74.

MCCOLLOUGH M A, BHARADWAJ S G, 1992. The recovery paradox: an examination of consumer satisfaction in relation to disconfirmation, service quality and attribution-based theory[G]// ALLEN C T. Marketing theory and applications. Chicago: American Marketing Association.

MCCOLLOUGH M A, BERRY L L, YADAV M S, 2000. An empirical investigation
of customer satisfaction after service failure and recovery[J]. Journal of service research, 3(2): 121-137.

MCCULLOUGH M E, FINCHAM F D, TSANG J A, 2003. Forgiveness, forbearance, and time: the temporal unfolding of transgression-related interpersonal motivations[J]. Journal of personality and social psychology, 84 (3): 540-557.

MCDOUGALL G H G, LEVESQUE T, VANDERPLAAT P, 1998. Designing the service guarantee: unconditional or specific?[J]. Journal of services marketing, 12(4): 278-293.

MCFARLAND C, ROSS M, 1982. Impact of causal attributions on affective reactions to success and failure [J]. Journal of personality and social psychology, 43(2): 937-946.

MCGILL A L, 2000. Counterfactual reasoning in causal judgments: implications for marketing[J]. Psychology and marketing, 17(4): 323-343.

MEDVEC V H, SAVITSKY K, 1997. When doing better means feeling worse: the effects of categorical cutoff points on counterfactual thinking and satisfaction[J]. Journal of personality and social psychology, 72(6): 1284-1296.

MEDVEC V H, MADEY S F, GILOVICH T, 1995. When less is more: counterfactual thinking and satisfaction among Olympic medalists[J]. Journal of personality and social psychology, 69(4): 603-610.

MEI A W O, DEAN A M, WHITE C J, 1999. Analysing service quality in the hospitality industry[J]. Managing service quality, 9(2): 136-143.

MENSAH A F, NIMAKO S G, 2012. Influences of demographic variables on complaining and non-complaining motives and responses in Ghana's mobile telephony industry[J]. European journal of business and management, 4(12): 3-28.

METZ C, 2000. Customer support: service on the fly[J]. PC Magazine, 19(13): 143-144.

MICHEL S, MEUTER M L, 2008. The service recovery paradox: true but overrated?[J]. International journal of service industry management, 19(4): 441-457.

MILLER J L, CRAIGHEAD C W, KARWAN K R, 2000. Service recovery: a framework and Empirical investigation[J]. Journal of operations management, 18(4): 387-400.

MILLER J A, 1997. Exploring satisfaction, modifying models, eliciting expectations, posing problems and making meaningful measurements [G]//HUNT H K. Conceptualization and measurement of consumer satisfaction and dissatisfaction. Cambridge, MA: Marketing Science Institute.

MIRSADEGHI S, 2013. A review on the attribution theory in the social psychology[J]. Journal of humanities and social science, 8(6): 74-76.

MITTAL V, ROSS W T, BALDASARE P M, 1998. The asymmetric impact of negative and positive attribute-level performance on overall satisfaction and repurchase intentions[J]. Journal of marketing, 62 (1): 33-47.

MIZERSKI R, GOLDEN L L, KERNAN J B, 1979. The attribution process in consumer decision making[J]. Journal of consumer research, 6(2): 123-140.

MOREL K P N, POIESZ T B C, ANDWILKE H A M, 1997. Motivation, capacity and opportunity to complain: towards a comprehensive model of consumer complaint behavior[J]. Advances in consumer research(24): 464-469.

MUELLER R D, PALMER A, MACK R, MCMULLAN R, 2003. Service in the restaurant industry: an American and Irish comparison of service failures and recovery strategies[J]. International journal of hospitality management, 22(4): 395-418.

N

NA J H, PARK J, SUK K, 2008. Unsuccessful purchase experiences and future consumer decisions: effects of initial goal setting processes and counterfactual thoughts[J]. Advances in consumer research. association for consumer research (U.S.)(35): 276-281.

NADIRI H, HUSSAIN K, 2005a. Perceptions of service quality in North Cyprus hotels[J]. International journal of contemporary hospitality management, 17(6): 469-480.

NADIRI H, HUSSAIN K, 2005b. Diagnosing the zone of tolerance for hotel services[J]. Managing service quality, 15(3): 259-277.

NARAYANDAS D, 1998. Measuring and managing the benefits of customer retention: An empirical investigation. Journal of Service Research, 1(2): 108-128.

NATALIA L, BARBARA R L, 2004. Service recovery in the airline industry: a cross-cultural comparison of the attitudes and behaviors of British and Italian frontline personnel[J]. Managing service quality, 14(1): 11-25.

NAVEH E, KATZ-NAVON T, 2014. Antecedents of willingness to report medical treatment errors in health care organizations: a multilevel theoretical framework [J]. Health care manage review, 39(1): 21-30.

NEK-KAMAL Y Y, SALOMAWATI I, SURAINI R, 2012. Critical service incidents: analyzing service failure and recovery in hotels, restaurants and transportations in Malaysia[J]. Journal of global business and economics, 5(1): 18-37.

NIKBIN D, ISMAIL I, MARIMUTHU M, JALALKAMALI M, 2010. Perceived justice in service recovery and recovery satisfaction: the moderating role of corporate image[J]. International journal of marketing studies, 2(2): 47-56.

NIMAKO S G, MENSAH A F, 2012. Motivation for customer complaining and non-complaining behavior towards mobile telecommunication services[J]. Asian journal of business management, 4(3): 310-320.

NUNNALLY J C, BERNSTEIN I H, 1994. Psychometric theory. 3rd ed. New York: McGraw-Hill.

NYER P U, 1997. A Study of the relationships between cognitive appraisals and consumption emotions[J]. Journal of the academy of marketing science, 25(4): 296-304.

NYER P U, 1997. Modeling the cognitive antecedents of post consumption emotions[J]. Journal of consumer satisfaction, dissatisfaction and complaining behavior(10): 80-90.

NYQUIST J D, BITNER M J, BOOM B H, 1985. Identifying communication difficulties in service encounter: a critical incident approach [G]//CZEPIEL J A, SOLOMON M, SURPRENANT C. Service encounter: managing employee/customer interaction in service businesses. Lexington: Mass, Lexington Books: 195-212.

O

O'DONOHOE S, TURLEY D, 2007. Fatal errors: unbridling emotions in service failure experiences[J]. Journal of strategic marketing, 15(1): 17-28.

O'NEILL J W, MATTILA A S, 2004. Towards the development of a lodging service recovery strategy [J]. Journal of hospitality and leisure marketing, 11 (1): 51-64.

OH H, 1999. Service quality, customer satisfaction, and customer value: a holistic perspective [J]. International journal of hospitality management, 18(1): 67-82.

OK C, BACK K, SHANKLIN C, 2005. Dimensional roles of justice on post-recovery overall satisfaction and behavioral intentions: test of casual dining experiences[J]. Journal of foodservice business research, 8(3): 3-22.

OK C, BACK K, SHANKLIN C W, 2007. Mixed findings on the service recovery paradox[J]. Service industries journal, 27(6): 671-686.

OLIVER R L, 2010. Satisfaction: a behavioral perspective on the consumer[M]. 2nd ed. Washington D. C.: M.E. Sharpe, Inc.

OLIVER R L, 1977. A theoretical reinterpretation of expectation and disconfirmation effects on post purchase product evaluations: experience in the field[G]//DAY R L. Consumer satisfaction, dissatisfaction and complaining behavior. Bloomington, IN: Indiana University.

OLIVER R L, 1999. Whence consumer loyalty? [J]. Journal of marketing, 63 (special issue): 33-44.

OLIVER R L, 1980. A cognitive model of the antecedents and consequences of satisfaction decisions[J]. Journal of marketing research, 17(4): 460-469.

OLIVER R L, 1981. Measurement and evaluation of satisfaction processes in retail settings[J]. Journal of retailing, 57(3): 25-48.

OLIVER R L, 1989. Processing of the satisfaction response in consumption: a suggested framework and research propositions [J]. Journal of consumer satisfaction, dissatisfaction, and complaining behavior(2): 1-16.

OLIVER R L, 1993a. Cognitive, affective and attribute bases of the satisfaction response[J]. Journal of consumer research, 20(3): 418-430.

OLIVER R L, 1997. Satisfaction: a behavioral perspective on the consumer[M]. New York: McGraw-Hill.

OLIVER R L, BEARDEN W O, 1985. Disconfirmation processes and consumer evaluations in product usage[J]. Journal of business research, 13(3): 235-246.

OLIVER R L, BURKE R R, 1999. Expectation processes in satisfaction formation: a field study[J]. Journal of service research, 1(3): 196-214.

OLIVER R L, DESARBO W S, 1988. Response determinants in satisfaction judgements[J]. Journal of consumer research, 14(4): 495-507.

OLIVER R L, SWAN J E, 1989. Consumer perceptions of interpersonal equity and satisfaction in transaction: a field survey approach [J]. Journal of marketing, 53(2): 21-35.

OLIVER R L, BEARDEN W O, 1983. The role of involvement in satisfaction processes[J]. Advances in consumer research, 10(4): 250-255.

OLSEN L L, JOHNSON M D, 2003. Service equity, satisfaction and loyalty: from transaction-specific to cumulative evaluations [J]. Journal of service research, 5(3): 184-197.

OLSEN S O, 2002. Comparative evaluation and the relationship between quality, satisfaction and responses loyalty [J]. Journal of the academy of marketing science, 30(3): 240-249.

OLSHAVSKY R W, MILLER J A, 1972. Consumer expectations, product performance, and perceived product quality[J]. Journal of marketing research, 9 (1): 19-21.

OLSON J C, DOVER P, 1979. Disconfirmation of consumer expectations through product trial[ ]J. Journal of applied psychology, 64(2): 179-189.

OSTROM A, IACOBUCCI D, 1995. Consumer trade-offs and the evaluation of services. Journal of marketing, 59(1): 17-28.

OWUSU-FRIMPONG N, NWANKWO S, DASON B, 2010. Measuring service quality and patient satisfaction with access to public and private healthcare delivery[J]. International journal of public sector management, 23(3): 203-220.

P

PARASURAMAN A, BERRY L L, ZEITHAML V A, 1991a. Refinement and reassessment of the SERVQUAL scale[J]. Journal of retailing, 67(4): 420-450.

PARASURAMAN A, BERRY L L, ZEITHAML V A, 1991b. Understanding customer expectations of service[J]. Sloan management review, 32(3): 39-48.

PARASURAMAN A, ZEITHAML V A, BERRY L L, 1985. A Conceptual model of service quality and its implications for future research[J]. Journal of marketing, 49 (3): 41-50.

PARASURAMAN A, ZEITHAML V A, BERRY L L, 1988. SERVQUAl: a multiple-item scale for measuring consumer perceptions of service quality[J]. Journal of retailing, 64(1): 12-40.

PARASURAMAN A, ZEITHAML V A, BERRY L L, 1994a. Reassessment of expectations as a comparison standard in measuring service quality: implications for further research[J]. Journal of marketing, 58(1): 111-124.

PARASURAMAN A, ZEITHAML V A, BERRY L L, 1994b. Alternative scale for measuring service quality: a comparative assessment based on psychometric and diagnostic criteria[J]. Journal of retailing, 70(3): 201-230.

PATRICK V M, LANCELLOTTI M, HAGTVEDT H, 2009. Getting a second chance: the role of imagery in the influences of inaction regret on behavioral intent[J]. Journal of the academy of marketing science, 37(2): 181-190.

PATTON M, STEVENS P, KNUTSON B J, 1994. Internationalizing LODGSERV as a measurement tool: a pilot study[J]. Journal of hospitality and leisure marketing, 2(2): 39-55.

PETER J P, OLSON J C, 2007. Consumer behavior and marketing strategy[M]. 8th ed. NY: McGraw Hill.

PETER J, CHURCHILL G, BROWM T, 1993. Caution in the use of difference scores in consumer research[J]. Journal of consumer research, 19(4): 655-662.

PETERSON R A, WILSON W R, 1992. Measuring customer satisfaction: fact and artifact[J]. Journal of the academy of marketing science, 20(1): 61-71.

PING R, 1993. The effects of satisfaction and structural constrains on retailer exiting, voice, loyalty, opportunism, and neglect[J]. Journal of retailing, 69(3): 320-352.

PITT L F, JEANTROUT B, 1994. Management of customer expectations in service firms: a study and checklist[J]. The service industries journal, 14(2): 170-189.

PIZAM A, ELLIS T, 1999. Customer satisfaction and its measurement in hospitality enterprises [J]. International journal of contemporary hospitality management, 11(7): 326-339.

PRAHALAD C K, RAMASWAMY V, 2000. Co-opting customer competence[J]. Harvard Business Review, 78(1): 79-87.

PREACHER K J, RUCKER D D, HAYES A F, 2007. Assessing moderated mediation hypotheses: strategies, methods, and prescriptions [J]. Multivariate behavioral research(42): 185-227.

PRILUCK R, LALA V, 2009. The impact of the recovery paradox on retailer-customer relationships[M]. Managing service quality, 19(1): 42-59.

PRUITT D J, INSKO C A, 1980. Extension of the Kelley attribution model: The role of comparison-object consensus, target-object consensus, distinctiveness, and consistency[J]. Journal of personality and social psychology, 39(1): 39-58.

Q

QLIVER R L, 1993. A conceptual model of service quality and service satisfaction, a compatible goals, different concepts [J]. Advances in services marketing and management, 2(l): 65-85

QUICK R, 2000. The lessons learned[J]. Wall Street journal(17): R6.

R

RAVALD A, GRÖNROOS C,1996. The value concept and relationship marketing [J]. European journal of marketing, 30(2): 19-30.

REICHHELD F F, 1993. Loyalty-based management [J]. Harvard business review, 71(2): 64-73.

REICHHELD F F, JR SASSER W E, 1990. Zero defections: quality comes to services[J]. Harvard business review, 68(5): 105-111.

REICHHELD F F, 1993. Loyalty-based management [J]. Harvard business review, 71(2): 64-74.

RESNIK A J, HARMON R, 1983. Consumer complaints and managerial response: a holistic approach[J]. Journal of marketing, 47(1): 21-28.

RICHINS M L, 1983. Negative word-of-mouth by dissatisfied consumers: a pilot study[J]. Journal of marketing, 47(1): 68-78.

RICHINS M L, 1987. A multivariate analysis of responses to dissatisfaction[J]. Journal of the academy of marketing science, 15(3): 24-31.

RICHINS M L, 1985. The role of product importance in complaint initiation[C]// DAY R L, HUNT H K. Proceedings of the conference on consumer satisfaction, dissatisfaction and complaining behavior. Bloomington, IN: Indiana University Press.

RINGBERG T, ODEKERKEN-SCHRÖDER G, CHRISTENSEN G L, 2007. A cultural models approach to service recovery[J]. 71(3): 194-214.

ROBBINS T L, MILLER J L, 2004. Considering customer loyalty in developing service recovery strategies[J]. Journal of business strategies, 21(2): 95-100.

ROBERTSON N, MCQUILKEN L, KANDAMPULLY J, 2012. Consumer complaints and recovery through guaranteeing self-service technology [J]. Journal of consumer behavior, 11(1): 21-30.

ROBERTSON T S, ROSSITER J R, 1974. Children and commercial persuasion: an attribution theory analysis[J]. Journal of consumer research, 1(1): 13-20.

ROBINSON J P, SHAVER P R, WRIGHTSMAN L S, 1991. Criteria for scale selection and evaluation[M]// ROBINSON J P, SHAVER P R, WRIGHTSMAN L S. Measures of personality and social psychological attitudes. San Diego: Academic Press: 1-15.

ROESE N J, 1997. Counterfactual thinking [J]. Psychological bulletin, 121(1): 133-148.

ROESE N J, OLSON J M, 1993. Self-esteem and counterfactual thinking[J]. Journal of personality and social psychology, 65(1): 199-206.

ROSS M, FLETCHER G J O, 1985. Attribution and social perception [M]// LINDZEY G, ARONSON E. The handbook of social psychology (2). New York: Oxford University Press: 73-114.

ROSCHK H, GELBRICH K, 2018. Compensation revisited: a social resource theory perspective on offering a monetary resource after a service failure[J]. Journal of service research(spring).

ROSCHK H, GELBRICH K, 2014. Identifying appropriate compensation types for service failures: a meta-analytic and experimental analysis[J]. Journal of service research, 17(2): 195-210.

ROTTER, J. B. (1966). Generalized expectancies for internal versus external control of reinforcement. Psychological monographs, 80(1): 1-28.

RUSSELL D, 1982. The causal dimension scale: a measure of how individuals perceive causes[J]. Journal of personality and social psychology, 42(6): 1137-1145

RUSSELL-BENNETT R, HAERTEL C E J, BEATSON A, 2011. Affective events theory as a framework for understanding third-party consumer complaints[J]. What have we learned? ten years on(7): 167-195.

RUST R T, ZAHORIK A, KEININGHANI T, 1996, Service marketing[M]. New York, Harper Collins.

RUST R T, OLIVER R C, 1994. Service quality: insights and managerial implications from the frontier [M]// RUST R T, OLIVER R C. Service quality: new directions in theory and practice. Thousand Oaks, CA: Sage Publications: 72-94.

RUYTER K, WETZELS M, 2000. Customer equity considerations in service recovery: a cross-industry perspective [J]. International journal of service industry management, 11(1): 91-108.

S

SABHARWAL N, SOCH H, KAUR H, 2010. Are we satisfied with incompetent services? A scale development approach for service recovery [J]. Journal of services research, 10(1): 125-142.

SALEH F, RYAN C, 1991. Analysing service quality in the hospitality industry using the SERVQUAL model[J]. The service industries journal, 11(3): 324-345.

SALO M, MAKKONEN M, 2014. Why not complain? A paradoxical problem for mobile service and application providers [C]//Twenty Second European Conference on Information Systems. Tel Aviv.

SANCHEZ-GUTIERREZ J, GONZALEZ-URIBE E, COTON S G H, 2011. Customer satisfaction in the hospitality industry in Guadalajara, Mexico [J]. Advances in Competitiveness Research, 19(3-4): 17-31.

SANDOR S D, RABOCA H M, 2007. Determinants and outcomes of citizens' satisfaction with public services in Cluj-Napoca [J]. Transylvania review of administrative sciences(21): 103-112.

SCHNEIDER B, BOWEN D E, 1995. Winning the service game[M]. Boston, MA: Harvard Business School Press.

SCHOEFER K, DIAMANTOPOULOS A, 2009. A typology of consumers' emotional response styles during service recovery encounters [J]. British journal of management, 20(3): 292-308.

SCHWEIKHART S B, STRASSER S, KENNEDY M R, 1993. Service recovery in health services organizations[J]. Hospital and health administration, 38(1): 3-21.

SEIDERS K, BERRY L L, 1998. Service fairness: what it is and why it matters [J]. Academy of management executive, 12(2): 8-20.

SEKARAN U, BOUGIE R, 2010. Research methods for business: a skill building approach. 5th ed. New York, USA: John Wiley and Sons.

SETH N, DESHMUKH S G, VRAT P, 2005. Service quality models: a review [J]. International journal of quality and reliability management, 22(9): 913-949.

SETTLE R B, 1972. Attribution theory and acceptance of information [J]. Journal of marketing research, 9(1): 85-88.

SHAHIN A, DABESTANI R, 2010. Correlation analysis of service quality gaps in a four-star hotel in Iran[J]. International business research, 3(3): 40-46.

SHAPIRO T, NIEMAN-GONDER J, 2006. Effect of communication mode in justice-based service recovery[J]. Managing service quality, 16(2): 124-144.

SHARMA A, 2008. Improving customer service and profitability through customer intervention in service relationships [J]. Journal of relationship marketing, 7(4): 327-340.

SHARMA P, MARSHALL R, REDAY P A, et al., 2010. Complainers versus non-complainers: a multi-national investigation of individual and situational influences on customer complaint behavior[J]. Journal of marketing management, 26(1-2): 163-180.

SHAVER K G, 1975. An introduction to attribution processes[M]. Cambridge, Mass.: Winthrop.

SHEMWELL D J, YAVAS U, BILGIN Z, 1998. Customer – service provider relationship: an empirical test of a model of service quality, satisfaction and relationship-oriented outcome [J]. International journal of service industry management, 9(2): 155-168.

SIDDIQUI M H, 2010. An analytical study of complaining attitudes: with reference to the banking sector [J]. Journal of targeting, measurement and analysis for marketing, 18(2): 119-137.

SINGH J, 1988. Consumer complaint intentions and behavior: definitional and taxonomical issues[J]. Journal of marketing, 52(1): 93-107.

SINGH J, 1989. Determinants of consumers' decisions to seek third party redress: an empirical study of dissatisfied patients [J]. Journal of consumer affairs, 23(2): 329-363.

SINGH J, 1990. A typology of consumer dissatisfaction response styles [J]. Journal of retailing, 66(1): 57-97.

SINGH J, 1990. Voice, exit, and negative word-of-mouth behaviors: an investigation across three service categories [J]. Journal of the academy of marketing science, 18(1): 1-15.

SINGH J, HOWELL R D, 1985. Consumer complaining behavior: a review and prospectus[C]//DAY R, HUNT K. Proceedings of the conference on consumer satisfaction / dissatisfaction and complaining behavior. Bloomington: Indiana University.

SINGH J, WIDING II R, 1991. What occurs once consumers complain? A theoretical model for understanding satisfaction / dissatisfaction outcomes of complaint responses[J]. European journal of marketing, 25(5): 30-46.

SINGH J, PANDYA S, 1991. Exploring the effects of consumers' dissatisfaction level on complaint behaviors[J]. European journal of marketing, 25(9): 7-21.

SINGH J, WILKES R E, 1996. When consumers complain: a path analysis of the key antecedents of consumer complaint response estimates[J]. Journal of the academy of marketing science, 24(4): 350-365.

SJOVALL A M, TALK A C, 2004. From actions to impressions: cognitive attribution theory and the formation of corporate reputation [J]. Corporate reputation review, 7(3): 269-281.

SMITH A K, BOLTON R N, 2002. The effect of customers' emotional responses to service failures on their recovery effort evaluations and satisfaction judgments[J]. Journal of the academy of marketing science, 30(1): 5-23.

SMITH A K, BOLTON R N, 1998. An experimental investigation of customer reactions to service failure and recovery encounters: paradox or peril? [J]. Journal of service recovery, 1(1): 65-81.

SMITH A K, BOLTON R N, WAGNER J, 1999. A model of customer satisfaction with service encounters involving failure and recovery[J]. Journal of marketing research, 36(3): 356-372.

SMITH A M, 1995. Measuring service quality: is SERVQUAL now redundant? [J]. Journal of marketing management, 11(1-3): 257-276.

SMITH E R, MILLER F D, 1982. Latent-variable models of attributional measurement[J]. Personality and social psychology bulletin, 8(2): 221-225.

SMITH R A, HOUSTON M J, 1983. Script-based evaluations of satisfaction with services [G]//BERRY L L, SHOSTACK G L, UPAH G D. Emerging perspectives on services marketing. Chicago, Illinois: American Marketing Association, Proceeding Series: 59-62.

SNELLMAN K, VIHTKARI T, 2003. Customer complaining behavior in technology-based service encounters[J]. International journal of service industry management, 14(2): 217-231.

SÖDERLUND M, 1998. Customer satisfaction and its consequences on customer behavior revisited: the impact of different levels of satisfaction on word-of-mouth, feedback to the supplier and loyalty[J]. International journal of service industry management, 9(2): 169-188.

SOLOMON S, 1978. Measuring dispositional and situational attributions [J]. Personality and social psychology bulletin, 4(4): 589-593.

SOUTAR G N, 2001. Service quality, customer satisfaction and value: An examination of their relationships[G]// KANDAMPULLY J, MOK C, SPARKS B. Service quality management in hospitality, tourism and Leisure. Binghamton, NY: The Haworth Press Inc.: 97-110.

SPARKMAN R M, LOCANDER W B, 1980. Attribution theory and advertising effectiveness[J]. The journal of consumer research, 7(3): 219-224.

SPARKS B A, MCCOLL-KENNEDY J R, 2001. Justice strategy options for increased customer satisfaction in a services recovery setting[J]. Journal of business research, 54(3): 209-218.

SPARKS B A, CALLAN V J, 1996. Service breakdowns and service evaluations: the role of customer attributions. Journal of hospitality and leisure research, 4 (2): 3-24.

SPARKS B A, MCCOLL-KENNEDY J R, 1998. The application of procedural justice principles to service recovery attempts: outcomes for customer satisfaction[J]. Advances in consumer research, 25(1): 156-161.

SPECTOR P E, 1982. Behavior in organizations as a function of employee's locus of control[J]. Psychological bulletin, 91(3): 482-497.

SPRENG R A, MACKOY R D, 1996. An empirical examination of a model of perceived service quality and satisfaction. Journal of retailing, 72(2): 201-214.

SPRENG R A, HARRELL G D, MACKOY R D, 1995. Service recovery: impact on satisfaction and intentions[J]. Journal of services marketing, 9(1): 15-23.

SPRENG R A, OLSHASKY R W, 1992. A desire as standard model of consumer satisfaction: implications for measuring satisfaction[J]. Journal of consumer satisfaction, dissatisfaction and complaining behavior, 5(2): 54-63.

SPRENG R A, MACKENZIE S B, OLSHAVSKY R W, 1996. A reexamination of the determinants of consumer satisfaction[J]. Journal of marketing, 60(3): 15-32.

STEENKAMP J, HOFSTEDE F, WEDEL M, 1999. A cross national investigation into the individual and national culture antecedents of consumer innovativeness [J]. Journal of Marketing, 63(2): 55-69.

STEPHENS N, 2000. Complaining[M]//SWARTZ T, IACOBUCCI D. Handbook of service marketing and management. Thousand Oaks: Sage Publication.

STEPHENS N, GWINNER K P, 1998. Why don't some people complain? A cognitive-emotive process model of consumer complaint behavior[J]. Journal of the academy of marketing science, 26(3): 172-189.

STEVENS P, KNUTSON B J, PATTON M, 1995. DINESER: a tool for

measuring service quality in restaurant[J]. Hospitality, 36(2): 56-60.

STRAUSS C, QUINN N, 1997. A cognitive theory of cultural meaning[M]. New York: Cambridge University Press.

STRICKLAND L S, 1958. Surveillance and trust[J]. Journal of personality, 26 (1): 200-215.

SU W, BOWEN J T, 2001. Restaurant customer complain behavior[J]. Journal of restaurant and foodservice marketing, 4(2): 35-65.

SURESHCHANDAR G S, CHANDRASEKHARAN R, KAMALANABHAN T, 2001. Customer perceptions of service quality: a critique[J]. Total quality management, 12(1): 111-124.

SWAN J E, TRAWICK F I, 1981. Disconfirmation of expectations and satisfaction with a retail service[J]. Journal of retailing, 57(3): 49-67.

SWAN J E, TRAWICK F I, CARROLL M G, 1982. Satisfaction related to comparison level and predictive expectations[G]//DAY R L, HUNT H K. New findings on consumer satisfaction and complaining. Bloomington: Indiana University:15-22.

SWAN J E, COMBS L J, 1976. Product performance and consumer satisfaction: a new concept[J]. Journal of marketing, 40(2): 25-33.

SWANSON S R, KELLEY S W, 2001. Attributions and outcomes of the service recovery process[J]. Journal of marketing theory and practice, 9(4): 50-65.

SWANSON S R, KELLEY S W, 2001. Service recovery attributions and word-of-mouth intentions[J]. European journal of marketing, 35(1/2): 194-211.

SZYMANSKI D M, HENARD D H, 2001. Customer satisfaction: a meta-analysis of the empirical evidence[J]. Journal of the academy of marketing science, 29(1): 16-35.

T

TABACHNICK B G, FIDELL L S, 2001. Using multivariate statistics[M]. 4th ed. New York: Harper Collins.

TAX S S, BROWN S W, 1998. Recovering and learning from service failure [J]. Sloan management review, 40(1): 75-88.

TAX S S, BROWN S W, CHANDRASHEKARAN M, 1998. Customer evaluations of service complaint experiences: implications for relationship marketing[J]. Journal of marketing, 62(2): 60-76.

TAX S S, CHANDRASHEKARAN M, CHRISTIANSEN T, 1993. Word-of-mouth in consumer decision-making: an agenda for research[J]. Journal of consumer satisfaction, dissatisfaction and complaining behavior(6): 74-80

TAYLOR S, 1994. Waiting for service: the relationship between delays and evaluations of service[J]. Journal of marketing, 58(2): 56-69.

TAYLOR S A, BAKER T L, 1994. An assessment of the relationship between service quality and customer satisfaction in the formation of consumers' purchase intentions[J]. Journal of retailing, 70(2): 163-178.

TEAS R K, MCELROY J C, 1986. Causal attributions and expectancy estimates: a framework for understanding the dynamics of salesforce motivation [J]. Journal of marketing, 50(1): 75-86.

TECHNICAL ASSISTANCE RESEARCH PROGRAMS, 1979. Consumer complaint handling in America: summary of findings and recommendations[M]. Washington, D. C.: U.S. Office of Consumer Affairs.

TECHNICAL ASSISTANCE RESEARCH PROGRAMS, 1986. Consumer complaint handling in America: an updated study [M]. Washington, D. C.: Office of Consumer Affairs.

THALER R H, 1985. Mental accounting and consumer choice[J]. Marketing science, 4(3): 199-214.

THIBAUT J W, LAURENS W, 1975. Procedural justice: a psychological analysis [M]. Hillsdale, NJ: Lawrence Erlbaum Associates.

THIBAUT J W, KELLY H H, 1959. The social psychology of groups[M]. New York: Wiley.

THOMAS K W, PONDY L, 1977. Toward an intent model of conflict management among principal parties[J]. Human Relations, 30(12): 1089-1102.

TING L H, BOO H C, OTHMAN M, 2011. Development of service quality dimensions in Malaysia—the case of multicultural society[J]. SEGi review, 4 (1): 93-108.

TRIBE J, SNAITH T, 1998. From SERVQUAL to HOLSAT: holiday satisfaction in Varadero, Cuba[J]. Tourism management, 19(1): 25-34.

TRONVOLL B, 2008. Customer complaint behavior in service [D]. Karlstad: Karlstad University Studies.

TRONVOLL B, 2011. Negative emotions and their effect on customer complaint behavior[J]. Journal of service management, 22(1): 111-134.

TSANG N, QU H, 2000. Service quality in China's hotel industry [J]. International journal of contemporary hospitality management, 12(5): 316-326.

TSE D K, WILTON P C, 1988. Models of consumer satisfaction formation: an extension[J]. Journal of marketing research, 25(2): 204-212.

TSIROS M, MITTAL V, 2000. Regret: a model of its antecedents and consequences in consumer decision making[J]. Journal of consumer research, 26(4): 401-417.

TSIROS M, MITTAL V, ROSS W T, 2004. The role of attributions in customer satisfaction: a re-examination [J]. Journal of consumer research, 31(2): 476-483 .

TYLER T R, 1994. Psychological models of the justice motive—Antecedents of distributive and procedural justice [J]. Journal of personality and social psychology, 67(5): 850-863.

V

VÁZQUEZ-CASIELLES R, IGLESIAS V, VARELA-NEIRA C, 2012. Service recovery, satisfaction and behavior intentions: analysis of compensation and social comparison communication strategies[J]. The service industries journal, 32(1): 83-103.

VALENZUELA F, PEARSON D, EPWORTH R, 2005. Influences of switching barriers on service recovery evaluation[J]. Journal of services research (special issue): 239-257.

VALLE V A, WALLENDORF M, 1977. Consumers' attributions of the cause of their product satisfaction and dissatisfaction[G]//DAY R L. Consumer satisfaction, dissatisfaction, and complaining behavior. Bloomington: School of Business, Indiana University: 26-30.

VAZQUEZ-CASIELLES R, ÁLVAREZ L S, MARTIN A M, 2010. Perceived justice of service recovery strategies: impact on customer satisfaction and quality relationship[J]. Psychology and marketing, 27(5): 487-509.

VÁZQUEZ-CASIELLES R, DEL RÍO-LANZA A B, DÍAZ-MARTÍN A M, 2007. Quality of past performance: impact on consumers' responses to service failure [J]. Marketing letters, 18(4): 249-264.

VIJAYADURAI J, 2008. Service quality, customer satisfaction and behavioral intention in hotel industry[J]. Journal of marketing and communication, 3(3): 14-26.

VOORHEES C M, BRADY M K, HOROWITZ D M, 2006. A voice from the silent masses: an exploratory and comparative analysis of noncomplainers[J]. Journal of the academy of marketing science, 34(4): 514-527.

W

WALL M, DICKEY L E, TALARZYK W W, 1977. Predicting and profiling consumer satisfaction and propensity to complain [G] DAY R L. Consumer satisfaction, dissatisfaction and complaining behavior. Bloomington: Indiana University: 20-22, 91-101.

WANG D, LIN C J, PHONGKUSOLCHITN K, 2010. The keys to e-service recovery: a fast and fair fix[J]. Business studies journal, 2(1): 21-34.

WANG Y J, 2008. The application of attribution theories in marketing research: a critique[J]. Review of business research, 8(3):174-180.

WEBSTER C, SUNDRAM D S, 1998. Service consumption criticality in failure recovery[J]. Journal of business research, 41(2): 153-159.

WEINER B, 1974. Motivational psychology and educational research [J]. Educational psychologist, 11(2): 96-101.

WEINER B, 1979. A theory of motivation for some classroom experiences[J]. Journal of educational psychology, 71(1): 3-25.

WEINER B, 1980. Human Motivation [M]. New York: Holt Rinehart, and Winston.

WEINER B, 1985. Human Motivation[M]. New York: Springer-Verlag.

WEINER B, 1985a. Attributional theory of achievement motivation and emotion [J]. Psychological review, 92(4): 548-573.

WEINER B, 1985b. Spontaneous causal thinking[J]. Psychological bulletin, 97 (1): 74-84.

WEINER B, 1986. An attributional theory of motivation and emotion[M]. New York: Springer-Verlag.

WEINER B, 1990. Attribution in personality psychology [M]// PERRIN L A. Handbook of personality: theory and research. New York: Guilford Press: 465-485.

WEINER B, 1992. Human motivation: metaphors, theories and research. Newbury Park, CA: SAGE Publications.

WEINER B, 1997. Satisfaction: a behavioral perspective on the consumer [M]. New York: McGraw-Hill.

WEINER B, 1997. Satisfaction: a behavioral perspective on the consumer [M]. New York: McGraw-Hill.

WEINER B, 2000. Attributional thoughts about consumer behavior[J]. Journal of consumer research, 27(3): 382-387.

WEINER B, 1985. An attributional theory of achievement motivation and emotion [J]. Psychological review, 92(4): 548-573.

WEINER B, KUKLA A, 1970. An attribution analysis of achievement motivation [J]. Journal of personality and social psychology, 15(1): 1-19.

WEINER B, FRIEZE I H, KUKLA A, et al., 1972. Perceiving the causes of success and failure [G]//JONES E E. Attribution: perceiving the causes of behavior. Morristown, NJ: General Learning Press.

WEINER B, RUSSELL D, LERMAN D,1979. The cognition-emotion process in achievement-related contexts [J]. Journal of personality and social psychology, 37(7): 1211-1220.

WEINER B, 1980. Human motivation[M]. New York: Holt, Rinehart and Winston.

WENG M H, HA J L, WANG Y C, TSAI C L, 2012. A study of the relationship among service innovation, customer value and customer satisfaction: an empirical study of the hotel industry in Taiwan [J]. The international journal of organizational innovation, 4(3), 98-112.

WESTBROOK R A, 1980. Intrapersonal affective influences upon consumer satisfaction with products[J]. Journal of consumer research, 7(1): 49-54.

WESTBROOK R A, 1987. Product / consumption-based affective responses and post purchase processes. Journal of marketing research, 24(3): 258-270.

WESTBROOK R A, OLIVER R L, 1991. The dimensionality of consumption emotion patterns and consumer satisfaction[J]. Journal of consumer research, 18(1): 84-92.

WESTBROOK R A, REILLY M D, 1983. Value-percept disparity: an alternative to the disconfirmation of expectations theory of consumer satisfaction [J]. Advances in consumer research association for consumer research (U.S.), 10 (4): 256-261.

WEUN S, BEATTY S E, JONES M A, 2004. The impact of service failure severity on service recovery evaluations and post-recovery relationships [J]. Journal of services marketing, 18(2): 133-146.

WIND Y, 1978. Issues and advances in segmentation research[J]. Journal of marketing research, 15(3): 317-337.

WIRTZ J, MATTILA A S, 2004. Consumer responses to compensation, speed of recovery and apology after a service failure[J]. International journal of service industry management, 15(2): 150-166.

WIRTZ J, KUM D, 2001. Designing service guarantees—is full satisfaction the best you can guarantee?[J]. Journal of service marketing, 15(4): 282-297.

WIRTZ J, MATTILA A, 2001. Exploring the role of alternative perceived performance measures and needs-congruency in the consumer satisfaction process[J]. Journal of consumer psychology, 11(3): 181-192.

WIRTZ J, KUM D, LEE K S, 2000. Should a firm with a reputation for outstanding service quality offer a service guarantee?[J]. Journal of service marketing, 14(6): 502-512.

WOFFORD J C, GOODWIN V L, 1990. Effects of feedback on cognitive processing and choice decision style[J]. Journal of applied psychology, 75(6): 603-612.

WOLAK R, KALAFATIS S, HARRIS P, 1998. An investigation into four characteristics of services[J]. Journal of empirical generalisations in marketing science, 3(2): 22-43.

WOLAK R, KALAFATIS S P, HARRIS P, 1998. An investigation into four characteristics of services[J]. Journal of empirical generalisations in marketing science(3): 22-43.

WONG J Y, TSAUR S H, WANG C H, 2009. Should a lower-price service offer a full-satisfaction guarantee?[J]. The service industries journal, 29(9): 1261-1272.

WONG O M A, DEAN A M, WHITE C J, 1999. Analysing service quality in the hospitality industry[J]. Managing service quality, 9(2): 136-143.

WOODRUFF R B, CADOTTE E R, JENKINS R L, 1983. Modeling consumer satisfaction processes using experience-based norms[J]. Journal of marketing research, 20(3): 296-304.

WORSFOLD K, WORSFOLD J, BRADLEY G, 2007. Interactive effects of proactive and reactive service recovery strategies: the case of rapport and compensation[J]. Journal of applied social psychology, 37(11): 2496-2517.

WU C C, LO Y H, 2012. Customer reactions to encountering consecutive service failures[J]. Journal of consumer behavior, 11(3): 217-224.

Y

YE G, 2005. The locus effect on inertia equity[J]. Journal of product and brand management, 14(3): 206-210.

YI Y, 1990. A critical review of consumer satisfaction[G]//ZEITHAML A V. Review of marketing. Chicago: American Marketing Association: 68-123.

YILMAZ I, 2010. Do hotel customers use a multi-expectation framework in the evaluation of services? [J]. A study in Cappadocia, Turkey, tourism and hospitality research, 10(1): 59-69.

YOON S, VARGAS P T, 2010. Feeling happier when paying more: dysfunctional counterfactual thinking in consumer affect [J]. Psychology and marketing, 27(12): 1075-1100.

YUKSEL A, KILINC U, YUKSEL F, 2006. Cross-national analysis of hotel customers' attitudes toward complaining and their complaining behaviors [J]. Tourism Management, 27(1): 11-24.

YÜKSEL A, YÜKSEL F, 2001. The Expectancy-disconfirmation paradigm: a critique, Journal of hospitality and tourism research, 25(2): 107-131.

Z

ZEITHAML V A, BITNER M J, 2000. Services marketing: integrating customer focus across the firm[M]. New York: McGraw-Hill.

ZEITHAML V A, BITNER M J, 2003. Services marketing: integrating customer focus across the firm[M]. 3rd ed. New York: McGraw Hill.

ZEITHAML V A, BERRY L L, PARASURAMAN A, 1996. The behavioral consequences of service quality[J]. Journal of marketing, 60(2): 31-46.

ZEITHAML V A, 1981.How consumer evaluation processes differ between goods and services [C]//Proceedings, marketing of services conference. Chicago: AMA: 186-190.

ZEITHAML V A, BERRY L L, PARASURAMAN A, 1988. Communication and control processes in the delivery of service quality[J]. Journal of marketing, 52 (2): 35-48.

ZEITHAML V A, BERRY L L, PARASURAMAN A, 1996. The behavioral consequences of service quality[J]. Journal of marketing, 60(2): 31-46.

ZEITHAML V A, BITNER M J, 1996. Service marketing [M]. New York: McGraw Hill.

ZEITHAML V A, 1988. Consumer perceptions of price, quality, and value: a means-end model and synthesis of evidence[J]. Journal of marketing, 52(3): 2-22.

ZEITHAML V A, BERRY L L, PARASURAMAN A, 1993. The nature and determinants of customer expectations of service [J]. Journal of the academy of marketing science, 21(1): 1-12.

ZEITHAML V A, PARASURAMAN A, BERRY L L, 1990, Delivering quality service: balancing customer perceptions and expectations[M]. New York: Free Press.

ZEITHAML V A, PARASURAMAN A, BERRY L L, 1985. Problems and strategies in services marketing[M]. Journal of marketing, 49(2): 33-46.

ZEMKE R, 1993. The art of service recovery: fixing broken customers and keeping them on your side [M]//The service quality handbook. New York: American Management Association: 463-476.

ZEMKE R, 1994. Service recovery[J]. Executive excellence, 11(9): 17-18.

ZEMKE R, BELL C R, 1990. Service recovery[J], Training, 27(6): 42-48.

ZHAO X, BAI C, HUI Y, 2002. An empirical assessment and application of servqual in a mainland Chinese department store[J]. Total quality management, 13 (2): 241-254.

ZHU Z, SIVAKUMAR K, PARASURAMAN A, 2004. A mathematical model of service failure and recovery strategies[J]. Decision sciences, 35(3): 493-525.